Oxford AQA History

A LEVEL AND AS

Tsarist and Communist Russia 1855–1964

REVISION GUIDE

 RECAP   APPLY   REVIEW   SUCCEED

Margaret Haynes

OXFORD

OXFORD

UNIVERSITY PRESS

Great Clarendon Street, Oxford, OX2 6DP, United Kingdom

Oxford University Press is a department of the University of Oxford. It furthers the University's objective of excellence in research, scholarship, and education by publishing worldwide. Oxford is a registered trade mark of Oxford University Press in the UK and in certain other countries

British Library Cataloguing in Publication Data
Data available

978-0-19-842144-3

5 7 9 10 8 6 4

Digital edition: 978-019-842145-0

Paper used in the production of this book is a natural, recyclable product made from wood grown in sustainable forests. The manufacturing process conforms to the environmental regulations of the country of origin.

Printed and bound by CPI Group (UK) Ltd, Croydon, CR0 4YY

Acknowledgements

The publisher would like to thank Sally Waller for her work on the Student Book on which this Revision Guide is based and Kat O'Connor for reviewing this Revision Guide.

The publishers would like to thank the following for permissions to use copyright material:

D. Christian: *Imperial and Soviet Russia*, (Palgrave Macmillan, 1986). Reproduced with permission from Pr D. Christian.

S. E. Cohen: *Bolshevism and Stalinism, from Stalinism, Essays in Historical Interpretation*, edited by R. Tucker (W. W. Norton, 1977). Reproduced with permission from Stephen E. Cohen.

J. Davis: *Stalin from Grey Blur to Great Terror*, (Hodder, 2008). Reproduced, in adapted form, by permission of Philip Allan (for Hodder Education).

O. Figes: *A People's Tragedy*, (Jonathan Cape Random House, 1996). Copyright © 1996 by Orlando Figes. Used by permission of Viking Books, an imprint of Penguin Publishing Group, a division of Penguin Random House LLC. All rights reserved. Reproduced by permission of The Random House Group Ltd. © 1996.

L. Holmes: *Communism, a very short introduction*, (Oxford University Press, 2009)> Reproduced with permission from Oxford University Press.

M. Lynch: *Reaction and Revolutions, Russia 1881–1924*, (Hodder, 1992). Reproduced with permission from Hodder Education.

M. McCauley: *The Soviet Union 1917-1991*, (Longman, 1993). Reproduced with permission from Taylor & Francis Group.

S. S. Montefiore: *STALIN: The Court of the Red Tsar*, (Phoenix, 2003). Used by permission of Alfred A. Knopf, an imprint of the Knopf Doubleday Publishing Group, a division of Penguin Random House LLC. All rights reserved. UK copyright holder not established at time of going to print.

J. P. Nettl: *The Soviet Achievement*, (Thams & Hudson, 1967). © J. P. Nettl. Reproduced with permission from Thames & Hudson Ltd., London.

R. Service: *The Penguin History of Modern Russia: from Tsarism to the 21st Century*, (Allen Lane, 1997). Copyright © Robert Service, 1997, 2003, 2009. Reproduced by permission of Penguin Books Ltd.

R. Service: *The Russian Revolution 1900-1927*, (Palgrave Macmillan, 2009). Reproduced with permission of Palgrave Macmillan

D. Volkogonov: *The Rise and Fall of the Soviet Union*, (Harper Collins, 1999). Reproduced with permission from HarperCollins.

P. Waldron: *The End of Imperial Russia, 1855-1917*, (Palgrave Macmillan, 1997). Reproduced with permission from Macmillan Higher Education.

Although we have made every effort to trace and contact all copyright holders before publication this has not been possible in all cases. If notified, the publisher will rectify any errors or omissions at the earliest opportunity.

Cover illustrations: Popova Valeriya/Shutterstock

Artwork: Aptara

Links to third party websites are provided by Oxford in good faith and for information only. Oxford disclaims any responsibility for the materials contained in any third party website referenced in this work.

Contents

PART ONE AS AND A LEVEL

Autocracy, Reform and Revolution: Russia 1855–1917

RECAP   APPLY   REVIEW

SECTION 1 Trying to preserve autocracy, 1855–1894

SECTION 2 The collapse of autocracy, 1894–1917

Political authority, opposition and the state of Russia in wartime.

Economic, political and social problems of wartime

Contents *continued*

Introduction

The *Oxford AQA History for A Level* textbook series has been developed by a team of expert teachers and examiners led by Sally Waller. This matching Revision Guide offers well-researched, targeted revision and exam practice advice on the new AQA exams.

This guide offers you step-by-step strategies to master your AQA History exam skills, and the structured revision approach of **Recap**, **Apply and Review** to prepare you for exam success. Use the progress checklists on pages 3–4 as you work through the guide to keep track of your revision, and use the traffic light feature on each page to monitor your confidence level on each topic. Other exam practice and revision features include the **'How to…' guides** for each AQA question type on pages 6–7 and a **Timeline** of key events to help you see the themes.

RECAP

Each chapter recaps key events and developments through a variety of concise points and visual diagrams. **Key terms** appear in bold and red; they are defined in the glossary. indicates the relevant Oxford AQA History Student Book pages so you can easily cross-reference for further revision.

SUMMARY highlights the most important points at the end of each chapter.

Key Chronology provides a short list of dates to help you remember key events.

APPLY

Carefully designed revision activities help drill your grasp of knowledge and understanding, and enable you to apply your knowledge towards exam-style questions.

Apply Your Knowledge activity tests your basic comprehension, then helps apply what you know to exam questions.

Plan Your Essay activity prepares you for essay exam questions with practical essay plans and techniques.

Improve an Answer activity shows you one or more sample student answers, and helps you to evaluate how the answers could be improved.

A Level essay activities (for example, **To What Extent** or **Assess the Validity of This View**) are extension activities that help you practise the A Level essay question.

Revision Skills provides different revision techniques. Research shows that using a variety of revision styles can help cement your knowledge and understanding.

Examiner Tip highlights key parts of an exam question, and gives you hints on how to avoid common mistakes in exams.

Extract Analysis activity helps you practise evaluating extracts and prepares you for the extracts question in your exam.

Key Question covers the six thematic questions, which are strongly linked to the essay questions you might find in your exams. This activity helps to drill your understanding of the Tsarist and Communist Russia key themes:

- How was Russia governed and how did political authority change and develop?
- Why did opposition develop and how effective was it?
- How and with what results did the economy develop and change?
- What was the extent of social and cultural change?
- How important were ideas and ideology?
- How important was the role of individuals and groups and how were they affected by developments?

REVIEW

Throughout each chapter, there will be opportunities to reflect on the work you have done, and support on where to go for further revision to refresh your knowledge. You can tick off the Review column from the progress checklist once you've completed this. **Activity Answers Guidance** and the **Exam Practice** sections with full sample student answers also help you review your own work. Also, don't forget to refer to the **Top Revision Tips for A Level History** on page 143 to help you organise your revision successfully.

The topic Tsarist and Communist Russia is a **Component 1: Breadth Study**, which means you should be familiar with the Key Questions relating to the topic and the skill of evaluating differing historical interpretations.

The **AS LEVEL** exam lasts 1.5 hours (90 minutes), and you have to answer two questions.

The **A LEVEL** exam lasts 2.5 hours (150 minutes), and you have to answer three questions.

On these pages, you will find guidance on how to tackle each type of question in your exam.

How to master the extracts question

In **Section A** of your Tsarist and Communist Russia exam, you will encounter one extracts question that you must answer. Here are the steps to consider when tackling the extracts question:

1 **Look at the question posed**
Note (underline or highlight) the topic in relation to which the extracts need to be evaluated.

EXAMINER TIP

AS LEVEL You have to answer one extracts question on two interpretations (worth 25 marks). Try to spend about 50 minutes on this question.

A LEVEL You have to answer one extracts question on three interpretations (worth 30 marks). Try to spend about 60 minutes on this question.

2 **Read the first extract carefully**
Keep the topic in mind. Underline or highlight the parts of the extract that provide an argument in relation to this topic (remember this will not always be in the first sentence). These parts should give you the 'overall' argument.

EXAMINER TIP

Look again at the extract: see if there are any sub-arguments or interpretations. Underline or highlight these in a different colour.

3 **Begin your evaluation**
Identify the overall argument of the extract, then evaluate the argument. Refer to your own knowledge. You should cite material which both supports and challenges the view the extract puts forward.

EXAMINER TIP

To provide a fully convincing answer, repeat step **3** for any sub-arguments.

4 **Make a judgement**
Provide some supporting comment on how convincing the argument in the extract is in relation to the topic of the question.

5 **Repeat steps 2–4 for the next extract or extracts.**
At **AS LEVEL** you will need a further paragraph in which you **compare** the two extracts directly and give a judgement on which is the more convincing.

At **A LEVEL** you **don't** need to make any comparative judgements and there is no need for an overall conclusion.

REVIEW

Take a look at the Exam Practice sections starting on pages 68 and 97 of this guide to reflect on sample answers to the extracts question.

No comparison !

How to master the essay question

In **Section B** of your Tsarist and Communist Russia exam, you will encounter a choice of essay questions. Here are the steps to consider when tackling an essay question:

1 Read the question carefully
Note (underline or highlight) key words and dates.

EXAMINER TIP

AS LEVEL You have to answer one essay question (worth 25 marks) from a choice of two questions. Try to spend about 40 minutes on this question.

A LEVEL You have to answer two essay questions (each worth 25 marks) from a choice of three questions. Try to spend about 45 minutes on each answer.

2 Plan your essay and form a judgement
Decide which approach will best enable you to answer the question – this may be chronological or thematic.

State a clear judgement, don't stray from that view!!!

PLAN

EXAMINER TIP

Plans can be in the form of columns, spider diagrams, mind-maps, flow charts and other styles, but should help you to both form a judgement and to devise a coherent structure for your answer.

3 Introduce your argument
State your judgement (view) in the introduction. The introduction should also be used to show your understanding of the question, particularly key terms and dates, and to acknowledge alternative views and factors.

State your opinion but include the question in your argument.

4 Develop your argument
The essay should proceed logically, supporting your balanced argument through the opening statements of the paragraphs. Remember: comment first, then provide specific and precise supporting information.

Comment → Specific details

↓

Supporting information

EXAMINER TIP

Don't forget to write analytically. Your job is to argue a case and evaluate events, developments and ideas, rather than simply describing what happened in a story-telling (narrative) fashion.

EXAMINER TIP

A good essay will have a balanced argument. You should examine alternative ideas and factors, and explain why they are less convincing than those you are supporting.

5 Conclude your argument
Your conclusion should repeat the judgement given in the introduction and summarise your argument. A good conclusion will not include any new information and will flow naturally from what has gone before.

Don't add new information !

REVIEW

In the Exam Practice sections starting on pages 37 and 126, you will find sample answers and helpful examiner tips to the essay exam question.

AQA AS and A Level History mark schemes

Below are simplified versions of the AQA mark schemes, to help you understand the marking criteria for your **Component 1: Breadth Study** History exam paper.

AS LEVEL	Section A: Extracts	Section B: Essay
5	Good understanding of interpretations. Very good knowledge. Comparison contains a substantiated judgment. [21–25 marks]	Good understanding of the question. Range of knowledge, with specific supporting information. Analytical, well-argued answer. Structured effectively. Substantiated judgement. [21–25 marks]
4	Good understanding of interpretations. Good knowledge. Partly substantiated comparison. [16–20 marks]	Good understanding of the question. Range of knowledge. Analytical, balanced answer. Structured effectively. Some judgement. [16–20 marks]
3	Reasonable understanding of interpretations. Adequate own knowledge. Partial comparison. [11–15 marks]	Reasonable understanding of the question. Some knowledge, with limited scope. Answer contains some balance. Structured adequately. Partial judgement. [11–15 marks]
2	Partial understanding of interpretations. Some knowledge. Undeveloped comparison. [6–10 marks]	Partial understanding of the question. Some knowledge, with very limited scope. Answer contains limited balance, or is descriptive. There is some structure. Undeveloped judgement. [6–10 marks]
1	Little understanding of interpretations. Limited knowledge. Vague or too general comparison. [1–5 marks]	Limited understanding of the question. Limited knowledge. Answer is vague or too general. Structure is weak. Unsupported judgement. [1–5 marks]

A LEVEL	Section A: Extracts	Section B: Essays
5	Very good understanding of interpretations. Strong and well-supported evaluation of arguments. Very good knowledge, used convincingly. [25–30 marks]	Very good understanding of the question and of the issues/concepts. Range of knowledge, with specific and precise supporting information. Full analytical, balanced answer. Good organisation, structured effectively. Well-substantiated judgement. [21–25 marks]
4	Good understanding of interpretations. Good and mostly well-supported evaluation of arguments. Good knowledge, used convincingly. [19–24 marks]	Good understanding of the question and of the issues/concepts. Range of knowledge, with specific and precise supporting information. Analytical, balanced answer. Good organisation, structured effectively. Some judgement. [16–20 marks]
3	Reasonable understanding of interpretations. Some evaluation of arguments, may contain some imbalance or lack of depth. Knowledge is present, used accurately. [13–18 marks]	Reasonable understanding of the question, with some awareness of the issues/concepts. Range of knowledge, may contain imprecise supporting information. Answer links to the question and contains some balance. Structured effectively. Partial judgement. [11–15 marks]
2	Partial understanding of interpretations (accurate for at least two extracts). Little evaluation of arguments, may contain some generalisations. Some knowledge is present. [7–12 marks]	Partial understanding of the question, with some awareness of the issues/concepts (may contain generalisations). Some knowledge, with limited scope. Answer contains limited balance, or is descriptive. There is some structure. Undeveloped judgement. [6–10 marks]
1	Partial understanding of interpretations (accurate for one extract, or limited accuracy for two to three extracts). Evaluation of arguments is too general and inaccurate/irrelevant. Limited knowledge is present. [1–6 marks]	Limited understanding of the question, with inaccurate or irrelevant understanding of issues/concepts. Limited knowledge. Answer is vague or too general. Structure is weak. Unsupported judgement. [1–5 marks]

Timeline

The colours represent different types of events and developments as follows:

● Blue: economic events   ● Red: political events
● Black: international events (including foreign policy)   ● Yellow: social events

1855	● Alexander II becomes Tsar
1856	● Crimean War ends
1861	● Abolition of serfdom
1863–64	● Polish revolt
1866	● Attempted assassination of Alexander II
1881	● Alexander II assassinated; Alexander III succeeds
1882	● May Laws
1883	● Peasants' Land Bank created
1885	● Nobles' Land Bank created
1889	● Land Captains established
1891–92	● Famine
1894	● Death of Alexander III; Nicholas II succeeds
1898	● Social Democratic Workers' Party founded
1899	● Social Revolutionary Party established
1904	● Russo-Japanese War begins
1905	● **July** – Bloody Sunday massacre
	● **Aug** – Russo-Japanese War concluded
	● **Oct** – October Manifesto
1914	● Germany declares war on Russia
1915	● Tsar assumes command of army
1916	● Murder of Rasputin
1917	● **Feb** – February Revolution
	● **April** – April Theses
	● **July** – July Days
	● **Aug** – Kornilov attempted coup
	● **Oct** – October Revolution
	● **Nov** – Armistice ends war
1918	● Constituent Assembly dissolved
	● Treaty of Brest-Litovsk
	● Civil War begins
1921	● Ban on factions

	● Treaty of Riga; Civil War ends
1921–22	● Great Famine
1922	● Constitution of USSR adopted
1924	● Lenin dies
1926	● United Opposition formed
1928–32	● First Five Year Plan
1929	● Final defeat of opposition brings Stalin to power
	● Call for collectivisation and dekulakisation
1932–33	● Famine in Ukraine and elsewhere
1933–37	● Second Five Year Plan
1934	● Assassination of Kirov
1936	● New Soviet constitution
1936–38	● Stalin's purges
1937–38	● Height of Great Terror
1938–42	● Third Five Year Plan
1941	● Nazi invasion of USSR
1945	● End of Second World War
1946	● Beginning of Zhdanovshchina
1946–50	● Fourth Five Year Plan
1951–55	● Fifth Five Year Plan
1953	● Death of Stalin
	● Khrushchev becomes First Secretary of Party
1954	● Virgin Lands Scheme adopted
1956	● Khrushchev's 'Secret' Speech
	● Sixth Five Year Plan (abandoned 1958)
1957	● 'Anti-Party' group defeated
	● Economic decentralisation adopted
1959	● Seven Year Plan adopted
1961–65	● Seventh Five Year Plan
1964	● Removal of Khrushchev

1 Trying to preserve autocracy, 1855–1894

REVISION PROGRESS

1 The Russian autocracy in 1855

RECAP

In 1855, Russia was a vast empire covering around 21 million square kilometres. It contained many ethnic groups, each with its own culture, customs, language and, in some cases, religion. The Empire was predominantly held together by the power of the Tsar and the Russian **Orthodox Church** to demand obedience.

Key
The Russian Empire in 1855

N

St Petersburg
POLAND   R U S S I A N   E M P I R E   MANCHURIA
Moscow
Caspian   Aral
Sea   Sea
Black Sea   MONGOLIA
OTTOMAN
EMPIRE
                    Kabul   CHINA
PERSIA   ●
AFGHANISTAN

The calendar in Russia

The Russians used the Julian calendar until 31 January 1918, rather than the Gregorian calendar, in use elsewhere in Europe. Consequently, by 1918, Russia was 13 days behind Western Europe. This book uses the old-style Julian calendar for dates to 1 February 1918 and the new-style Gregorian calendar thereafter.

The political context

Russia was an **autocracy**. At its head was a tsar (emperor), who enjoyed unlimited powers. The Tsar's imperial edicts were law.

The Tsar was supported by:

- **The Church:** The Tsar was regarded as the embodiment of God on earth, controlling the Russian Orthodox Church. Russian lands were his property and the Russian people were his children. Russians were taught to show devotion to their tsar and accept their conditions on earth as God's will. Church and State were closely entwined.

- **Advisers and ministers:** These were chosen by the Tsar himself.

- **The nobility:** They kept order on their estates, and might serve as provincial governors, or in special committees appointed by the Tsar.

- **The bureaucracy:** These civil servants were paid noble officials, each holding a 'rank'. Through this bureaucracy, orders were passed down from the central government to the provinces and, in turn, to the districts and towns. It was riddled by corruption and incompetence.

- **The army:** This included around 1.5 million conscripted **serfs**, each forced into service for 25 years. The military absorbed around 45% of the government's annual expenditure. It could be used to fight in wars or to put down internal disturbances. The higher ranks were prestigious posts for nobles; for the lower ranks, army life was hard. In addition, elite regiments of mounted Cossacks, with special social privileges, acted both as a personal bodyguard to the Tsar and as police reinforcements.

- **The police:** Russia had developed into a **police state**. Freedom of speech, freedom of the press and travel abroad were prevented. Political meetings and strikes were forbidden. Censorship was enforced. The secret state security network was run by the 'Third Section' of the Emperor's Imperial Council. Its agents had unlimited powers to carry out raids, arrest and ensure the imprisonment or exile of anyone suspected of anti-tsarist behaviour.

Over 50% of the Russian population were peasant-serfs – men, women and children who were classified as the 'property' of their owners. Just over half were privately owned; the remainder were 'state serfs' who paid taxes and rent. Most serfs worked on the land in village communes (*mirs*). The serfs' working and living conditions were primitive. Most peasants were illiterate but deeply religious, superstitious and hostile to change.

Political developments

By the 19th century, liberal ideas were spreading from the West and many Russian intellectuals were arguing for a civil society based on the rule of law. However Tsar Nicholas I (reigned 1825–55) had followed a path of repression. He sought to maintain autocracy and to distance Russia from the West. His reign culminated in military defeat in the Crimea, which finally brought the need for change to the new Tsar's attention.

The economic and social context

Economic situation

In 1855, Britain, Belgium, France and the German states were industrially advanced. Meanwhile, the Russian economy remained predominantly rural. This was partly because the inhospitable territory and climate in much of Russia limited economic progress. However the main reason for Russian backwardness was the serf-based economy. This limited the forces that drive change (wage-earners, markets and entrepreneurs):

- **Wage-earners:** The serfs were poor. Most only just managed to survive on the produce they grew, and starvation was common in winter. Land management systems meant that individual serf families worked scattered strips, following communal farming patterns. There was little opportunity for them to develop into 'wage-earners'.

- **Internal market demand:** Although markets existed, few goods were 'purchased'; instead, goods were exchanged. In some areas, market forces were beginning to develop as peasants sought wage-work in towns when farming was slack, but for most, money was irrelevant and there was no internal market demand.

- **Entrepreneurs:** At the other end of the scale, the small landowning elite could largely obtain what they needed by squeezing it from their serfs through service and feudal dues. Although many landowners were in debt, money was of little use to them. There was therefore little incentive to seek alternative ways of making money.

Social context

Socially, Russia was divided between the privileged land-owning elite and the serf majority – also known as the non-productive and the productive classes.

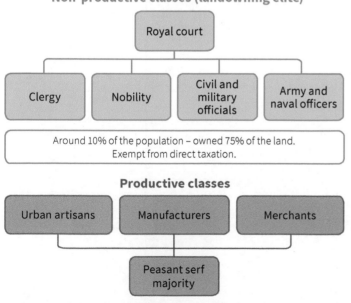

Non-productive classes (landowning elite)

Royal court → Clergy, Nobility, Civil and military officials, Army and naval officers

Around 10% of the population – owned 75% of the land. Exempt from direct taxation.

Productive classes

Urban artisans, Manufacturers, Merchants → Peasant serf majority

Provided around 90% of imperial finance.
Liable for direct and indirect taxes (and private serfs paid feudal dues to their masters).

There was no coherent 'middle class', as elsewhere in Europe. There were a small number of professionals (e.g. doctors, teachers and lawyers), some of whom comprised an educated '**intelligentsia**', but the educated were predominantly the sons of nobles.

Society therefore remained essentially 'feudal' (based on birth, land and service).

The impact of the Crimean War 1853–56

The Ottoman (Turkish) Empire stretched from the Middle East across the Black Sea Straits and into the Balkans. Nicholas I's attempts to increase Russian influence there had caused the Turks to declare war in October 1853. The British and French, to protect their trading interests, entered the war in defence of Turkey. The Russians proved no match for the West and suffered defeats at Balaclava (October 1854) and Inkerman (November 1854).

Alexander II became Tsar in March 1855. By September, the fortress of Sebastopol, in the Russian Crimea, had fallen to its enemies. Russia was shocked. The concluding Treaty of Paris (1856) added the final humiliation by preventing Russian warships from using the Black Sea in peacetime.

The Crimean War had revealed Russia's military and administrative inadequacies, including:

- outdated technology
- poor transport
- inadequate leadership
- the problems of having a conscripted army.

Trade had been disrupted, peasant uprisings had escalated and much of the intelligentsia were appealing for action to close the gap between Russia and the West.

Russia's failure in the Crimean War proved a 'wake-up call'. 1855 marked the accession of a new tsar, Alexander II, and a new generation of liberal-minded nobles and officials who would strongly influence his reign.

SUMMARY

- In 1855 the vast Russian Empire was characterised by geographic, social, intellectual, economic and religious divisions.
- It was ruled by the Tsar, an autocrat with unlimited powers, in a regime backed by the Russian Orthodox Church and based on a feudal system of government.
- Politically, economically and socially, Russia remained undeveloped and 'backward' in comparison with the West.
- Failure in the Crimean War highlighted Russian inadequacies. This was to prove the catalyst for change under the new Tsar, Alexander II.

 **APPLY**

APPLY YOUR KNOWLEDGE

a Look at the text and define or briefly explain the following terms (in relation to mid 19th-century Russia).

Autocracy	
Russian Orthodox Church	
Bureaucracy	
Conscript army	
Police state	
Serfdom	
Liberal intellectuals	
Productive and non-productive classes	

b How might these terms contribute to an understanding of the weaknesses of Russia in c1855?

EXAMINER TIP

This activity will help you in any essay requiring you to analyse the strengths and weaknesses of Russia from 1855. Use of terms such as these will show your depth of knowledge.

REVIEW

Look back at Chapter 1 and see if there are any other key terms or concepts that it would be useful to record and use in your essays.

TO WHAT EXTENT?

 A LEVEL **To what extent was economic backwardness the most important factor weakening the Russian State in c1855?**

In order to plan an answer to this question, draw up a three-column chart as follows:

Economic factors weakening the State	Other factors weakening the State	Ways in which the State remained strong

EXAMINER TIP

In answering this essay question, you would need to think carefully about the meaning of 'weakness' in relation to a state.

REVISION SKILLS

Prepare a set of 6 cards – one for each of the Key Questions for this component. As you revise each chapter, consider what Key Questions it addresses. Write no more than 3 bullet points per chapter on each of the relevant cards, so that you can see how the material you have studied links to these Key Questions.

EXAMINER TIP

This revision exercise will enable you to address the key themes that will be asked about in the exam questions. Many chapters focus on one specific Key Question, but some address more than one. For example, a chapter that primarily discusses political authority may also contain information relevant to the Key Question on opposition.

KEY QUESTION

One of the Key Questions asks:

How and with what results did the economy develop and change?

Complete this diagram on the state of the Russian economy in 1855 as a basis for this:

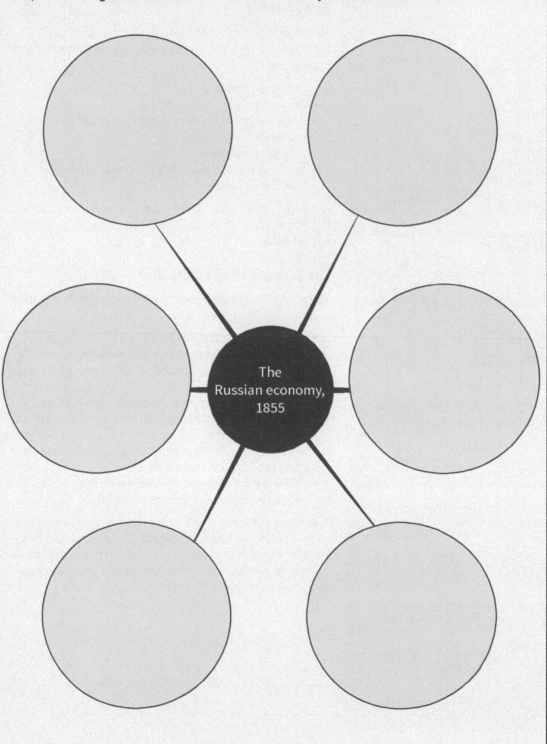

2 Alexander II, the 'Tsar Reformer'

RECAP

Tsar Alexander II has been called the 'Tsar Liberator'. This is because of his decision to **emancipate** (free) Russia's 51 million serfs in 1861. However, there is historical debate as to whether he deserves such a title, as it can be argued that his main aim in granting emancipation was to strengthen the tsarist autocracy.

The emancipation of the serfs

Motives for reform

Alexander may have been influenced by some or all of the following:

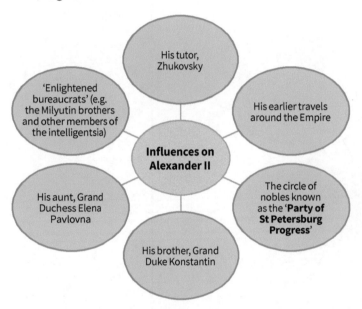

Supporters of emancipation argued that serfdom was morally wrong. In addition, there were strong economic motives to abolish it:

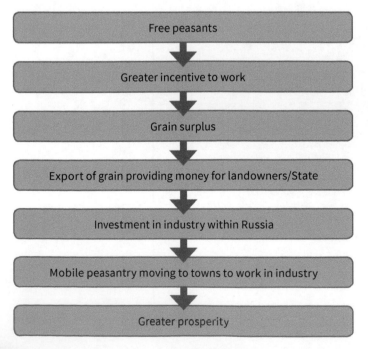

There were also social reasons for reform – peasant uprisings had increased since the 1840s and this may have encouraged Alexander to concede that emancipation should be granted.

However the main trigger was Russia's defeat in the Crimean War. Dmitry Milyutin argued that only a 'free' population would provide the labour needed to improve the army.

Early reforms

Alexander was determined to maintain the autocracy. Nevertheless, he felt the pressure for reform. In the first year of his reign he:

- released political prisoners
- relaxed controls on censorship
- lessened restrictions on foreign travel and university entrance
- cancelled tax debts
- restored some of the rights of Poland and the Catholic Church.

Alexander began looking into emancipation in March 1856, but it took him until 1861 before his edict was ready to be implemented.

The Emancipation Edict, 1861

This applied to privately owned serfs immediately and state serfs from 1866.

- Serfs were granted freedom and a land allotment.
- Landlords were compensated by the government. They kept some lands but open fields were given to the peasant commune (*mir*).
- Freed serfs had to pay 'redemption payments' over 49 years to the government for their land. They were to remain within their *mir* until these had been paid. The *mir* would distribute the allotments, control the farming and collect and pay the peasants' taxes.
- ***Volosts*** were established to supervise the *mirs*; from 1863, the *volosts* ran their own courts.

There was, in theory, a two-year period of 'temporary obligation' before freedom was granted, while allocations were arranged. In practice, around 15% of peasants remained 'temporarily obligated' to their landlords until 1881, when redemption was made compulsory.

Positive results of emancipation	Negative results of emancipation
Peasants were no longer subject to their masters' whim and had free status.	Land allocations were rarely fair.
Some peasants, the prosperous *kulaks*, did well out of the land allocations, buying up extra land and exporting surplus grain.	• Since the land in each *mir* had to be divided between all male peasants, most peasant holdings grew increasingly smaller as the population grew. • The allotments were small, allowing little opportunity to adopt new farming methods. • The *mir* system was highly traditional – subsistence farming and technical backwardness persisted.
Some peasants sold their land, obtained a passport to leave the *mir*, and raised their living standard by finding work in the cities.	• The loss of former benefits, restrictions on travel and the burden of the redemption payments made rural life difficult. • Resentment of *kulaks* and disputes over landholding and redemption payments led to further violence.
Some landowners used the compensation offered to get out of debt.	Noble bankruptcies continued, as landowners had to sell or mortgage their own allocated land.
Enterprising landlords made profits through investment in industrial enterprises.	Landowners resented their loss of influence. The newspapers ran articles about their disappointments and a wave of student protests and riots occurred in St Petersburg, Moscow and Kazan.

Other domestic reforms

The changes to the rights and position of peasants and landowners had wide implications for society and government. Further reforms followed.

Local government reforms (1864–70)

Elected local councils (*zemstva*) replaced the rights and obligations of the serf-owning gentry:

- These were chosen through 'electoral colleges'; there was a separate college for nobles, townspeople, Church and peasants, allowing a degree of popular representation.
- They were composed of men who understood the locality and its needs.
- They were given power to improve public services, develop industrial projects and administer poor relief. In 1870 elected town councils called **dumas** were set up in the towns.

However:

- The power of the *zemstva* was strictly limited.
- They had no control over taxes.
- The voting procedure favoured the nobility.
- Provincial governors continued to appoint officials, took responsibility for law and order and could overturn *zemstvo* decisions.
- The councils were never truly 'people's assemblies'. They attracted doctors, lawyers, teachers and scientists who used meetings to debate political issues.

Judiciary reforms (1864)

Emancipation required changes to the law and to the administration of local justice. Previously a judge had examined written evidence usually prepared by the landowner and police. There had been no jury system, no lawyers and no examination of witnesses. The accused was considered guilty until proven innocent and the judge's decision was final.

The new system was modelled on the West:

- A single system of courts established equality before the law. The accused was presumed innocent until proven guilty and could employ a lawyer.
- Criminal cases were heard before barristers and a jury, selected from lists of property owners. Judges were appointed by the Tsar and given improved training and pay.

- Local Justices of the Peace were elected every three years by the *zemstva*, and were to be independent from political control.
- Courts were opened to the public and proceedings could be reported.

The new system was fairer. However:

- Articulate lawyers could criticise the regime.
- The new juries sometimes acquitted the guilty out of sympathy. A new decree was therefore issued permitting political crimes to be tried by special procedures.
- There were limitations and exclusions.

Education reforms (1863–64)

Emancipation increased the need for basic literacy and numeracy among peasants.

Under Golovnin (Minister for Education from 1862–67):

- Universities could govern themselves and appoint their own staff.
- Responsibility for schools was transferred from the Church to the *zemstva*.
- Primary and secondary education was extended.
- Schools were declared open to boys and girls of all classes.
- The numbers of those attending schools and universities grew.

However:

- The universities' new independence increased the number of radical thinkers. After 1866, government control was reasserted.

Military reforms (1874–75)

Dmitry Milyutin's reorganisation of the armed forces improved efficiency and reduced cost.

- Conscription became compulsory for all classes from the age of 21 but the length of service was reduced.
- Punishments were made less severe.
- The system of military colonies was abandoned.
- Better provisioning, medical care and education were provided.
- Modern weaponry was introduced.
- A new command structure was created.
- Military Colleges were set up to provide better training for the non-noble officer corps.

However:

- Richer people often found substitutes to serve for them.
- The officer class remained largely aristocratic.
- Problems of supply and leadership continued.

Other reforms

- Between 1858 and 1870, press censorship (which had extended to all books and newspapers) was relaxed.
- There were attempts to eliminate corruption in the lower levels of the Church.
- Some reform of the condition of the Jews and ethnic minorities was initially undertaken.
- Some economic liberalisation was granted.

However:

- After critical writing increased, government control was tightened again in the 1870s.
- Church reform stopped in the reactionary years of the 1870s.
- The lenient treatment of Poles and Jews was reversed after the 1863 Polish rebellion.
- Economic liberalisation remained, but it was largely at the peasants' expense.

SUMMARY

- Alexander II's reforms altered Russia's social, economic, political, and military structure.
- There was some continuity with before; the noble class remained dominant and peasant society changed little.
- However, the reforms, though limited, changed patterns of land ownership and brought about wide-ranging social changes.
- These may have increased instability in Russia by setting expectations for further change.

 **APPLY**

APPLY YOUR KNOWLEDGE

For each of Alexander II's reforms, answer the following questions. (You may like to answer in chart form.)

- What ideas/motives were behind the reforms?
- What beliefs or ideas limited them?
- Which group benefited most from this reform?
- Which lost power or prestige?

Reform	Ideas/motives behind the reform	Beliefs or ideas that limited the reform	Group or groups that benefited most	Group or groups that lost power
Emancipation				
Local government				
Judiciary				
Education				
Military				
Other				

EXAMINER TIP

You could use your chart to answer an exam question on the causes, detail and/ or consequences of Alexander II's reforms.

REVIEW

Look back to Chapter 1 to extend your understanding of the motives behind Alexander II's reforms.

ASSESS THE VALIDITY OF THIS VIEW

A LEVEL **'Alexander II's reforms transformed Russia into a liberal state.' Assess the validity of this view.**

a Complete the diagram below to show ways in which the reforms were liberal and ways in which they were not.

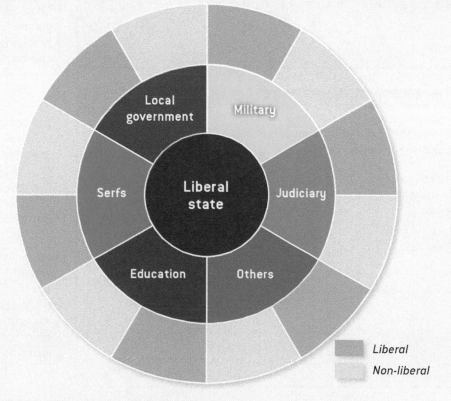

Liberal
Non-liberal

REVIEW

Were you able to recall this information without looking back? If not, you may like to create a word-play (or mnemonic) to help you to remember the range of Alexander II's reforms. What about the name – 'Sir Joe Milo' (Serfs (Sir), Judiciary, Other, Education (Joe), Milo (Military and Local government))?

b Now use your diagram to answer the question above.

IMPROVE AN ANSWER

Here are 2 exemplar paragraphs from different students answering an essay question asking,

 To what extent were Alexander II's reforms the result of Russian defeat in the Crimean War?

Answer 1

After the Crimean War, Dmitry Milyutin helped Alexander II to reform the military. He reduced military service and extended conscription to all classes. This meant nobles as well as peasants would have to serve. He banned extremely severe punishments and he increased opportunities for education in the services. This strengthened Russia's army, although the officer class remained almost exclusively noble and the well-off could usually buy their way out of service. Weapons were upgraded and transport improved. These new reforms improved efficiency and reduced cost.

Answer 2

The Crimean War had shown profound weaknesses in both the Russian army itself and its organisation and Alexander II's reforms went some way towards addressing these. Conscription was extended to all classes, conditions of service were improved and the oppressive system of military colonies abandoned. Furthermore, improvements were made to weaponry, command and training, all of which had proved inadequate from 1853 to 1855. Although the reforms had limitations and problems of aristocratic leadership and difficulties of supply remained, the reforms addressed key military and administrative inadequacies, improving technology, transport, leadership and service. Overall, the reforms provided for a much stronger army than that which had fought in the Crimean War and lost so disastrously at Inkerman and Balaclava.

Which is the better answer and why?

EXAMINER TIP

Take care to distinguish between description and analysis. The first sentence of every paragraph in an essay is crucial. This is what moves an argument forward.

REVIEW

Look back to Chapter 1 to remind yourself of the problems of the Crimean War.

PLAN YOUR ESSAY

 'Alexander II's reforms were the result of Russian defeat in the Crimean War.' Explain why you agree or disagree with this view.

All AS essay questions will require you to balance points of agreement against points of disagreement. It is a good idea to use a two-column chart to prepare for this. See if you can create a plan for this question for your revision.

Agree	Disagree

EXAMINER TIP

Before you begin to write you will need to decide whether you will agree or disagree with the statement. This two-column chart should help you to decide.

Planning your exam essay is essential, so you should practise writing essay plans as much as you practise writing full answers.

3 The autocracy of Alexander II and Alexander III

Alexander II and reaction

In 1866, following an attempt on his life, Alexander adopted a more repressive policy (although in some areas, especially the military, reforming legislation continued). There was a short period of further constitutional reform in the late 1870s. However, from 1881, the reign of Alexander II's son, Alexander III, was similarly characterised by **reaction**.

Reasons for reaction

- In 1865 Alexander's eldest son and heir died. Thereafter the Tsar spent more time with his mistress and less with the reformist Grand Duke Konstantin and Grand Duchess Elena.
- Reactionary conservatives emphasised that the reforms had gone too far and were weakening the Church and the nobility (upon whom the monarchy relied).
- Four assassination attempts on Alexander between 1866 and 1880 reinforced the need for reaction.

Alexander therefore replaced four reformist ministers with conservatives in 1866.

Education

Tolstoy, the new Minister for Education, wanted tight control over education, to eradicate Western liberal ideas and growing criticism of the autocracy.

- The *zemstva's* powers over education were reduced.
- The Church regained its authority over rural schools.
- The higher *gimnazii* schools were ordered to follow a traditional classical curriculum, and the new modern schools could no longer send students to university.
- In the universities, more liberal courses were replaced by a traditional curriculum. Censorship was tightened and student activities firmly controlled.
- More state teacher-training colleges were set up, but to increase tsarist control, rather than improve education. Tolstoy frequently vetoed university appointments.

Police, law and control

Shuvalov, the new head of the Third Section (secret police) strengthened the police and increased the persecution of ethnic and religious minorities. Pahlen, the new Justice Minister, ensured that the judicial system made an example of 'political agitators'.

Searches and arrests increased; political offenders could be prosecuted under emergency powers and exiled; radicals who had fled Russia could be tracked down and recalled to face justice.

'**Show trials**' were held, which were aimed at deterring others from revolutionary activity. However this had the opposite effect and in 1878, political crimes were transferred to special secret courts.

Pressures in the late 1870s

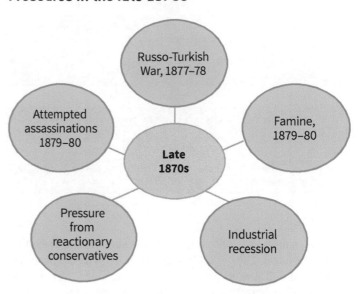

As political crisis deepened in the late 1870s, Alexander II tried to reduce unrest by widening democratic consultation. Count Loris-Melikov was appointed Minister for Internal Affairs. He relaxed many restrictions and abolished the Third Section; however its powers were transferred to a new special section of the regular police known as the 'Okhrana' (which became just as oppressive).

In 1880, Loris-Melikov produced a report which became known as 'Loris-Melikov's Constitution'. It recommended including elected representatives in debating some state decrees. Alexander II accepted the report in the morning of 13 March 1881, but was killed by a bomb the same day.

Alexander III as Tsar

Alexander III (reigned 1881–94) was terrified of revolutionary activity. He was strongly influenced by his tutor, Pobedonostsev, who believed firmly in absolutism, nationalism and **anti-Semitism**.

Alexander believed that he alone could decide what was right for his country; the duty of his subjects was not to question, but to love and obey. At the start of his reign he:

- publicly hanged the conspirators involved in his father's assassination
- issued the 1881 'Manifesto of Unshakable Autocracy' and a Law on Exceptional Measures
- abandoned Loris-Melikov's proposals
- accepted the resignations of reforming ministers, including Dmitry Milyutin, and instead relied heavily on conservatives.

Local government

Nobles were reinstated to positions of authority and state authority increased.

1889 – Office of noble 'Land Captain' created

- State-appointed
- Could over-ride elections to the *zemstva* and disregard *zemstvo* decisions
- Responsible for law enforcement and government in the countryside and could overturn court judgements

⬇

1890 – *Zemstvo* election arrangements and *zemstvo* powers altered

- Peasants' vote reduced
- *Zemstva* placed under central government control

⬇

1892 – town councils' election arrangements altered

- Electorate reduced to the owners of property above a certain value
- Mayor and town councils became state employees, directed by central government

---

Policing

The Department of Police (including the Okhrana), was led by Plehve between 1881 and 1884, and from 1884 by Durnovo. The number of police was increased; new branches of the criminal investigation department were set up; and spies and 'agents provocateurs' were recruited. The Okhrana investigated communists, socialists and trade unionists and also watched members of the civil service and government.

The 1882 Statute on Police Surveillance gave the police tremendous power over people's lives. Any area of the Empire could be deemed an 'area of subversion' and police agents could search, arrest, detain, question, imprison or exile anyone who had committed a crime, who was thought likely to commit crimes or who knew, or was related to, people who had committed crimes.

Judicial system

The judicial reforms of Alexander II were partially reversed:

- Decrees of 1885, 1887 and 1889 gave greater powers to the Ministry of Justice.
- In 1887, the property and educational qualifications needed by jurors were raised.
- In 1889 the *volost* (peasant) courts were put under the direct jurisdiction of the Land Captains in the countryside and judges in the towns.

Education

Alexander II's education reforms were similarly eroded:

- In 1884, university appointments became subject to the approval of the Education Ministry. They were now based on 'religious, moral and patriotic orientation', rather than academic grounds.

- Universities for women were closed, separate university courts were abolished and university life was closely supervised.
- Low-class children were restricted to primary education, which was under Church control.

Although the number of schools and the numbers of those receiving some education increased, nevertheless, only 21% of the population were literate by 1897.

These education policies ran counter to the government's attempts to promote economic modernisation. They also failed to prevent student involvement in illegal political movements, particularly in the 1890s.

Censorship

From 1882 powers of censorship were increased and censors became more active.

Extent and impact of counter-reform

These changes greatly increased central government control over local matters and restored some of the influence of the nobility. However some reforms remained in place and there was some positive change. For example:

- May 1881 – redemption fees were reduced and arrears were cancelled in the central provinces.
- May 1885 – the poll tax was abolished; inheritance tax was introduced, which helped shift the burden of taxation away from the lowest classes.
- The right of appeal to higher courts was allowed.
- The Peasants' Land Bank was established in 1883.
- Some reformist factory legislation was introduced.

SUMMARY

- From 1866, Alexander II adopted a more reactionary policy. Education reforms were partially undone, while policing was strengthened and the judicial system changed in an attempt to prevent political agitation and unrest.
- A renewed attempt to improve democratic consultation ended with the assassination of Alexander II in 1881. After this, Alexander III reversed many of his father's reforms and stepped up repression.

APPLY

APPLY YOUR KNOWLEDGE

Summarise the effect and extent of counter-reform in the years 1866–94 using the following table.

Reactionary changes	Positive Reforming signs and changes
1866–81	**1866–81**
From 1881	**From 1881**

EXAMINER TIP

Essays often require you to consider consequence. Think carefully about each reform to assess and evaluate its impact.

REVIEW

Was the tsarist autocracy crumbling or strengthening itself in the second half of the 19th century? Look back through the chapters so far and reflect on this breadth question. You could be asked to evaluate a question such as this in an exam.

To refresh your memory on Alexander II's military reforms, look back to Chapter 2.

IMPROVE AN ANSWER

AS LEVEL **'Alexander III was an entirely different type of ruler from Alexander II.' Explain why you agree or disagree with this view.**

Consider the following paragraph from a mediocre essay. This comes immediately after the introduction:

Answer

Alexander III became Tsar in 1881 after the assassination of Alexander II. All the reforming ministers which Alexander II had chosen to work with were dismissed, which shows how different Alexander III was. His motto was absolutism and nationalism, but Alexander II had been a Tsar liberator. Alexander II had been planning to provide some democracy in Russia but Alexander III would not allow the reform proposals even to be considered. Alexander III was certainly not a liberal like his father. He was a total autocrat. He showed this through his extremely repressive actions, which were a complete contrast to Alexander II's concern for reform. Alexander III's actions included the public execution of the conspirators involved in his father's assassination and the 'Manifesto of Unshakable Autocracy'. His reign was a disaster.

Consider this paragraph both as a whole and one sentence at a time and assess its strengths and weaknesses. Consider both the style and the content and comment on whether the allegations made are fair. Could you produce a better paragraph?

EXAMINER TIP

A good paragraph will begin with a comment, linked to the question, which is then supported by precise and specific information. Dates and detail help to convince and enable high exam marks.

REVIEW

Paragraph construction is very important in essays. What have you learnt about paragraph construction from this exercise? Look at any essay you have written and see if your paragraphs follow the formula suggested above. If not, could you rearrange your text to make them more analytical?

ASSESS THE VALIDITY OF THIS VIEW

A **LEVEL** 'The years 1870 to 1894 were exclusively a period of conservatism and reaction.' **Assess the validity of this view.**

a Complete the mind-map below to help you to answer this question. You might like to start by looking at aspects of the later years of Alexander II's and also of Alexander III's reign and then break each of these down to examine the extent of reaction and conservatism. Your map should extend to allow you to consider non-conservative aspects of the reign.

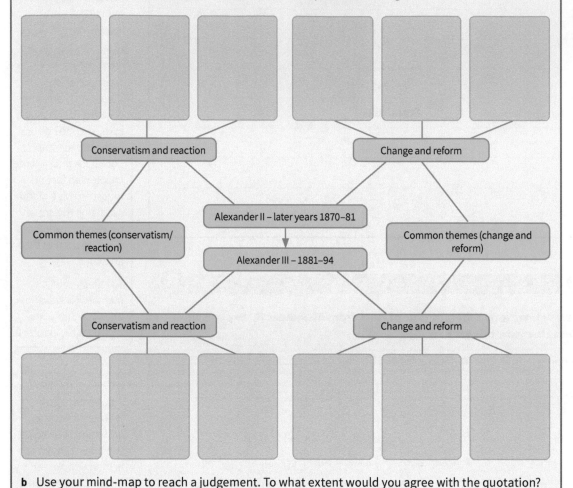

Conservatism and reaction

Change and reform

Alexander II – later years 1870–81

Common themes (conservatism/reaction)

Alexander III – 1881–94

Common themes (change and reform)

Conservatism and reaction

Change and reform

b Use your mind-map to reach a judgement. To what extent would you agree with the quotation?

EXAMINER TIP

Exam questions often contain a provocative word – in this case 'exclusively'. Use a diagram such as this to help you to formulate your judgement by clarifying the facts that support and challenge a statement visually.

Exam questions at A Level will cover a minimum 20-year span. This question therefore covers the latter end of Alexander II's reign as well as that of Alexander III.

KEY QUESTION

One of the Key Questions asks:

How important was the role of individuals?

Reflect on Alexander III as an individual and make a bullet point list of ways in which his personality and outlook shaped his actions.

- _____
- _____
- _____
- _____
- _____
- _____
- _____

EXAMINER TIP

You might find it helpful to go further and balance the importance of Alexander III as an individual against other factors shaping policies in the years 1881–94. This would be helpful for any discursive essay on the policies of Alexander III.

4 Political authority in action

Russification

Tsarist Russia was a multi-national empire inhabited by over 100 different ethnic groups. Although the Slavs in Russia, Ukraine and Belorussia comprised two thirds of the population, the remaining peoples were a mixture of many different nationalities, languages, religions and cultural traditions.

This posed a continual challenge for the tsarist autocracy, as the various ethnic groups asserted their distinctive identities.

Alexander II and the ethnic minorities

Alexander used a mixture of repression and concessions to maintain Russian control over the states of the Empire.

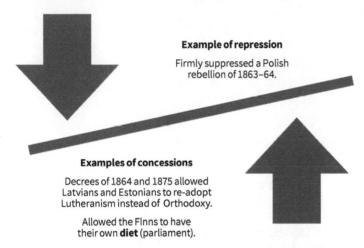

Example of repression

Firmly suppressed a Polish rebellion of 1863–64.

Examples of concessions

Decrees of 1864 and 1875 allowed Latvians and Estonians to re-adopt Lutheranism instead of Orthodoxy.

Allowed the Finns to have their own **diet** (parliament).

There was no systematic persecution of racial minorities. However, in the period of increased reaction towards the end of Alexander's reign, intolerance of national differences increased. For example, in 1876, the use of the Ukrainian language in publications or performances was banned.

Russification under Alexander III

Alexander III and his ministers extended this intolerance. They adopted a systematic policy of cultural 'Russification'. This sought to merge all the Tsar's subjects into a single nation with a feeling of shared identity, controlled by the autocracy and the Orthodox Church. The destruction of non-Russian national cultures was particularly marked in Poland and Finland but affected the whole of the Empire:

Finland – the 'diet' was weakened; the use of the Russian language was increasingly demanded; the Finnish postal service was abolished; and Russian coinage replaced the local currency.

Poland – the administration was changed; the Polish National Bank was closed; schools and universities had to teach almost all subjects in Russian; and literature had to be studied in a Russian translation.

The Baltic – the Baltic Germans had been loyal to Russia and had enjoyed special protection. However, Russification was aggressive here too. Russian was enforced in all state offices, at school and university level, and in the police force and judicial system.

Ukraine – the use of the Ukrainian language was limited, and all the theatres were closed.

In addition:

- Military conscription was extended into areas previously exempt and conscripts were dispersed to prevent national groupings developing in the army, where business was entirely conducted in Russian.
- Ethnic uprisings were crushed throughout the Empire.
- Adherence to the Orthodox Church was encouraged everywhere. Laws benefited people of Orthodox faith, while the freedom of non-Orthodox believers such as Catholics or Muslims was restricted.

Results of Russification

Russification had a de-stabilising effect:

- Unrest and mass disturbances broke out in many of Russia's provinces and districts. These were quickly suppressed.
- Resentment grew among the more educated and wealthy Finns, Poles and Baltic Germans in the west of the Empire. Here, national groups constantly petitioned the tsars for more liberties; local language books were secretly published; and some ethnic schools survived.

Supporters of Russification believed that it was necessary, in order to 'unite' the country, improve its administration and allow for modernisation. However, in the longer term, it seems to have failed in its objectives, increased national feeling among the ethnic nationalities and fuelled political opposition.

Anti-Semitism

The Jews were the racial group worst affected by Russian nationalism. There were around 5 million Jews within the Empire, mostly confined to the 'The Pale of Settlement'.

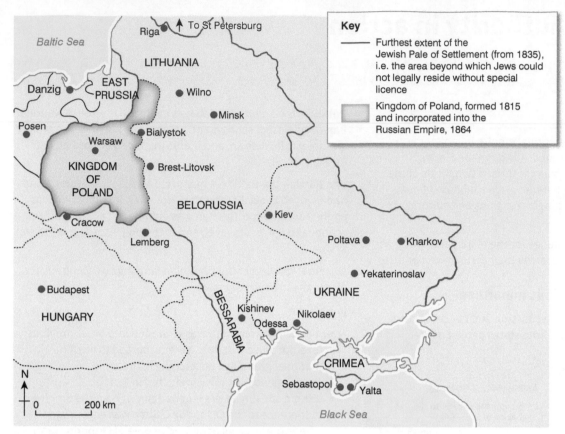

The Jewish 'Pale of Settlement'

Alexander II initially allowed wealthier Jews to settle elsewhere. However, following the Polish revolt of 1863–64, he withdrew his concessions and reduced the Jews' participation in town government. This action resulted in the growth of anti-Semitism.

Anti-Semitism was further encouraged in the reign of Alexander III. Both the Tsar and many of his ministers, including Pobedonostsev, were **anti-Semitic**. This was for both religious and political reasons, including a fear of Jewish involvement in the growing opposition movements.

The Jewish pogroms of 1881–84

In April 1881 a series of anti-Jewish **pogroms** broke out in Yelizavetgrad in Ukraine. The authorities did little to stop the attacks (the Okhrana may even have encouraged them). The violence spread to other Ukrainian towns and beyond, affecting around 16 major cities. Jewish property was burned, shops and businesses were destroyed, and there were many incidences of rape and murder. Many Jews fled into western Europe. The main outbreaks continued to 1884, but sporadic pogroms occurred after this.

Anti-Semitic legislation

In the years 1882–94 a series of laws were passed that increasingly curtailed the rights of Jews. These included the May Laws of 1882 which confined the Jews to living in ghettoes in towns and cities even within the Pale of Settlement and the 1886 decree that prevented Jews from running inns, by restricting their right to sell alcohol. Jews were even forbidden from participation in local elections in 1892.

The impact of anti-Semitism

- After the pogroms, many Jews left the country – either voluntarily or else forcibly expelled.
- From 1890, foreign Jews and Jews who had settled outside the Pale began to be deported from Russia.
- In 1891–92 around 30,000 Jewish artisans were expelled from Moscow.

The effect was to drive many of the Jews who remained towards revolutionary groups.

SUMMARY

- Alexander II governed Russia's diverse national and ethnic groups using both force and concessions.
- Under Alexander III, growing intolerance of national cultures hardened into a policy of Russification. Russian language and culture was imposed throughout the Empire.
- The Jews suffered particularly badly, as concessions made under Alexander II were withdrawn and discrimination against them increased.

APPLY

APPLY YOUR KNOWLEDGE

Indicate which ethnic groups were affected by the following measures.

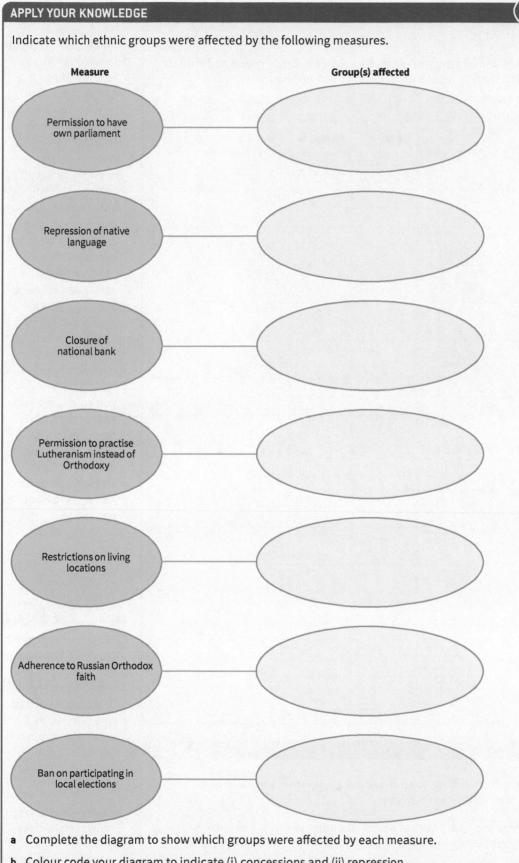

Measure	Group(s) affected
Permission to have own parliament	
Repression of native language	
Closure of national bank	
Permission to practise Lutheranism instead of Orthodoxy	
Restrictions on living locations	
Adherence to Russian Orthodox faith	
Ban on participating in local elections	

a Complete the diagram to show which groups were affected by each measure.

b Colour code your diagram to indicate (i) concessions and (ii) repression.

c Use this diagram to help you plan an answer to the question:

 'Policies towards the ethnic minorities in the reigns of Alexander II and Alexander III helped to strengthen the empire.' Explain why you agree or disagree with this view.

REVIEW

You may need to look back at previous chapters for contextual material on the strength of the Empire in this period.

EXAMINER TIP

Using the information in the diagram, consider how the policies might be considered to have strengthened the Empire. You would, of course, need to consider the ways in which they weakened the Empire also, in order to produce a balanced answer.

APPLY YOUR KNOWLEDGE

A LEVEL **How important were Alexander III's own ideas and ideology about other nationalities within the Russian Empire in strengthening the opposition to Tsarist autocracy from 1881 to 1900?**

One aspect of Alexander III's ideas and ideology would be his policies of Russification and anti-Semitism. Complete the following chart to record the details of these policies:

Russification policies		Anti-Semitic policies	
Date	Example	Date	Example

PLAN YOUR ESSAY

A LEVEL **'The ethnic minorities suffered more than any other group from the policies of Alexander III.'** **Assess the validity of this view.**

Use the information in this chapter and look back at Chapter 3 in order to assess the impact of Alexander III's reign on other groups in the population. Now write an introduction to this question. Remember that you will need to:

- show your view in relation to the statement
- make your understanding of 'ethnic minorities' and the other groups you intend to look at clear.

---

5 The growth of opposition to tsarist rule

 **RECAP**

Alexander II's reforms brought hope of further change. The increased freedom they provided allowed radical ideas to spread, and permitted a growth in the number of educated intellectuals with better opportunities to challenge the regime. The period of repression that followed reinforced the demands for change.

Moderate liberal opposition

Russia contained comparatively few literate and educated Russians, but their numbers and influence grew with the changes of the later 19th century. These intellectuals had the wealth and time to consider political matters; many had travelled abroad and despaired at Russia's political and social stagnation.

Some believed in philosophical ideas such as nihilism or anarchism. However most were either Westernisers or Slavophiles.

Westernisers	Slavophiles
Wanted Russia to adopt Western values.	Wanted to preserve Russia's culture and heritage as the country modernised.
Hoped for Western-style economic and military reform.	Preferred to retain the peasant-based society.
Favoured representative assemblies, with civil liberties and less power to the Orthodox Church.	Wanted to preserve the principles of the Orthodox Church.
Expressed their views through the *zemstva* and hoped that the increase in local decision-making would lead to greater national representation. Were disappointed by Alexander III's restriction of *zemstvo* powers in 1890.	Declined in influence in the 1890s, as industrialisation progressed and Western-style socialist movements began to grow.

The famine of 1891–92 marked a significant point in the growth of opposition. When the government failed to provide adequate relief, the *zemstva* largely assumed responsibility for improving conditions and the intelligentsia demanded a greater role in public affairs. By the mid 1890s there were renewed *zemstva*-led calls for a national body to advise the government.

By the 1890s, the intelligentsia were split. Some remained moderate liberals and continued to hope for a reform of tsardom; others were attracted by Marxist theory and socialism.

Radical opposition

More radical opposition developed among the younger generation. 'Nihilism' became popular in the 1860s, and in 1862, a group of students calling themselves 'Young Russia' published a manifesto, in which they argued for 'bloody and merciless revolution'. In 1863 'The Organisation' was set up by students at Moscow University and also called for radical reform. Student idealism and determination was heightened by the repression of the later 1860s onwards and the influence of radical socialist writers.

Radical thinkers

These included:

Nikolai Chernyshevsky: author whose writings suggested that the peasants should be leaders of revolutionary change.

Alexander Herzen: editor of the illegal radical journal *The Bell*, who advocated a new peasant-based social structure.

Mikhail Bakunin: anarchist and socialist who proposed that private ownership of land should be replaced by collective ownership, with income based on hours worked. Bakunin helped to introduce Marxism into Russia.

Sergei Nechaev: radical activist whose *Catechism of a Revolutionary* exhorted revolutionaries to be merciless in their aims.

The Tchaikovsky Circle

Set up in 1868–69 in St Petersburg, this was primarily a literary society which organised the printing, publishing, and distribution of scientific and revolutionary literature. It sought social (although not political) revolution. From 1872, it organised workers with the intention of sending them to work among the peasants in the countryside.

The Narodniks (Populists)

The idea of 'going to the people' became known as 'Narodnyism' or 'Populism'. In 1874 Pyotr Lavrov encouraged around 2000 young men and women, mainly from the nobility and intelligentsia, to travel to the countryside in order to exploit peasant discontent and persuade the peasantry that Russia's future depended on developing the peasant commune. However the peasants' ignorance, superstition, and loyalty to the Tsar ensured that the incomers were reported to the authorities. 1600 were arrested.

A second attempt to 'go to the people' in 1876 also failed and a series of show trials was held in 1877–78. Nevertheless, Narodnyism did spread radical opposition into the countryside, and showed the government the depth of feeling of its opponents.

'Land and Liberty'

This group, set up in 1877, continued the Populist tradition. Its members sought work within the peasant communes but more discreetly. Some carried out political assassinations (the head of the Third Section was murdered in 1878). They gained much public sympathy and sometimes talked with the *zemstva* in order to press for constitutional reform. However, the tsarist government failed to respond to the growing pressure for change.

In 1879 Land and Liberty split into two groups:

Tsarist reaction and the radical opposition after 1881

Following Alexander II's assassination, security and repression were increased. The Populist movement effectively ceased to exist, though some of its supporters managed to meet in secret and commit terrorist acts.

- Underground societies continued to translate and reproduce the writings of foreign socialists.
- Contact with radicals in exile and in the West was maintained.
- 1883 – Georgi Plekhanov (in exile in Switzerland) established the Emancipation of Labour group, which translated and arranged for Marxist tracts to be smuggled into Russia. Plekhanov suggested that revolutionaries should concentrate their activities among the workers in the cities, as it was the proletariat that would drive a socialist revolution. However he believed that the proletariat would first need to cooperate with the bourgeoisie to destroy autocracy.
- 1886 – students in St Petersburg tried to reform the People's Will.
- March 1887 – a group who had made bombs in order to assassinate Alexander III was arrested. Five members, including Lenin's elder brother, were later hanged.
- By 1890s – the growth of industrialisation led to the development of workers' organisations, illegal trade unions, Marxist discussion circles and other groups. These spread radical Marxist ideas more widely.

SUMMARY

- Alexander II's reforms set expectations for further change.
- When these expectations were not met, opposition to the tsarist regime grew.
- Much of the opposition was moderate, led by liberals seeking non-violent constitutional change. However, the onset of industrialisation in the 1890s brought the emergence of a more radical opposition, fuelled by Marxism. These radicals were prepared to use extreme methods to achieve their goals.

Land and Liberty split 1879

Black Partition

Wanted to share the black soil provinces of Russia among the peasants.

Worked peacefully among the peasantry.

Hoped to stimulate social change without violence.

Ceased to exist following arrests in 1880–81; some of its leaders turned to Marxism.

The People's Will

Bigger group than Black Partition.

Advocated violent methods, undermining government by assassinating officials.

Tried unsuccessfully several times to kill Alexander; finally succeeded in March 1881.

APPLY

APPLY YOUR KNOWLEDGE

EXAMINER TIP

Precise information on the various opposition movements will enable you to support answers to questions on the growth of opposition fully.

Here is a list of radical opposition groups and movements.

◯ Narodniks
_____
_____
_____

◯ Land and Liberty
_____
_____
_____

◯ The Organisation
_____
_____
_____

◯ Emancipation of Labour
_____
_____
_____

◯ Black Partition
_____
_____
_____

◯ People's Will
_____
_____
_____

◯ Tchaikovsky Circle
_____
_____
_____

a Write numbers in the small circles to order the groups chronologically.

b Give a one-sentence explanation of each on the lines provided. Try to include the group's ideology, aims and methods.

REVIEW

Reflect on why these opposition movements had limited success. Try to produce 1 or 2 generic reasons as well as a specific reason for the failure (or limited success) of each.

TO WHAT EXTENT?

 A LEVEL **To what extent was the emergence of opposition in Russia during the reign of Alexander III due to the influence of Marxism?**

Draw a mind-map which should bring together the various factors which influenced the development of opposition and show the connections between these. For example, whilst the Narodniks (Populists) were influenced by Marxist ideas, they were also the product of the Slavophile tradition.

REVIEW

Look back to Chapters 3 and 4 to identify other political reasons for the growth of opposition.

EXTRACT ANALYSIS

In the AS and A Level exam, you will be given 2 or 3 extracts to study. You will need to identify the arguments put forward in each extract and evaluate these, with reference to your own knowledge. This task helps you analyse related interpretations.

EXTRACT A

The reaction that began under Alexander III and continued into the reign of Nicholas II oppressed but did not destroy opposition to the tsarist regime. Indeed, despite greater police surveillance, opposition became more organised. A number of political parties, ranging from moderate reformers to violent revolutionaries, came into being. The government's policies of reaction and Russification combined to produce a situation in which many political and national groups were becoming increasingly frustrated by the mixture of coercion and incompetence that characterised the tsarist system. The rapid industrial growth in the 1890s had created a special problem. It had brought to the cities large numbers of peasants, who were attracted by the prospect of relatively well-paid factory work. When a depression followed in the first decade of the 20th century, it left many of these new industrial workers unemployed and angry. Their bitterness made them a serious threat to public order.

Adapted from Michael Lynch, *Reaction and Revolutions, Russia 1881–1924*, 1992

EXTRACT B

Russian political life before 1917 was overwhelmingly the preserve of social elites. The formal structures of government and bureaucracy were dominated by educated noblemen. The middle classes which were making their mark on the politics of Western Europe were much slower to emerge in Russia. In addition, the groups and individuals who manifested opposition to the autocracy came in large part from the same social background as those who made up the regime which they sought to reform or destroy. The ordinary people of the Russian Empire played almost no part in institutional politics, and it was revolt – whether threatened or real – which most forcefully reminded the patriarchal tsarist autocracy of their existence.

Adapted from Peter Waldron, *The End of Imperial Russia, 1855–1917*, 1997

EXTRACT C

Could the development of social forces – abundant and many-sided – be fitted into an autocracy? All Russian experience denied this possibility. It is certainly true, of course, that there is no contradiction between industrialisation and an authoritarian political system. On the contrary, industrialisation supplies its own, improved methods of social control. Yet, to suppose that an emerging capitalism, beset with social problems of great magnitude, could somehow be integrated into a fundamentally unchanged socio-political pattern, geared to an agrarian order, especially if the Tsar saw no need for change, was surely utopian.

Adapted from Lionel Kochan, *Russia in Revolution,* 1970

EXTRACT ANALYSIS

Consider the following A Level question:

 Using your understanding of the historical context, assess how convincing the arguments in Extracts A, B and C are in relation to the reasons behind the various types of opposition to tsarist rule in the reigns of Alexander III and Nicholas II.

a Read each extract in turn. For each:

- Summarise in your own words the argument it puts forward in relation to the question.

- Using your own knowledge, make a short list of bullet points to support or challenge the argument.

b Using your answers to **a**, plan your answer to the question.

Consider the following AS question:

 With reference to Extracts A and B and your understanding of the historical context, which of the extracts provides the more convincing interpretation of the opposition to tsarist rule in the reigns of Alexander III and Nicholas II?

a Read Extracts A and B in turn. For each:

- Summarise the interpretation in your own words.

- Using your own knowledge, complete the short list of bullet points below to support or challenge the argument.

Extract A: _____

_____

_____

_____

- _____

- _____

- _____

- _____

Extract B: _____

_____

_____

_____

- _____

- _____

b Using your answers to **a**, plan your answer to the question.

6 Economic and social developments

Economic change

The beginnings of state-promoted industrial growth

Industrialisation in Russia was largely driven by the State, to try match the economic development of Western Europe. Following emancipation in 1861, von Reutern, Alexander II's Minister of Finance (1862–78), produced a series of reforms to boost the economy and drive industrial growth:

- The Treasury and taxation were reformed; tax-farming was abolished.
- A state bank was set up in 1860.
- Import duties (tariffs) were reduced from 1863 to promote trade.
- Government subsidies were offered to railway entrepreneurs.
- Foreign investment was encouraged by state-guaranteed annual dividends.
- Joint-stock companies were made subject to new regulations to protect investors.
- Government support was offered for development of the cotton and mining industries.

Strengths of the reforms	Limitations of the reforms
The reforms encouraged investment and enterprise.	Russia's economy remained comparatively weak.
Foreign technical expertise and capital supported industrial expansion.	A third of all government expenditure went on the repayment of debts.
The railway network expanded markedly.	The Russian currency (the rouble) remained unstable.
Although textiles were still the dominant industry, new developments took place, including coal and oil extraction, iron mining and iron working.	Tariff reductions led to a decline in government revenues, so these were raised again from 1878.
There was an annual average growth rate of 6% during Reutern's term of office.	The peasantry was still poor and the domestic market small.

The industrial 'take-off'

Vyshnegradsky was Finance Minister from 1887 to 1892. In order to raise capital, reduce the budget deficit and boost home production, he:

- introduced a high tariff of 30% of the value of imported raw materials
- negotiated loans and increased indirect taxes
- mounted a drive to swell grain exports.

Between 1881–91, grain exports increased by 18%, as a percentage of total Russian exports. By 1892, the Russian budget was in surplus. However, the peasants suffered badly – they had to pay the taxes and give their grain to the State. Many were left with no reserve stores for the winter. In 1891–92 bad harvests brought widespread famine and thousands died. Vyshnegradsky was dismissed in 1892.

Witte was Finance Minister from 1892 to 1903. He:

- maintained protective tariffs, heavy taxation and forced exports
- sought further loans and presided over a huge increase in foreign investment
- encouraged engineers, managers and workers from Western Europe to oversee industrial developments and advise on planning and techniques.

By 1897 Russia had become the world's fourth-largest industrial economy. Exports and foreign trade increased, although Russia still exported mainly grain rather than industrial goods, and the railway network was vastly expanded.

Agriculture and the land issue

Agriculture changed little following emancipation. Grain production remained low compared to Western Europe. Although the government established Land Banks for both peasants (1883) and nobles (1885) to facilitate land purchase, their benefits were limited.

Although the richer peasants (*kulaks*) responded positively to Vyshnegradsky's export drive, increasing overall agricultural production in the 1870s and 80s, the famine of 1891–92 showed that most peasants had too little land to prosper.

Social divisions: nobles, landowners and position of the peasantry

As industrialisation spread, Russia's traditional land-based society slowly began to move towards one more focused on money, capital and wages. Although society was still strongly divided before 1895, a new middle class and urban working class began to emerge.

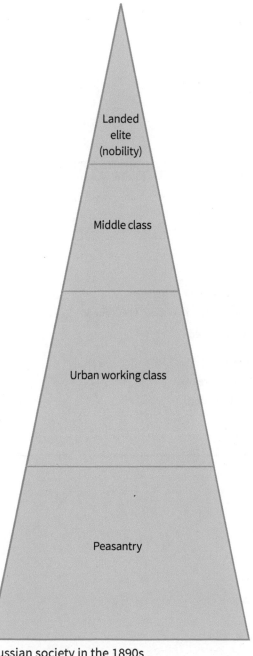

Russian society in the 1890s

The landed elite (former serf-owners)

- Small but diverse group, mostly of noble status.
- Personal landholdings had declined since emancipation.
- Might be employed in:
    - professional activities (e.g. university professors)
    - business, commerce, transport or industry
    - state service
    - *zemstva* and/or the provincial governorships.
- Often retained much of their previous wealth and status.

The middle class

- Growing class, resulting from urban/industrial expansion and education.
- Included bankers, doctors, teachers and administrators.
- Enterprises included building railways or starting factories.
- Lower middle class could become managers or workshop owners and traders.

The urban working class

- Around 2% of the population by the 1890s:
    - Some peasants worked in towns temporarily, returning to the villages at peak farming times.
    - Others became urban workers or worked in migrant groups building railways.
- Growing class – by 1864 one in three of the inhabitants of St Petersburg were peasants by birth.
- Suffered poor living and working conditions (despite some reforming welfare legislation in the years 1882–90).

The peasantry

- Richer peasants (*kulaks*)
    - did well out of emancipation
    - bought up land and employed labour
    - might buy grain from poorer peasants in autumn and sell it back at a profit in spring.
- Poorer peasants
    - suffered more after emancipation
    - became landless labourers, often in debt
    - experienced varying but generally poor living standards
    - experienced poor health and low life expectancy.

The cultural influence of the Church

Russia was a strongly Orthodox state (70% of the population were Orthodox believers). Religion and superstition were an integral part of peasant culture. Priests had close ties with both village and State; they were expected to read out imperial manifestos and decrees and to inform the police of any suspicious activity.

The Church also possessed strict censorship controls and the Church courts judged moral and social 'crimes' and awarded punishments to the guilty.

The government was highly conscious of the power of the Orthodox Church.

- 1862 – an Ecclesiastical Commission was established to look into the Church organisation and practice.
- 1868 – reforms were introduced to improve the education of priests.
- Under Alexander III and Minister for Education Delyanov, the Orthodox Church was given increased control over primary education.
- Alexander III's Russification policy promoted Orthodoxy throughout the Empire. It became an offence to convert from the Orthodox faith, or to publish criticisms of it. Radical sects were persecuted. Some regions saw enforced baptisms while thousands of Muslims, Catholics and pagans were converted to Orthodoxy.

There is, however, evidence that the control of the Orthodox Church over people's lives was weakening. It was becoming less relevant for workers in the industrialising towns, and even in the countryside superstition was sometimes stronger than trust in the priests. Some liberal clergy wanted to regenerate the Church and reform its relations with the tsarist State but their demands were suppressed by senior conservatives including Pobedonostsev.

SUMMARY

- From the 1860s, state-driven financial policies and the encouragement of overseas investment and expertise helped to bring about industrialisation and economic progress.
- Emancipation and industrialisation also brought social change.
- The Orthodox Church maintained a strong cultural influence and was used by the State to control the population.

KEY CHRONOLOGY

Political developments

1855	Alexander II becomes Tsar
1856	Crimean War ends
1861	Emancipation Edict
1863–64	Polish rebellion
1866	Attempted assassination of Alexander II
1881	Alexander II assassinated; Alexander III succeeds
1889	Land Captains established

Economic and social developments

1883	Peasants' Land Bank created
1885	Nobles' Land Bank created
1891–92	Famine
1894	Death of Alexander III

⚙ APPLY

APPLY YOUR KNOWLEDGE

Look back at the work of Vyshnegradsky and Witte. Create a balance between successes and failures.

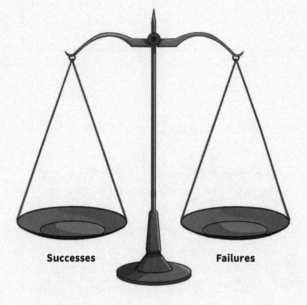

Successes   Failures

EXAMINER TIP

This activity should enable you to answer any question requiring an evaluation of the economic policies of Vyshnegradsky and Witte or of economic development in Russia in the late 19th century.

REVIEW

You might like to reflect on the weighting of the successes and failures. Should the scales remain perfectly balanced or tip in one direction?

 'A time of impressive economic and social progress.' Assess the validity of this view of the years 1881 to 1894 in Russia.

a To answer this question you will need to think about 'progress' in its broader sense. Use the chart below to help organise your arguments:

Examples of progress
- •
- •
- •

No progress (i.e. things that stayed much the same)
- •
- •
- •

Examples where matters got worse
- •
- •
- •

b Now decide the argument you will adopt and write a suitable introduction to this question.

REVIEW

If you had to answer an exam question which asked about economic and social progress in the second half of the 19th century, you would also need to include material from the reign of Alexander II – most notably the emancipation of the serfs. Look back to Chapter 2 to revise this. You could follow up your work above by writing a plan for this broader essay.

EXAMINER TIP

Remember, an introduction should make your view clear. In order to do this, you will also need to explain what you understand by 'progress' and perhaps break this down into economic and social 'progress'.

KEY QUESTION

Consider the Key Question:

What was the extent of social change?

a Copy the pyramid diagram from page 33 and for each section of society add 2 bullet points to show change and 2 to show continuity.

b Below your diagram explain

- which section of society changed the most and

- which changed the least.

REVISION SKILLS

Change and continuity

Having studied Section 1, make a large revision chart on a sheet of A3 paper. For each chapter you should select and record no more than 6 key facts. These should be the most important in the chapter.

When you have filled in the first row, try to identify the main points of change and continuity in the two rows below.

Topics	The Russian autocracy in 1855	Alexander II, the Tsar Reformer	The autocracy of Alexander II and Alexander III	Political authority in action	The growth of opposition to tsarist rule	Economic and social developments
Key facts to remember						
Change						
Continuity						

AS Level essay sample answer

REVISION PROGRESS

REVIEW

On these Exam Practice pages you will find a sample student answer for an AS Level essay question. What are the strengths and weaknesses of the answer? Read the answer and the corresponding Examiner Tips carefully. Think about how you could apply this advice in order to improve your own answers to questions like this one.

 'Alexander II only introduced reforms because of Russia's defeat in the Crimea.' Explain why you agree or disagree with this view.

25 marks

Sample student answer

Alexander II is known as the 'Tsar Reformer' because of the many changes he introduced in Russia. He carried out the emancipation of the serfs, military, local government, judiciary, education and censorship reforms as well as stimulating economic development. Many of Alexander's reforms were linked to Russia's defeat in the Crimea, but there were other reasons, too. These include the pressure from intellectuals, Alexander's own background, and economic motives.

Russia's failures in the Crimea deeply humiliated the country. Reliance on an army of conscripted serfs, outdated weaponry and poor transport systems, added to military incompetence at the top, all contributed to defeat. The peasants were not committed to the fight and discipline was so harsh, they were often more scared of their officers than the enemy. The war also disrupted supplies of food within Russia and brought a large number of peasant uprisings.

Alexander proclaimed the emancipation of the serfs in 1861. He said, 'It is better to abolish serfdom from above rather than wait until it abolishes itself from below.' Freeing the serfs was intended to promote economic growth. Free peasants would travel to towns to work in industry and would also provide a market for industrial goods. However, this did not happen. Under the Emancipation Edict, the freed peasants had to pay redemption dues for 49 years, and stay in their village 'mir' until they had done so. This prevented free movement and although industry did begin to take off and emancipation led to new forms of army conscription, the reform did not really tackle the issue of failure in the Crimean

REVISION SKILLS

AS essay questions will contain a quotation advancing a judgement followed by 'Explain why you agree or disagree with this view'. Read page 7 of this Revision Guide for details on how to master the essay question.

EXAMINER TIP

The introduction provides an overview of Alexander II's reforms and provides good detail both on the reforms and on the 'other' reasons for them. It could, however, have given a clearer 'view'.

EXAMINER TIP

The second and third paragraphs show good knowledge, but they need to be more closely linked to the question. Each should begin with an opening sentence that relates directly to the question – this will prevent the paragraph becoming too descriptive. The third paragraph in particular is largely a narrative account of the emancipation of the serfs with some add-on comment on its failure to tackle the issues of the Crimean War. There is reference to the need to promote economic growth, but the argument needs to be much clearer – if the Crimean War was not the only motivation behind emancipation, what were the other reasons?

War. There were actually more peasant risings after it was passed than before.

Alexander's military reforms, introduced by the ex-Crimean army general, Dmitry Milyutin, were a direct result of defeat. Conscription was extended to all classes and the length of service reduced from 25 to 15 years. Military colonies were abolished and harsh punishments banned. This reform was accompanied by improvements in training, weaponry and communications, and military service was no longer given as a punishment. Although the upper classes were generally able to buy their way out of conscription, these reforms definitely addressed problems thrown up by the Crimean War.

Some of Alexander's other reforms can also be linked to the Crimea. Economic reforms promoting investment in industry and the expansion of Russia's railway network, for example, could be seen as a response to the problems of the Crimea. Through his finance minister, Reutern, Alexander also encouraged the development of banks and foreign investment to help promote economic growth.

However, not all of Alexander's reforms were directly linked to defeat in the Crimea. For example, the reforms of local government and the setting up of the zemstva were more the result of emancipation than the Crimean defeat. Although the welfare services provided by the zemstva and Alexander's education reforms and reduction in censorship may have had helped to modernise society, the link is not direct. Similarly, Alexander's legal reforms, which introduced a jury system, seem to have been more driven by a desire to compete with the West than to address failure in war.

Other motives for reform were therefore important. Intellectuals had been pressing for reform for some time. They were divided between the Westernisers and Slavophiles and generally argued that Russia was failing its people morally. Alexander's own background was also important. He had travelled the Empire and served on his father's Council of State and several serfdom committees before he had even become tsar. Pressure from his brother, the Grand Duke Konstantin and his aunt, the Grand Duchess Elena, is also likely to have had a major effect on Alexander II, as well as the enlightened bureaucrats with which he was surrounded at court. Russia's debts and rural poverty were also not new and the need to industrialise was becoming crucial even without the war failure.

EXAMINER TIP

This paragraph begins well, answering the question directly. However it then lists the military reforms. The paragraph would have done better by exploring specifically why the reforms were implemented – e.g. to make the army less expensive and more efficient, in an attempt to avoid repeating the humiliations of the Crimean War.

EXAMINER TIP

This paragraph shows knowledge of Alexander's economic reforms, and attempts to link them to the question. However the link is asserted rather than argued. It does not address the question as to why investment in industry and the railway network, or the development of banks and foreign investment, should be seen as a result of the Crimean War rather than other economic factors.

EXAMINER TIP

This paragraph offers balance to the argument and correctly identifies some areas that were not directly the consequence of failure in the Crimean War.

EXAMINER TIP

Again, this paragraph provides balance, directly answering the question by setting out the 'other' motivations behind Alexander's reforms, with good supporting detail.

It is true that the war encouraged Alexander's reforms, but it was more a catalyst than their sole cause. Defeat by the West probably gave more weight to the arguments of the Westernisers who argued that Russia needed to adopt Western ways if it was to equal its rivals. Reforms that had been discussed for some time became more urgent and the opposition of the nobility to change was undermined by the failures of the noble army officers. Whilst it cannot be said that Alexander II 'only' introduced reforms because of Russia's defeat in the Crimea, it can be agreed that he introduced reforms when he did largely because of the Crimean defeat.

EXAMINER TIP

This is a strong conclusion. The first sentence demonstrates depth of understanding and the whole is well-focused and shows judgement.

OVERALL COMMENT

This essay would achieve Level 4. For the most part, it is well-focused, effectively organised and clearly written, with analytical comment and a range of accurate supporting information showing a good understanding. Whilst the conclusion has hints of Level 5 in its judgement, other parts are more descriptive and there is some assertion.

OVER TO YOU

Give yourself 25 minutes to answer this question on your own. Consider this checklist when reviewing your answer:

☐   Did you provide details on Alexander II's reforms due to the Crimean War?

☐   Did you also provide details on his reforms due to other reasons?

☐   Did you write a conclusion showing a judgement on whether you agree or disagree with the statement?

Go back and look at pages 10–18 to help refresh your knowledge on Alexander II's reforms.

2 The collapse of autocracy, 1894–1917

7 Nicholas II and the challenge to autocracy

RECAP

Political authority and government under Nicholas II, 1894–1904

Nicholas II had little interest in politics. However he believed in his God-given right to rule. Tutored by Pobedonostsev, he set out to maintain the autocracy, continue the policy of Russification and suppress demands for reform.

Demands for change and the government reaction

The years after 1894 were a time of serious unrest in Russia.

- Following the government's failure to deal with the famine of 1891–92, support for reform had broadened.

- New outbreaks of trouble in universities were firmly crushed by the Okhrana.

- In the years 1902–07 there were widespread disturbances in both towns and countryside. These were fiercely suppressed by Stolypin.

- Industrial strikes escalated in the towns.

- In 1904, Father Gapon formed an 'officially approved' trade union, the Assembly of St Petersburg Factory Workers, to 'channel' workers' grievances.

The Russo-Japanese War

In January 1904 the Japanese attacked the Russian naval base at Port Arthur. Plehve (Minister for Internal Affairs 1902–04) encouraged the Tsar to launch a swift and successful war to divert attention from the unrest at home. There was an initial outburst of patriotism, but a series of defeats in the war led to further opposition. Plehve was assassinated in July 1904.

There were renewed cries for a representative National Assembly Duma and in November 1904 the new Minister for Internal Affairs, Mirsky, agreed to invite *zemstvo* representatives to discussions in St Petersburg. However Nicholas refused to allow representative government. He only conceded an expansion of the *zemstva*'s rights.

The events and outcome of the 1905 Revolution

KEY CHRONOLOGY

The 1905 Revolution

1904 Dec	The Russians surrendered Port Arthur to the Japanese	**Sept**	*Zemstvo* Conference demanded a Duma elected by universal suffrage
1905 Jan	A strike began at the Putilov Iron Works		Wave of strikes in Moscow
Jan	Bloody Sunday – Father Gapon led a peaceful march to the Winter Palace to petition the Tsar for reform. The demonstration was broken up by military force; hundreds were killed or wounded	**Oct**	A soviet (workers' council) was set up in St Petersburg and directed a General Strike
Feb	Grand Duke Sergei, the Tsar's uncle, was assassinated; Nicholas promised an elected consultative assembly		The Tsar signed the 'October Manifesto' promising a constitution, civil rights and the establishment of a State Duma (representative assembly) with the power to approve laws
			The General Strike was called off
March–May	Numerous illegal trade unions were formed	**Oct–Dec**	Mutinies, strikes and peasant unrest were firmly repressed; leaders of the St Petersburg Soviet were exiled to Siberia
June	Mutiny on the battleship *Potemkin*		
Aug	Treaty of Portsmouth concluded the Russo-Japanese War	**Dec**	The Moscow revolt was crushed. Peasant unrest continued

The era of the Dumas

The new constitution

In accordance with the Tsar's October Manifesto, a new constitutional arrangement was drawn up as follows:

Lower chamber (State Duma)
- Deputies elected through **indirect voting** (weighted in favour of nobility and peasants).
- Deputies elected for five-year term.

Upper chamber (State Council)
- Deputies half elected by *zemstva*, half appointed by the Tsar.
- Representatives of nobility from the major institutions.

The two houses had equal legislative power and all legislation also had to be approved by the Tsar.

Government (Council of Ministers under the Prime Minister)
- Appointed by the Tsar and responsible to the Crown, not the Duma.

The Fundamental Laws

On 23 April 1906, five days before the first Duma met, Nicholas issued a series of Fundamental Laws. These reasserted his **autocratic** power and his right to:

Rule by decree in an emergency or when the Duma was not in session

Direct foreign relations and declare war

Veto legislation

Tsar's rights

Overturn verdicts given in a court of law

Dissolve the Duma

Control the Orthodox Church

Command Russia's army and navy

Political groupings

There were to be four Dumas between 1905 and 1917. The main political parties which stood in the elections were:
- Social Democrats (SDs) – divided since 1903 between the Bolsheviks and Mensheviks.
- Social Revolutionaries (SRs)
- Trudoviks (Labour group)
- Kadets (Constitutional Democrats)
- Octobrists (Union of 17 October)
- Progressives
- Rightists – including the Union of the Russian People
- Nationalist groupings.

The first two Dumas were dominated by Kadets and left-wing groups; by the Third Duma, Octobrists were in the majority; the Fourth Duma predominantly consisted of those on the right-wing.

The four Dumas

There were four Dumas between 1906 and 1914.

The First Duma, May–July 1906:
- was boycotted by the Bolsheviks, SRs and the extreme right
- was mostly radical-liberal; a third were peasants
- requested radical reforms; when these were refused, it passed a 'vote of no confidence' in the government
- was dissolved in July (the hard-line Stolypin became Prime Minister)
- sent 200 delegates to Vyborg and tried to organise protest. This failed and its leaders were imprisoned.

The Second Duma, February–June 1907:
- was more left-wing, because the Bolsheviks, Mensheviks and SRs participated
- opposed the government
- was dissolved after refusing to support Stolypin's agrarian reform; some delegates were arrested and exiled
- changed in composition when Stolypin (illegally) increased the representation of the gentry.

The Third Duma, November 1907–June 1912:
- agreed to the majority of government proposals but disputed some reforms
- was suspended twice in 1911.

The Fourth Duma, November 1912–17:
- was largely ignored by the government.

Political developments by 1914

By 1914, autocracy appeared to have recovered:
- Stolypin had ruthlessly restored order in the countryside.
- Reform of agriculture meant that the agrarian situation had improved.
- The Duma's influence had become almost non-existent.
- Revolutionary groups had been weakened, partly because of police activity and exiles and partly because of their own internal quarrels.
- Pan-Slavism and, as war grew closer, patriotism, revived.

However, problems remained:
- From 1912, labour troubles resurfaced.
- The influence on the Tsar and Tsarina of the mystical 'faith-healer' Rasputin damaged Nicholas' reputation among his traditional supporters.

SUMMARY

- Demands for change, fuelled by Russian failures in the Russo-Japanese War, culminated in the '1905 Revolution'.
- Nicholas II's 'October Manifesto' promised constitutional reform and national representation through a State Duma.
- In practice the Duma's powers proved limited and the autocracy maintained control.
- Despite some development politically and economically along Western lines, Russian government remained reactionary and oppressive.

APPLY

APPLY YOUR KNOWLEDGE

a Annotate the timeline of the years 1900–14 in Russia below. You should indicate the key turning point of 1905 in red and include the events of both January and October of that year.

- 1900
- 1901
- 1902
- 1903
- 1904
- 1905
- 1906
- 1907
- 1908
- 1909
- 1910
- 1911
- 1912
- 1913
- 1914

b When your timeline is complete, use this information to address the question:

 To what extent was the survival of tsardom in the years 1900 to 1914 due to repression?

You might start by colour-coding your timeline to record when there was repression and when concessions were granted.

HOW SUCCESSFUL?

 How successful was opposition to tsarist authority in the years 1894 to 1914?

It is important that you make clear the criteria against which you will assess 'success'. One way of doing this would be to identify the aims of the various opposition groups. These aims might be referred to in the opening sentences of the paragraphs of your essay – so providing constant reference to the question and building up an argument.

a Consider the aims of the

- moderate liberal opposition.
- radical socialist opposition (SRs).
- radical Marxist opposition (SDs).
- other groups – e.g. ethnic minority groups.

b Plan an answer to this essay by looking at the aims and successes of each group.

c Write the first sentence of each paragraph (excluding the introduction and conclusion) in full. These first sentences should show the direction of your argument.

REVIEW

To remind yourself of some of the broader reasons for the survival of tsardom, look back at Section 1.

EXAMINER TIP

A full answer would require consideration of both long- and short-term factors.

However, specific reference to developments in the years specified in the question would be expected for high exam marks.

EXAMINER TIP

Remember that it is impossible to talk of 'success' without defining what success might look like. There are various ways of doing this and in some essays it might be more appropriate to assess success in a different way, for example, in relation to the strength of the country or the well-being of its people.

REVIEW

You might like to remind yourself of the different types of opposition in Russia by looking back at Chapter 5. You will be able to find further detail on opposition groups in Chapter 10.

EXTRACT ANALYSIS

Consider the following extract.

EXTRACT A

Nicholas had been blessed with neither his father's strength of character, nor his intelligence. That was Nicholas' tragedy. With his limitations, he could only play at the part of an autocrat, meddling in (and in the process, disrupting) the work of government, without bringing to it any leadership. He was far too mild-mannered and shy to command any real authority among his subordinates. Being only five feet seven inches tall and feminine in stature, he didn't even look the part of an autocrat. Yet it would be a mistake to assume that Nicholas' failure stemmed from a fundamental 'weakness of will'. Beneath his docile exterior, Nicholas had a strong sense of his duty to uphold the principles of autocracy. He stubbornly defended his autocratic rights against the encroachments of his ambitious ministers and even his own wife. It was not a 'weakness of will' that was the undoing of the last Tsar but, on the contrary, a wilful determination to rule from the throne, despite the fact that he clearly lacked the necessary qualifications to do so.

Adapted from Orlando Figes, *A People's Tragedy,* 1996

a Underline the key words of the extract that will help you to identify the overall argument which the extract puts forward about Nicholas II as Tsar.

b Underline (in a different colour) any references that it might be useful to quote in an answer, to illustrate this argument.

c Using the information you have identified above, write a paragraph in response to the question: Assess how convincing the argument in this extract is in relation to the tsardom of Nicholas II. In this paragraph you should show your understanding of the argument with reference to the extract only.

EXAMINER TIP ◎

This activity provides practice in the first step towards answering a full AS or A Level question. The next step would involve applying your own knowledge of the historical context to the arguments in the extract in order to respond to the instruction, 'how convincing'. You will get an opportunity to practise this skill in Chapter 12.

REVISION SKILLS

Complete the following chart to reflect the state of Russia in 1914.

Area	Strengths	Weaknesses
Position of Tsar		
Government		
Opposition		
Agriculture		
Industry		
International		

REVIEW ↻

You can add to your chart as you study Chapters 8, 9 and 10.

8 The economic development of Russia to 1914

From the mid 1890s, Russia's economy underwent a major transformation.

Developments in business and industry

Under Witte (Finance Minister 1892–1903):

- railway trackage almost doubled
- coal output in southern Russia nearly quadrupled
- a new rouble was introduced, backed by the value of gold, to strengthen the currency
- foreign investment soared
- industrial growth was strongly state-managed; capital, technical advisers, managers and skilled workers were sought from overseas.

Even after Witte, the State remained directly involved in economic growth to 1914.

By the early 20th century the State controlled 70% of Russia's railways and held extensive holdings in heavy industry. From 1903–13, the government received more than 25% of its income from its industrial investments.

The capital was used to:

- fund public works
- develop Russia's infrastructure
- develop mines, oil fields and forests for timber
- re-equip the army after the Russo-Japanese War.

From 1894–1913 Russia's annual growth rate was more than 8% per annum. This growth was particularly marked in the railways and heavy industry.

Railways

The State bought out smaller private railway companies and extended lines. The railway-building programme:

- helped open up the Russian interior, allowing more extensive exploitation of Russia's raw materials, and linked grain-growing areas to the Black Sea ports, assisting the export drive
- stimulated the development of the iron and coal industries
- permitted the development of new industries along the length of the expanding rail network
- caused a fall in transport costs, which in turn reduced the price of goods
- raised funds for the government from freight charges and passenger fares.

Although the rate of railway building slowed after 1908, by 1913 Russia had the second largest railway network in the world.

Heavy industry

In the early stages of industrial growth, the lighter industries, particularly textiles, had led the way. However, Witte wanted to increase heavy goods production. To do this, he concentrated production in key areas and developed large factory units of over 1000 or so workers. This pattern continued to 1914.

The policies produced some impressive results:

- By 1914, Russia was the world's fourth-largest producer of coal, pig-iron and steel.
- Russian oil production trebled from 1885 to 1913; Russia became not only internally self-sufficient, but also able to compete with the USA on the international market.
- Russia became the world's second-biggest oil producer and fourth in gold mining.
- Light industry and textiles also grew.
- By 1914 Russia was the world's fifth-largest industrial power (after Britain, USA, France and Germany).

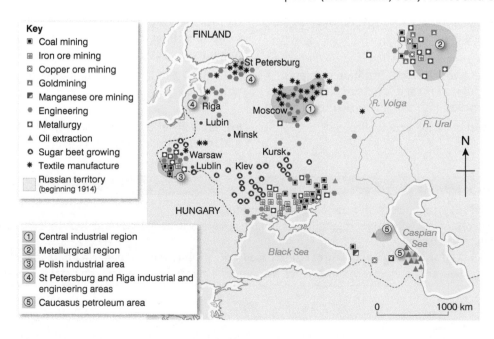

Key
- ▣ Coal mining
- ▦ Iron ore mining
- ▨ Copper ore mining
- ▤ Goldmining
- ▧ Manganese ore mining
- ● Engineering
- ▢ Metallurgy
- ▲ Oil extraction
- ○ Sugar beet growing
- ✳ Textile manufacture
- ▨ Russian territory (beginning 1914)

1 Central industrial region
2 Metallurgical region
3 Polish industrial area
4 St Petersburg and Riga industrial and engineering areas
5 Caucasus petroleum area

Developments in agriculture

The rural economy provided a livelihood for 80–90% of the population. However it was largely ignored in favour of industrialisation until 1906, when Stolypin was appointed Minister for Internal Affairs.

Before 1906, most farming had remained small-scale, in the hands of former serfs and state peasants. The earlier problems continued:

- The peasants were tied to their local *mir* by redemption dues and were heavily taxed.
- Estates continued to be subdivided by the *mir* as sons inherited. This, coupled with the rising population, meant that there was less land for each peasant to farm.
- Agricultural practices and tools were still traditional and grain yields were poor compared to the USA and Britain.

However some peasants, the *kulaks*, had prospered since emancipation by buying up land and farming more efficiently. Stolypin aimed to produce more *kulaks*, partly to win their loyalty to the tsarist regime and partly to develop the economy by improving agriculture, and creating an internal market for the products of industry.

Stolypin's land reforms

Stolypin wanted individual peasants to own their land, holding it in one piece, rather than as a collection of scattered strips; he believed they should be able to develop it as they wished, without interference by the *mir*. Accordingly, from 1903, the *mir* ceased to be responsible for paying taxes on behalf of the peasants. After 1906, Stolypin introduced a series of laws to reform agriculture.

KEY CHRONOLOGY

Stolypin's land reforms

1906	More state and Crown land was made available for peasants to buy
	Government subsidies to encourage settlement in Siberia were increased
	Peasants were granted equal rights in their local administration
	Peasants could leave the *mir*
	Collective ownership of land by a family was abolished; the land became the property of an individual
	A peasant could consolidate his strips of land into a compact farm
	A new Peasants' Land Bank was established to help fund land ownership
1907	Redemption payments were finally abolished
1910	Communes which had not redistributed land since 1861 were dissolved

Positive results of Stolypin's agrarian reforms	Limitations of Stolypin's agrarian reforms
Larger farms were developed as land was transferred and poorer peasants sold out to the more prosperous ones.	Changes in the land tenure arrangements took a long time to process.
Hereditary ownership of land by peasants increased.	By 1913, less than half of applications for the consolidation and hereditary tenure of individual farms had been processed.
Grain production rose annually; by 1909, Russia was the world's leading cereal exporter.	By 1914, only around 10% of land had been transferred from communal to private ownership and 90% of peasant holdings were still in traditional strips.
The emigration incentives moved 3.5 million peasants away from over-populated rural districts to Siberia, and helped Siberia to develop into a major agricultural region.	In 1914, 50% of the land remained in the hands of the nobility.
Kulaks prospered and became a rural elite.	Probably fewer than 1% achieved *kulak* status. Many others had to leave their farms and become migrant labourers.

SUMMARY

- Between 1894 and 1914, the Russian economy was transformed.
- State-managed economic development resulted in an annual growth rate of over 8% and by 1914 Russia was the world's fifth-largest industrial economy.
- From 1906 Stolypin's reforms to agriculture greatly increased grain production and began a fundamental transformation of Russian rural life. However changes were slow to take root, and the measures were not completely successful.

APPLY

APPLY YOUR KNOWLEDGE

a Create a mind-map to show the ways in which the development of the Russian economy, in the years 1894–1914, was linked to the growth of the railways.

b Use your diagram to help you plan an essay to answer either of these questions:

 AS LEVEL 'The growth of the Russian economy, in the years 1894 to 1914, was dependent on the expansion of the railway network.' Explain why you agree or disagree with this view.

 A LEVEL How significant was investment in railway construction in Russian economic growth in the years 1894 to 1914?

EXAMINER TIP

Your answer would also require a balance of other factors which helped to promote economic growth.

REVIEW

Look back at Chapter 6 to prompt your thinking on the other factors promoting economic growth in Russia.

ASSESS THE VALIDITY OF THIS VIEW

A LEVEL 'Problems of land ownership and use remained acute throughout the years 1894 to 1914.' Assess the validity of this view.

a This essay question addresses change and continuity so it would be helpful to complete the following diagram before you begin:

> **Land ownership and use 1894–1914**

Positive changes	**Continuity**	**Negative changes**

EXAMINER TIP

In addressing change and continuity, you should ensure you provide precise examples across the full date range of the question to support your comments. Take care not to slip into narrative, though, by focusing on the beginning and end of the period.

b Use your diagram to help you to decide whether problems remained acute, got better or got worse.

c Write a conclusion to this essay, offering a judgement on the view given.

REVIEW

You might find it helpful to look back to Chapters 2 and 6 for further contextual information on the position of the peasantry and the land issue.

IMPROVE AN ANSWER

 A LEVEL 'Between 1890 and 1914, Russia overcame its economic backwardness and became a strong and prosperous country.' Assess the validity of this view.

Here is an introduction to the question:

In 1855, Russia had lagged behind the West, as shown by its defeat in the Crimean War. It had many resources, but these had not been developed, largely because of its difficult geography. It had poor communication systems and a traditional social structure. This meant that serfs had worked the land, while noble landowners did not want to be involved in business. This all changed in the 1890s when industry really began to take off. By 1914 Russia was the world's fifth-largest industrial power, the world's fourth-largest producer of coal, pig-iron, steel and gold and the second-biggest oil producer. Even agriculture had developed, thanks to the work of Stolypin, even if his reforms were not complete in 1914.

a Review what you have learnt about writing an introduction and then identify the weaknesses and strengths in this introduction.

b Write an improved version of this introduction.

REVIEW

See Chapter 4, page 26 for further advice on how to write a good introduction to an essay.

EXAMINER TIP

The introduction should lead the reader into your essay so that what follows makes sense. Parts of this introduction are very detailed, yet not all is well-focused or clearly explained. Is your own version better?

KEY QUESTION

One of the Key Question asks:

How and with what results did the economy develop and change?

Now you have studied the growth of the economy in the years 1855–1914 (in this chapter and Chapter 6), you should be able to fill in the following revision chart which will help you to address this Key Question:

Developments 1855–1914	How (by what means) did this change?	What were the results of the change?
Industry		
Agriculture		

Leave room to add some further points in the results column, after you have studied Chapter 9.

9 Social developments to 1914

 RECAP

Developments in working and living conditions in towns

Between 1867 and 1917, Russia's urban population quadrupled from 7 to 28 million, as peasants arrived to seek work in the new factories and workshops. By 1914, three quarters of the population of St Petersburg were peasants by birth, and half the city's population had arrived in the previous 20 years. In Moscow the atmosphere was of a peasant village, where livestock roamed the streets.

Conditions in the towns were grim. Workers often lived in barrack-like buildings provided by the factory-owners, which were dangerously over-crowded and lacked sanitation; privately rented accommodation was little better. Rents were high and some people slept in the factories or on the streets. Wages varied but generally failed to keep pace with inflation. Women were especially poorly paid.

Between 1885 and 1912 a series of decrees attempted to improve conditions. These included:

- reducing working hours
- enforcing the use of contracts
- banning the employment of children under 12
- providing sickness and accident insurance
- increasing educational provision.

Political discontent spread easily in towns and cities. Strike activity was rare before and immediately after the events of 1905 but it escalated again in 1912 and in 1914 there were over 3000 stoppages. The government repressed these activities violently.

Developments in working and living conditions in the countryside

Conditions for peasant farmers did not improve substantially and there was still widespread rural poverty, despite Stolypin's agricultural reforms.

- Although the *kulak* class prospered, life became harsher for the poorest peasants.
- Many had to leave their farms and look for seasonal farming work or industrial employment. A minority migrated to Siberia.
- The commune remained at the heart of rural life.
- Living standards varied but in general were poor.
- Despite health care improvements provided through the *zemstva*, many peasants were classified unfit for military service. Mortality rates remained high and there were too few doctors.
- There were not enough teachers; most peasants received only basic education and in 1914 there was still around 60% illiteracy.
- The peasantry therefore remained at the bottom of the social ladder.

Social divisions

Russian society was becoming more complex as economic changes took place. However it was still strongly divided between the small noble class and the peasant majority.

The nobility

Around a third of nobles' land was transferred to the urban middle class or peasants between 1861 and 1905, with varying effects:

Continuity and change in the lives of nobles

Negative changes	Little change	Positive changes
Some nobles struggled to meet debts.	Taxes were not redistributed, so for most nobles, their income and way of life remained largely unchanged.	Some did well out of land distribution, consolidating the best land for themselves at minimum cost, and thus increasing income.
Some nobles proved unable to adapt to more modern business practices in managing their estates.	Nobles retained influence in government office, provincial governorships, the military and the *zemstva*.	Some prospered by turning to industrial enterprises and financial speculation.

The middle classes

Russia's traditional legal structure had been based on four groups – nobles, merchants, clergy and peasantry. However as demand for managers and professionals grew, the emerging 'middle layer' increased in influence. Its members expressed their views through the *zemstva* and the town and state dumas.

Social mobility began to occur as nobles' sons chose to join the business world or peasants' sons rose to become middle managers or factory managers.

Workers and peasantry

Population growth and economic development most affected the workers and peasantry.

In the countryside, traditional attitudes persisted; most peasant protest before 1914 was the result of traditional grievances. But by 1914 political activism was starting to take effect.

In urban areas, former peasants gradually lost their former identity. Instead they associated with others with whom they lived and worked, sharing grievances and becoming targets for political agitators. The large and discontented urban working class would provide the impetus to overthrow the regime in 1917.

Nobles' sons

↓

Businessmen / capitalists
Professionals (e.g. doctors, teachers, civil engineers)
Factory owners,
Managers

↑

Peasants' sons

Cultural changes

Culturally, Russia in 1914 might have appeared little changed. The fundamental patriarchal structure of Russian society, based on family ties, was still in place. Nevertheless, economic and political developments had led to cultural change:

- There were new opportunities for women, e.g. for education, or for independence though factory work.
- Improvements in education had reduced illiteracy (though secondary and higher education remained elitist).
- Books and publications increased; many writers and artists addressed problems in Russian society through their works.
- Censorship was relaxed from 1905, producing the 'silver age' of culture.

However, some aspects of Russian culture remained unchanged. The Orthodox Church continued to influence both government and community. There was an outpouring of patriotism and support for the Tsar when war broke out in 1914 and all social groups rallied to defend the Russian Motherland.

SUMMARY

- The urban population grew dramatically by 1914 as peasants migrated to the cities.
- Living and working conditions were harsh in both countryside and towns.
- Socially, Russia remained divided between nobles and peasantry; however the new middle class was growing in size and influence.
- By 1914, cultural changes were becoming apparent but Russian culture remained predominantly traditional.

APPLY

APPLY YOUR KNOWLEDGE

It is often said that 'living standards' were poor for the 'ordinary Russian people' at the beginning of the 20th century. However, not all 'ordinary people' experienced the same conditions. To understand 'living standards' better, use the information in Chapter 9 to complete the following chart:

	Income/possessions/ ability to live above subsistence level	Quality of life: living conditions, working conditions
Urban workers		
Peasants		

Based on your findings, would you argue that the peasants or the urban workers were better off?

EXAMINER TIP

The word, 'people' is rarely helpful in essays. It is far better to reflect on specific groups of people. In this exercise, you will find that even a category such as 'peasants' is quite broad and encompasses a variety of different experiences. Always try to be as specific as possible in your own writing.

REVIEW

Look back to Chapter 9 to consider how the lives of peasants and urban workers changed in the years 1855–94.

ASSESS THE VALIDITY OF THIS VIEW

 'The key social development of the years 1894 to 1914 was the change in the position of the peasants.' Assess the validity of this view.

a When asked to address a 'key' development, it is important to consider what other developments occurred and to create a hierarchy of importance. Here are some of the social developments of the years 1894–1914. Rank them in order of importance and add a brief comment alongside each to explain your choice.

- The *zemstva* provided increased amounts of health care.
- Half the population of St Petersburg arrived in the 20 years up to 1914.
- Many peasant farmers migrated to Siberia.
- Substantial amounts of nobles' land was transferred to townsmen or peasants.
- The *kulak* class prospered in the countryside.
- Many peasants' sons rose to become factory managers.
- There were new opportunities for women.
- Many nobles turned to industrial enterprises and financial speculation.

b Use your findings to make a judgement as to whether you agree or disagree with the premise of the quotation.

c Look again at Chapter 9 to select additional information that would be relevant in answer to this question, then plan and write the full essay.

EXAMINER TIP

Prioritisation is essential when analysing the importance of events and developments. Try also to show how such events and developments interrelate in your essay answers.

REVIEW

Look back to Chapter 6 to remind yourself of social divisions and developments up to 1894.

EXTRACT ANALYSIS

EXTRACT A

Between 1850 and 1914, Russian society saw both the creative and the destructive sides of modernisation. Slowly, Russia's social structures were assuming the familiar features of capitalism and the traditional social and economic structures of Russian society lost vitality. By 1900 many peasants and many nobles had abandoned their traditional way of life. It is no coincidence that in 1905, the tsarist government came close to collapse. Did this mean that the government had failed to solve the dilemma of modernisation? Not necessarily. To survive it had to preserve the traditional bases of its support. Yet to modernise, it had to allow the emergence of new social and economic forces. Eventually the government would have to start looking for support amongst these new groups without alienating its traditional supporters. This was a delicate political manoeuvre. The crises of the first decade of the twentieth century suggest that the Russian government lacked the insight or the skills needed to initiate success. The Russian government was drifting in very dangerous waters.

Adapted from David Christian, *Imperial and Soviet Russia*, 1986

This extract might be used in a question asking you to assess how convincing its argument is in relation to the importance of social change in undermining tsarist autocracy.

a To identify the author's argument:
- Try to pick out the part of the extract that puts forward a distinctive view on social change and the tsarist autocracy – this will be the overall argument.
- Identify any other views/interpretations/arguments in the extract.

b To assess how convincing the author's argument is:
- Find evidence that would support the overall argument and evidence that would contradict it.
- Find evidence to support or criticise the other views/interpretations/arguments.

c Now try writing an answer to the question which assesses how convincing the argument in the extract is, with reference to your contextual own knowledge.

_____

_____

_____

_____

_____

_____

_____

_____

_____

_____

IMPROVE AN ANSWER

Consider the extract opposite. In an extracts question at AS Level you will be asked which of two extracts is the more convincing about the same theme. Here, you will be looking at the beginning of an answer on one extract – and since each extract will be shorter than those at A Level, you should read only the first part of the extract given opposite (as far as 'forces' in line 8).

The answer below is responding to an AS extracts question that asks whether the extract provides a convincing interpretation of the impact of economic factors on social change.

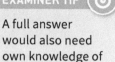

Answer

The extract's interpretation is that Russian society experienced the 'creative and destructive' sides of modernisation in the years 1850 to 1914. The extract says that Russian society was becoming more capitalist and peasants and nobles were abandoning their traditional way of life at this time. This shows the impact of economic factors on social change and how everything was breaking down. The extract also says that these changes caused the 1905 Revolution when the government nearly collapsed and that to modernise, the government 'had to allow the emergence of new social and economic forces.' So, this extract clearly shows the impact of economic factors on social change and its interpretation is very negative.

> **EXAMINER TIP**
>
> A full answer would also need own knowledge of context to support and criticise views.

Explain your views in the space provided below:

a Does this answer begin/end well?

_____

_____

_____

_____

_____

b What would you judge to be the overall strengths and weaknesses of this analysis (based on the extract only)? Could you improve on it?

_____

_____

_____

_____

_____

_____

_____

_____

_____

_____

_____

_____

_____

_____

10 Opposition: ideas and ideologies

The growth of liberal opposition to 1905

As education spread and a stronger middle class emerged, the number of liberals pressing for more representation and the rule of law grew.

KEY CHRONOLOGY

Growth of liberal opposition

1895	Nicholas rejected a petition from the Tver Zemstvo, calling for a national advisory body, but *zemstva* demands for an all-class *zemstvo* at district level and a National Assembly continued
1896	Shipov tried to set up an 'All-Zemstvo Organisation'
1899	Some radical liberals established the Beseda Symposium, which met secretly to discuss reform. This led the liberal movement
1900	Hundreds of liberals were dismissed from the elected boards of the *zemstva*
1903	Struve helped found the Union of Liberation. This pushed for a constitutional system through which urban workers could campaign legally to improve their conditions
1904	The Union invited representatives of the *zemstva* and other professional societies to a grand meeting, and arranged a series of banquets for the liberal elite

The liberals had limited political influence before 1905 but they contributed to the pressure for change. They achieved one of their aims in 1905, when the State Duma was established.

The development of socialism and the emergence of the Social Revolutionary Party

The Great Famine of 1891–92 highlighted the need to reform the rural economy. Students began to champion a new form of Populism, involving violent protest.

In 1899, the Social Revolutionary Party (SRs) was founded. This was a loose organisation comprising groups with a wide variety of views. Its most influential theorist was Chernov, a law graduate and editor of the party journal, who became leader of the SRs in the Second Duma of 1907.

> **Social Revolutionary Party**
>
> Combined Marxist teaching with Populist ideas in a specifically 'Russian' revolutionary programme
>
> Tried to unite peasants and workers (the 'labouring poor') in the fight against autocracy and for land redistribution
>
> Attempted to stir up discontent in the countryside and strikes in the towns
>
> Tried to disrupt government by political assassinations (2000 between 1901 and 1905)
>
> Played an active part in the 1905 Revolution
>
> Assassinated the Prime Minister, Stolypin, in 1911

The party developed a wide national base. 50% of its support came from the urban working class, but there was a large peasant membership. However, the secret police infiltrated the movement and over 4000 were sentenced to death between 1905 and 1909, although only a little over a half were actually executed.

The influence of Marxism and the development of the Social Democratic Party

Marxist theories became more attractive to many Russian intellectuals from the late 1890s as industrialisation took place.

In 1898 a new Social Democratic Workers' Party (SDs) was created out of various Marxist groups. It shared some basic principles with the SRs but adopted a different approach.

> **Social Democratic Workers' Party**
>
> Believed that:
> • the working classes had been, and were being, exploited by their masters
> • the future of Russia would be the product of the class struggle
> • impetus for change had to come from the working men themselves
>
> Split 1903

> **Bolsheviks (majority)**
> Led by Lenin
> Believed in:
> • a centralised and disciplined organisation of professional revolutionaries
> • total dedication to revolution not compromised by political alliances

> **Mensheviks (minority)**
> Led by Martov
> Supported by Trotsky
> Believed in:
> • a broad party with a mass working class membership
> • co-operation with liberal parties

At the 1903 Second Party Congress Lenin carried the vote in favour of having a centralised party structure, and claimed (falsely) that his supporters were in the majority. Between 1903 and 1906 divisions between Bolsheviks and Mensheviks hardened so that by 1906 there were effectively two separate Social Democratic parties.

The extent of opposition between 1905 and 1914

Trade unions

Trade unions were legalised after the 1905 Revolution. However, they were unable to achieve a great deal in the face of continued government repression.

- Hundreds of trade unions were closed down or denied registration after 1906.
- In 1912, the shooting of unarmed demonstrators at the Lena Goldfields Massacre triggered a wave of strikes but these were forcefully repressed.
- In practice, only 12% of enterprises experienced a strike.

Other opposition groups

The concessions of 1905–06 helped to reduce opposition.

- The moderate liberal opposition tried to co-operate with the Duma system, in the hope of further constitutional reform.
- After 1905 there was no single, strong opposition among the nationalities.
- Between 1905 and 1914, the revolutionary SR and SD parties were weakened by:
  - the exile of their leaders
  - the rivalry between the SR and SD parties
  - the split within the SDs
  - ideological divisions and disagreements over how to respond to the 1905 defeat
  - the success of the secret police in breaking revolutionary cells
  - organisational difficulties, including lack of finance and a shortage of secret printing presses.

The Bolsheviks succeeded in sending six workers' deputies to the Fourth Duma in 1912 and their newspaper, *Pravda* (*The Truth*) enjoyed a high circulation. However, their overall support was limited. Membership declined after 1905 and both SR and SD organisations survived at a local level only.

> **SUMMARY**
>
> - Liberal opposition grew to 1905, when it achieved its aim of national representation through the State Duma.
> - Meanwhile growing interest in socialism and Marxism gave rise to two new opposition parties, the SRs and the SDs.
> - These parties stirred up unrest and organised strike action.
> - However, before 1914, opposition in Russia was generally weak and labour protest was contained by repression and occasional concessions.

APPLY

APPLY YOUR KNOWLEDGE

On the left are the names of some important individuals who influenced or led opposition movements. On the right are the three main strands of opposition in the years 1894–1914. Match the individual to the group and give a one-sentence explanation of his contribution to the movement.

Lenin
_____
_____
_____

Chernov
_____
_____
_____

Trotsky
_____
_____
_____

Struve
_____
_____
_____

Martov
_____
_____
_____

Moderate liberal opposition

Social Revolutionary Party

Social Democratic Workers' Party

EXAMINER TIP

It is important to be aware of the role of key individuals in developments. Knowledge such as this should help you to write more precisely in your essays.

REVIEW

Look back to Chapter 5 in order to understand the origins of the different strands of opposition and the intellectual ideas which influenced them.

HOW IMPORTANT?

A LEVEL **How important were the opposition groups that emerged in Russia from the late 19th century in forcing governmental change in the years 1905 to 1914?**

a In the centre of a large sheet of paper, draw a box containing a two-bullet point explanation of governmental change between 1905 and 1914.

b Create a spider diagram around this box showing as many factors as you can think of, which helped to produce this governmental change after 1905.

c Highlight all the factors which relate to opposition groups.

EXAMINER TIP

Your diagram should help you to see the importance of the opposition groups (relative to other factors) visually and so help you to reach a judgement.

KEY QUESTION

Consider the Key Question:

How important was the role of groups and how were they affected by developments?

To answer this, it would help to chart the emergence of the various opposition groups in relation to the broader political, economic and intellectual developments in the years 1894–1914.

a Look at this horizontal timeline of the three key periods 1894–1900, 1900–05, 1905–14. Record the key political, economic and social developments in the first 2 rows.

b In the 3rd row, write down the intellectual developments.

c In the 4th row, give the dates, names and key aims of the various opposition movements.

	1894–1900	1900–05	1905–14
Political			
Economic and social			
Intellectual ideas			
Opposition movements			

d Can you see a link between the growth of opposition movements and the political and economic situation? What intellectual ideas were affecting opposition movements at this time? Write 1–2 paragraphs giving a summary of how opposition groups were affected by the key developments of 1894–1914.

PLAN YOUR ESSAY

AS LEVEL **'Opposition to Tsarist government failed in the years 1905 to 1914 because it was not united.'**

Explain why you agree or disagree with this view.

In order to plan your answer effectively you will need to look at a variety of reasons as to why opposition to tsarist government failed.

a Create a mind-map of reasons.

b Colour all the reasons that link to the lack of unity between the opposition groups in one colour.

c Use 3 different colours to 'group' your remaining reasons, e.g. repressive actions; tsarist concessions; any other factors.

d Now use your colour-coded diagram to plan and write an answer to the question above.

REVIEW

If you found it challenging to note the key political, economic and social events and intellectual ideas, you should revisit Chapters 7–9 to consolidate your knowledge.

REVISION SKILLS

You may find that making a visual diagram like this helps you to structure and remember key facts. Alternatively, you may find it more helpful to create a straight timeline with dates and events, using colour-coding to distinguish between types. Choose the revision method that works best for you – or use a variety of methods, to suit your own revision style.

EXAMINER TIP

Grouping factors in a suitable way helps clarify the argument in an essay and grouping is often more successful than seeing each factor separately.

REVIEW

Look back to Chapter 7 for details of tsarist concessions and the Duma experiment.

11 Political authority, opposition and the state of Russia in wartime

 **RECAP**

The political problems of tsardom in wartime

The Tsar's decision to go to war in August 1914 was greeted by a wave of patriotism.

- Strike activity stopped.
- The Duma voted **war credits**, then dissolved itself to avoid 'unnecessary politics' in wartime.
- 'St Petersburg' was renamed 'Petrograd'.
- A huge army (the Russian 'steam-roller') was quickly assembled.

However, heavy defeats at Tannenburg (August) and the Masurian Lakes (September) reignited discontent.

Wartime government and organisation

By the end of 1914, there were disputes over the organisation of the war effort. This resulted in some changes.

> **KEY CHRONOLOGY**
>
> **Wartime organisational changes**
>
> **1914 July** The government established 'military zones' where civilian authority was suspended
>
> **Aug** The *zemstva* established a 'Union of Zemstva' to provide medical facilities
>
> **1915 May** Factory owners and businessmen established a Congress of Representatives of Industry and Business to help co-ordinate production
>
> **June** The Zemstva Union joined with the cities to form the All-Russian Union of Zemstva and Cities (Zemgor). Chaired by Prince Lvov, it wanted to help in the war effort, but as it was never allowed any direct influence, it became a focus for liberal discontent
>
> **Aug** Some deputies from the Fourth Duma organised themselves into the 'Progressive bloc' and demanded that the Tsar establish a 'government of public confidence'. Nicholas refused

In September 1915, Nicholas appointed himself Commander-in-Chief of the Russian Army and Navy. This was a terrible decision. Nicholas lacked military experience and had already lost the confidence and support of the Russian General Staff. Moreover, he was even further distanced from developments in Petrograd and open to blame for all military failures.

In Petrograd, Rasputin wielded still more power and the Tsarina was accused of sabotaging the Russian war effort. Liberals and socialists began to demand changes in government. In December 1916, Rasputin was murdered by the Tsar's nephew, Prince Yusupov, and an accomplice, in an attempt to save the monarchy's reputation. Nicholas was horrified but he continued to ignore opposition demands.

The economic and social problems created by the war

The war had a disastrous effect on the Russian economy.

Military issues

- The government mobilised around 15 million men between 1914 and 1917 but soldiers lacked weapons, warm clothing and suitable footwear.
- By mid 1916, the munitions situation had improved, but most experienced officers had been killed.
- By the end of 1916, morale in the army had plummeted – 1.5 million deserted in 1916 alone.

Internal problems

The war brought mounting domestic problems:

- Military spending soared as the war progressed.
- Production slumped – yet greater production was needed to supply the army.
- German and Austro-Hungarian invasions of Poland and other parts of western Russia weakened industrial capacity.
- Naval blockades and the loss of overland routes severely damaged trade.
- The government paid low prices for grain and other goods, so many peasants hoarded their produce.
- Railways were requisitioned for the troops, so foodstuffs were often unable to reach the cities, where conditions became increasingly hard. The cost of living rose by 300% and thousands nearly starved. In January 1917, strike activity in Moscow and Petrograd escalated.

The opposition to the autocracy and the political collapse of February/March 1917

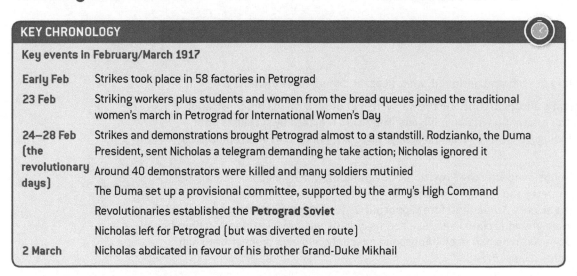

KEY CHRONOLOGY

Key events in February/March 1917

Early Feb	Strikes took place in 58 factories in Petrograd
23 Feb	Striking workers plus students and women from the bread queues joined the traditional women's march in Petrograd for International Women's Day
24–28 Feb **(the revolutionary days)**	Strikes and demonstrations brought Petrograd almost to a standstill. Rodzianko, the Duma President, sent Nicholas a telegram demanding he take action; Nicholas ignored it
	Around 40 demonstrators were killed and many soldiers mutinied
	The Duma set up a provisional committee, supported by the army's High Command
	Revolutionaries established the **Petrograd Soviet**
	Nicholas left for Petrograd (but was diverted en route)
2 March	Nicholas abdicated in favour of his brother Grand-Duke Mikhail

The development of Russia under the Dual Power of 1917

The Provisional Government

Grand-Duke Mikhail rejected the tsardom and passed political authority to a 'Provisional Government', under Prince Lvov. Its members represented the elites; they were men who had favoured constitutional monarchy.

The Provisional Government was intended to be temporary until elections could be held for a new Constituent Assembly. However it was accepted by the old tsarist civil service, army officers and police.

The Petrograd Soviet

The mass of workers, soldiers and peasants regarded the Provisional Government as a committee of the wealthy and preferred to be led by the Petrograd Soviet.

The Petrograd Soviet was elected by the capital's soviets. It was dominated by Mensheviks and SRs, with a few Bolsheviks. It was mainly composed of radical socialist intellectuals.

Alexander Kerensky (the only member of both the Provisional Government and the Petrograd Soviet) negotiated an agreement that the two bodies would work together, sharing '**Dual Power**'.

The Provisional Government promised:

- amnesty for political prisoners
- basic civil liberties
- the abolition of legal discrimination based on class, religion and nationality
- the right to organise trade unions and to strike
- elections to a Constituent Assembly.

The Soviet accepted these promises and did not demand land redistribution or the **nationalisation** of industry.

The Provisional Government also:

- allowed freedom of religion and the press
- abolished the death penalty at the front
- replaced the tsarist police force with a 'people's militia'
- dismissed Provincial Governors, giving their work to the *zemstva*.

The Dual Power in action

The alliance between liberals and radicals was marred by disagreements.

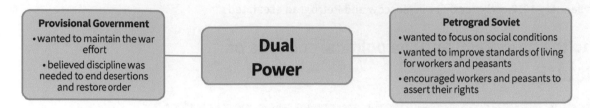

Workers' strikes and military desertions continued, while peasant disturbances increased.

The Provisional Government's efforts to continue the war were met by an anti-war demonstration in April 1917 which led to the resignation of two ministers. They were replaced by socialists from the Petrograd Soviet, including Kerensky as War Minister. In July 1917, Prince Lvov was replaced as Chairman by Kerensky.

The upper classes were disillusioned with the Provisional Government, which failed both to win the war and to protect their property and maintain order during the 'July Days', when riots, involving Bolsheviks, broke out in the streets. Some therefore supported General Kornilov, Commander-in-Chief of the army, who mounted a right-wing coup in August. Kerensky, who had initially supported Kornilov, panicked and released Bolsheviks who had been imprisoned after July, allowing them arms to halt Kornilov's advance. The coup collapsed.

By summer 1917, there was little support for the Provisional Government. Food supplies were chaotic. Pay and conditions were deteriorating. The continuation of the war and the government's failure to redistribute land led to suspicions that the 'bourgeois' government was postponing greater democracy in order to preserve its own power.

SUMMARY

- The war produced new political and economic problems, which culminated in the February/March Revolution of 1917.
- A liberal-dominated Provisional Government was established, which was forced to share authority with the socialist Petrograd Soviet in a system of 'Dual Power'.
- Disagreements between liberals and radicals meant that this arrangement was unstable. Unrest continued and by summer 1917 the Provisional Government had lost most of its support.

APPLY

APPLY YOUR KNOWLEDGE

Create a horizontal flow chart of developments in February/March 1917. Below each development, provide a comment on its importance for the collapse of tsarist autocracy. Use a colour to identify the 'turning point' in this sequence of events.

EXAMINER TIP

Although an A Level exam essay on the revolution would span 20 years or more, the events of February/March 1917 are likely to require close examination.

REVIEW

Consider how the events of February/March 1917 link to the breakdown of the tsarist autocracy after 1900 by looking back at Chapters 7 and 10.

ASSESS THE VALIDITY OF THIS VIEW

 'The collapse of tsarist authority in March 1917 was due to the First World War.' Assess the validity of this view with reference to the years 1894 to 1917.

a In order to ensure breadth coverage of the years addressed in the question, it might be helpful to break this essay down into 3 chronological sections. Use the following to consider the points you will need to cover:

Causes of diminishing tsarist authority	1894–1904	1905–14	1914–March 1917
Factors linked to the Tsar himself			
Factors linked to the growth of opposition			
Other factors, e.g. economic; social; military			

EXAMINER TIP

Looking at developments chronologically is sometimes necessary, although special care should be taken to avoid narrative. In this essay, it would probably be preferable to start with the 3rd column, looking at the impact of war on tsarist authority, and then reflect back on the ways in which that authority had already been diminished.

b Highlight points that you feel are particularly important and consider which you will wish to emphasise in your answer.

c Write an introduction to this essay which summarises these key factors and gives your judgement on the question.

REVIEW

For further detail about the influences on tsarist authority from 1894, look back at Chapters 7 and 10.

KEY QUESTION

Consider the Key Question:

How did opposition develop?

Complete the diagram to show the political, economic/social and military developments of the war years that contributed to the growth of opposition and would eventually ignite the spark of revolution in Russia.

1915

Political:

Economic and social:

Military:

1916

Political:

Economic and social:

Military:

1914

Political:

Economic and social:

Military:

1917

Political:

Economic and social:

Military:

War!

REVISION SKILLS

Divide a large sheet of paper into 6. Use the following section headings:

- Government and political authority
- Opposition
- Economy
- Society and culture
- Ideas and ideology
- Individuals and groups

In each section of your paper, write no more than 12 key facts to summarise the changes between 1894 and 1917. When you are satisfied with your chart, you might like to type it up and print off a copy for reference. You could repeat this activity for each section of your Specification. (There are 2 for AS and 4 for A Level.)

12 The establishment of Bolshevik government

Lenin's return and the growth of Bolshevik support

Lenin returned to Russia on 3 April 1917. His 'April Theses' demanded the following (often summed up as 'peace, bread, land'):

- Power should be transferred to the soviets.
- The war should be ended immediately.
- All land should be taken over by the state and re-allocated to peasants by local soviets.

Lenin also proposed that the Petrograd Soviet should refuse to co-operate with the Provisional Government. He argued that to allow the middle classes to continue in power would only delay the proletarian revolution.

Initially, the Bolsheviks' response to his reappearance was mixed.

- Some thought that his radical proposals would do more harm than good.
- Some believed that it would be unrealistic to oppose the Provisional Government as the Bolsheviks were still in a minority among the socialists.

By the end of April, Lenin had convinced the majority of the Central Committee of the Bolshevik Party. In July, Trotsky too decided to support the Bolshevik cause fully.

However:

- In June, the First 'All-Russian Congress of Soviets' passed an overwhelming vote of confidence in the Provisional Government.

- Uncontrolled rioting during the 'July Days' was blamed on the Bolsheviks; Lenin fled to Finland and other Bolshevik leaders, e.g. Trotsky, were imprisoned.

After their part in the **Kornilov coup** of August, the Bolsheviks' reputation rose and their support grew massively.

- In September, they won a majority in the Petrograd Soviet (they already controlled the Moscow Soviet), and Trotsky became chairman.
- By early October, membership stood at 200,000 (against 23,000 in February); the party was producing 41 newspapers and had a force of 10,000 Red Guards in the Petrograd factories.

From mid September, Lenin demanded (from Finland) that the Bolshevik Party's Central Committee should stage a revolution and seize power. On 15 September the Committee voted against this:

- Zinoviev and Kamenev feared that Russia was not yet economically ready for revolution. They did not want action until after the Provisional Government's promised elections.
- Trotsky wanted to work through the Petrograd Soviet and wait for the Congress of Soviets which was scheduled for 26 October. He hoped to win the support of all socialist parties for a soviet government without having to resort to violence.

The Bolshevik seizure of power, October 1917

KEY CHRONOLOGY

Bolshevik seizure of power, 1917

7–9 Oct	Lenin secretly returned to Petrograd to try to persuade the Central Committee to take power Kerensky sent some of the more radical army units out of Petrograd. The Soviet set up a 'Military Revolutionary Committee' (MRC), to defend the city
10 Oct	Lenin persuaded the Central Committee to vote for an armed rising. (The vote was 10–2, with Zinoviev and Kamenev opposed.)
24 Oct	Kerensky tried to close two Bolshevik newspapers, and raised the bridges linking the working-class areas to the centre of Petrograd. The Bolsheviks used this as an excuse to act
25 Oct	Kerensky left Petrograd for the front, hoping to gain support from loyal troops. The remaining members of the Provisional Government met in the Winter Palace. They were still there when armed Bolshevik supporters, coordinated by Trotsky, entered the palace. They were arrested

The consolidation of Bolshevik government, October–December 1917

On 26 October, the Second 'All-Russian Congress of Soviets' opened. Not all delegates approved the coup (even the Bolshevik Zinoviev and Kamenev opposed it); however the Congress voted overwhelmingly for a socialist government.

The majority of seats for a new executive committee went to Bolsheviks and more extreme left-wing SRs. In protest, many 'moderate' Mensheviks and right-wing SRs walked out of the Congress. This left a Bolshevik and left-wing Social Revolutionary coalition in control.

The executive committee established the 'Soviet of People's Commissars' (**Sovnarkom**) as the new government. All its members were Bolsheviks; Lenin was Chairman, Trotsky was Commissar for Foreign Affairs and Stalin was Commissar for Nationalities.

Lenin immediately announced a series of decrees:

27 October
Decree on peace
Decree on land
→
November
Workers' control decree
Nationality decree
New legal system (with elected people's courts)
Sex discrimination outlawed
→
December
Military decree
Decrees on the Church
Nationalisation of banks

Early decrees of the Bolshevik government, 1917

An armistice in November 1917 ended Russia's involvement in the war.

The suppression of opposition to the Bolshevik government, October–December 1917

The establishment of control

The Bolsheviks' position was still precarious:

- Many bankers refused to provide finance, and civil servants refused to work for them.
- Kerensky had assembled an army which outnumbered Lenin's forces.
- In Moscow and other cities there was fierce fighting between supporters of the Provisional Government and the Bolshevik revolutionaries.
- Railway and communications workers went on strike in protest against the emergence of a one-party government.

By the end of the year Kerensky's troops had defected or been held back on the outskirts of the city and the Bolsheviks dominated the major towns and railways. Nevertheless, large areas of the countryside were still outside Bolshevik control. It would take years of civil war before the Communists could claim full victory.

Other means of combating opposition

Lenin used a variety of methods to establish Bolshevik control:

- a propaganda campaign against political and 'class' enemies – particularly the bourgeoisie
- closure of anti-Bolshevik newspapers
- a **purge** of the civil service
- the establishment of a new secret police body, the **Cheka**.
- imprisonment of leading Kadets, right-wing SRs and Mensheviks.

He allowed elections to a Constituent Assembly to take place in November. However when the Bolsheviks received just under a quarter of the votes, he dissolved the Assembly after it had met for just one day (5 January 1918).

SUMMARY

- Following his return to Russia in April 1917, Lenin largely united the Bolshevik Party in favour of 'peace, bread, land' and a policy of non-cooperation with the Provisional Government.
- Initially the Bolsheviks seemed to have little success, but their part in preventing the Kornilov coup in August helped to increase their support.
- Having successfully deposed the Provisional Government in the October Revolution, the Bolsheviks moved quickly to consolidate their power, issuing decrees and suppressing opposition.

KEY CHRONOLOGY

Political and international events 1894–1917

1894	Accession of Nicholas II
1898	Social Democratic Workers Party founded
1899	Social Revolutionary Party established
1904	Russo-Japanese War begins
1905 July	Bloody Sunday massacre
Aug	Russo-Japanese War concludes
Oct	October Manifesto
1914	Germany declares war on Russia
1915	Tsar assumes command of army
1916	Murder of Rasputin
1917 Feb	February Revolution
April	Lenin returns; April Theses
July	July Days
Aug	Kornilov coup
Oct	October Revolution
Nov	Armistice ends war

 **APPLY**

APPLY YOUR KNOWLEDGE

Here are some of the problems which the Bolsheviks had to solve in their first months of power, October–December 1917.

1	Control of industry	
2	Land ownership	
3	Opposition/co-operation from other socialist parties	
4	Opposition from liberals and the right	
5	Peace with Germany	
6	Establishing an effective government	
7	Social issues	

a For each, indicate what they did in the box on the right.

b On the continuum line below, indicate how successful they were by inserting the number of the issue at an appropriate point along the line.

Continuum

Failure .... **Success**

EXAMINER TIP

This exercise should provide useful supporting material for an essay on the success of the Bolshevik takeover in 1917.

REVIEW

To look at the Bolshevik aims, ideas and ideology, look back to Chapter 10.

ASSESS THE VALIDITY OF THIS VIEW

Consider the following essay question:

> **A LEVEL** **'Social discontent was more important than Lenin's advancement of Bolshevik ideology in bringing the Bolsheviks to power in October 1917.'**
>
> **Assess the validity of this view with reference to the years 1894 to 1917.**

a This question requires an assessment of 2 very different factors about which you are required to make a judgement on relative importance. Note that you are not required to look at any other factors. Breaking the question down by filling in this chart will help you to consider the evidence and formulate an opinion.

Social discontent		Bolshevik ideology shown in	
Peasants		**Broad ideas**	
		Lenin's advancement of ideas	
Industrial workers		**Broad ideas**	
		Lenin's advancement of ideas	

REVIEW

Look back to Chapters 5, 9 and 10 for information on social developments and ideologies. Chapter 13 will further explore Bolshevik ideology, examining it with reference to the years following the Bolshevik takeover of power.

EXAMINER TIP

Always take a little time before making a judgement. Diagrams that help you to separate factors often help you to formulate a view by showing the balance of evidence.

b Study your chart carefully and choose one of the following judgements:

- Social discontent was more important than Lenin's Bolshevik ideology in bringing the Bolsheviks to power in October 1917.
- Lenin's Bolshevik ideology was more important than social discontent in bringing the Bolsheviks to power in October 1917.
- Social discontent was of equal importance to Lenin's Bolshevik ideology in bringing the Bolsheviks to power in October 1917.

c Write an introduction to this question in which you convey your judgement.

EXTRACT ANALYSIS

EXTRACT A

The tsarist government's failings in the war and its weakness at home led to the self-destruction of the autocracy on a wave of discontent. Had the democratic February Revolution managed to hold, most likely, Russia today would be a great democratic state, rather than one that has disintegrated. Soon after returning from exile to Petrograd in April 1917, Lenin embarked on a course of violent seizure of power. His slogans, primitive and rabble-rousing, worked without fail. The Bolsheviks promised the war-weary, land-starved and hungry people, peace and land and bread and told them that to achieve this they must first stick their bayonets into the ground, abandon the trenches and go home, where they should seize their allotments. The power of Kerensky's Provisional Government melted like ice in the spring thaw. Meanwhile, the Bolshevik demagogues promised the gullible and ignorant peasants-in-uniform prosperity, land, bread, hospitals and liberty.

Adapted from Dmitri Volkogonov, *The Rise and Fall of the Soviet Union*, 1999

a Use a highlighter to identify opinion (and potential bias) in this extract.

b Summarise the argument in this extract in 2 sentences. (Try to avoid repeating the words used in the extract.)

c Why might the argument in this extract be considered unconvincing?

PLAN YOUR ESSAY

 'The collapse of the Provisional Government in October 1917 was due to the growth in strength of the Bolshevik Party since 1903.'

Explain why you agree or disagree with this view.

This question is asking you to account for the collapse of the Provisional Government in October 1917. It would be helpful to produce a three-column plan, so that you can consider not only Bolshevik party strengths, but also their weaknesses as these are also important in evaluating the part played by other factors. This plan should enable you to decide what view you will adopt. Note that the question requires detail on the Bolsheviks from 1903.

a Complete the following:

Strengths of the Bolsheviks, 1903–Oct 1917	Weaknesses of the Bolsheviks, 1903–Oct 1917	Other factors, e.g. the failures of the Provisional Government

b Think about how you might address the strengths of the Bolsheviks, in the first section of your essay. You may need to reorder your points in order to argue clearly.

c Write 2 paragraphs of this essay, addressing Bolshevik strengths.

EXAMINER TIP

Since this is a breadth paper, you should be prepared for questions which look at the long-term causes of change in 1917.

REVIEW

To remind yourself of the development of the Bolsheviks from 1903 look back at Chapter 10. The workings of the Provisional Government from February 1917 are covered in Chapter 11.

AS Level extracts sample answer

REVISION PROGRESS

REVIEW

On these Exam Practice pages you will find a sample student answer for an AS Level extracts question. What are the strengths and weaknesses of the answer? Read the answer and the corresponding Examiner Tips carefully. Think about how you could apply this advice in order to improve your own answers to questions like this one.

> **AS**
> **LEVEL**
> **With reference to these extracts and your understanding of the historical context, which of these two extracts provides the more convincing interpretation of the growth of the Russian economy in the years c1890 to 1914?**
>
> 25 marks

REVISION SKILLS

The AS Level exam paper will have one extracts question which is compulsory; the question will be linked to two historical interpretations with different views. Read page 6 of this Revision Guide for details on how to master the extracts question.

EXTRACT A

Industrialisation was no new phenomenon in Russia. It had been in progress since the Crimean War; the emancipation of 1861 gave some further impetus to the movement. But not until the 1890s did it enjoy the whole-hearted encouragement of the State in a compulsive effort to have done with Russian backwardness and overcome decades of weakness. Much success was certainly achieved. In the heavy industries, the rate of development was particularly rapid. The decade of the 1890s marked the point when Russian industry took off into maturity. By 1914 Russia was annually producing some 5 million tons of pig-iron and exporting about 12 million tons of grain. Accompanying this was an unprecedented growth in the population, far outstripping that of any other European country.

Adapted from Lionel Kochan, *Russia in Revolution*, 1970

EXTRACT B

State ownership and state contracts contributed vitally to capitalise economic development in Russia in the 1890s and the decision, in 1897, to put the rouble on the gold standard also attracted investment from abroad. But there were dangers of relying so heavily upon injections of capital from Western Europe and the Russian imperial economy remained vulnerable to periodic recessions. The imperial population increased steeply and the benefit of agricultural expansion was less than it would have been. The appearance of advance in the years up to 1914 is deceptive. Although the Russian Empire's industrial output increased before 1914, the still higher rate of expansion in the US and Germany meant that the gap in productive capacity was widening.

Adapted from Robert Service, *The Russian Revolution 1900–1927*, 2009

Sample student answer

Extract A suggests that the Russian economy enjoyed a continuous advance from the 1890s to 1914 and 'much success' was achieved. The view in Extract A that the basis for growth from the 1890s had already been laid since the Crimean War and the emancipation of the serfs is valid. Reutern, Finance Minister under Alexander II, extended credit facilities, provided government subsidies and encouraged foreign investment. Similarly, the view that there was a take-off in the 1890s with the 'whole-hearted encouragement of the State' is also appropriate, since Vyshnegradsky and Witte vastly increased state and foreign investment and, in particular, contributed to the expansion of the railway network. This enabled the economy to take off 'into maturity' and the extract gives figures to exemplify its growth to 1914. The extract also mentions the unprecedented growth of the population, implying that it also contributed to economic development by providing a larger workforce and consumer base.

The positive interpretation of Extract A could, however, be challenged. Both Vyshnegradsky and Witte drove industrialisation at the expense of the heavily taxed peasantry and most of the export trade was in grain, rather than industrial goods, even in 1914. The internal market was limited by the poverty of the overwhelmingly rural and peasant-based society, so population growth was not an advantage. Russia was the least developed European power in 1914 and large areas of the Russian Empire were unaffected by the industrial growth, which makes the view of this extract less convincing.

Extract B largely focuses on the limitation to industrial growth before 1914. Whilst it acknowledges the part of the State in supporting growth in the 1890s, referring again to the work of Vyshnegradsky and Witte, it emphasises the dangers of reliance on foreign loans rather than seeing them as wholly positive. Extract B also views the population increase negatively, reflecting the fact that peasant 'land-hunger' weakened the economy. Even though Stolypin introduced a series of measures from 1906 to counter this, by 1914, only 10% of land had been transferred from communal to private ownership. Furthermore, the extract's comment that Russia's industrial output was inferior to that of the USA and Germany is borne out by the knowledge that Russia was only the world's fifth-largest industrial power in 1914.

EXAMINER TIP

This opening sentence attempts to identify the overall argument of Extract A, which is a good way to begin an answer. However, it slightly misunderstands the argument – the extract actually states that the Russian economy enjoyed a continuous advance from the Crimean War (1855–56), with the real take-off occurring from the 1890s.

There is good use of detail to support the view in Extract A – the answer both refers to supporting evidence in the text (the growth figures, and the sub-argument on the population growth) and provides detailed own knowledge.

EXAMINER TIP

Again, there is good use of supporting knowledge, this time to challenge the view in Extract A.

EXAMINER TIP

There is good detail here to support the argument in Extract B, although it does not always link clearly to the argument (e.g. the statement that Russia was only the world's fifth-largest power by 1914 does not clarify whether or not Russia had narrowed the gap in industrial production). Perhaps a little more detail could be provided on the issue of land hunger. The part played by state ownership and contracts and by foreign investment, as mentioned at the beginning of the extract, could also have been developed.

However, Extract B is in danger of making the situation sound worse than it was. State-sponsored industry was giving way to private capitalism in the early 20th century and Stolypin's reforms helped to create a class of independent landed proprietors in the countryside. There were many positive signs including growing internal demand and a growth rate of 8.5% per year from 1908. Indeed, Russian industrialisation had grown enough that, by 1914, the Germans sought war for fear that any delay would allow Russia to outstrip the massive German economy.

Despite its limitations, Extract B would seem to offer the more convincing interpretation of the growth of the Russian economy between c1890 and 1914. It pays due attention to the take-off in the 1890s and acknowledges the increase in industrial output, but it also offers some reservations and so produces a more balanced picture than Extract A. Awareness that the output was considerably less than that of the USA and Germany is more helpful to understanding than the figures of iron and grain exports offered in Extract A. Similarly, only Extract B makes reference to the problems of agriculture which, given its importance for the Russian population, must be considered in any appraisal of economic development in these years.

> **EXAMINER TIP**
>
> This paragraph is more focused and provides excellent detail in terms of evidence to challenge the argument in Extract B.

> **EXAMINER TIP**
>
> This is a good conclusion, which offers a clear judgement as to which extract is more convincing and substantiates that judgement with reference to both extracts.

OVERALL COMMENT

Despite a few criticisms, as given above, this is a very good response, and would achieve a strong Level 5. It shows good understanding of the interpretations and provides a well-substantiated judgement as to which is the more convincing. Contextual understanding is also impressive as a wide range of specific detail both supporting and criticising the arguments is provided.

OVER TO YOU

Give yourself 50 minutes to answer this question on your own. Consider this checklist when reviewing your answer. Have you:

- ☐ Identified the overall argument of each extract?
- ☐ Shown the strengths **and** limitations of each extract?
- ☐ Referred to the detail of the extracts and your own knowledge to support your comments?
- ☐ Provided a substantiated conclusion to show which extract is the more convincing?

Go back and look at Chapter 6 (pages 32–33) and Chapter 8 (pages 45–46) to help refresh your knowledge of the Russian economy between 1890 and 1914.

3 The emergence of Communist dictatorship, 1917–1941

REVISION PROGRESS

13 New leaders and ideologies

 **RECAP**

Lenin's Russia; ideology and change

Following the October Revolution of 1917, the Bolsheviks' priority was to consolidate control. Marxist ideology became less important. Later Soviet historians tried to explain the Bolsheviks' actions in terms of Marxist theory, but at the time, policies and decisions were often dictated by circumstances.

Initially the Bolsheviks were ideologically divided on:

- whether to end the war
- what type of government should be established.

Ideology and the end to war

The October Revolution had failed to spark workers' revolutions (as hoped) across Europe so, to honour their promise of 'peace', the Bolsheviks had to negotiate with the Kaiser's government in Germany. This caused divisions.

- Some (including Bukharin) wanted to pursue the war.
- Trotsky proposed 'neither peace nor war' – retreating further if necessary while waiting for the revolution in the West.
- Lenin was prepared to give in to German territorial demands to bring peace and consolidate his revolution.

Lenin's pragmatic approach won and the treaty of Brest-Litovsk was signed on 3 March 1918. This set a precedent: in future, 'socialism at home' would take priority over spreading international revolution.

Ideology and one-party government

The ideological division over the future government of Russia produced a divide between:

- those who favoured a broad socialist government, creating a coalition of Bolsheviks and other socialist parties (as proposed by Zinoviev and Kamenev)
- those who argued for an exclusively Bolshevik State.

Lenin advocated the latter, claiming that a strong party was necessary to establish the 'dictatorship of the proletariat'.

Again Lenin won. He established an exclusively Bolshevik 'Sovnarkom' (cabinet), his only concession being to allow a few left-wing SRs to join this in November 1917 after that month's election (as promised by the Provisional Government) in which the SRs received the most votes. However, in March 1918 the left-wing SRs walked out of Sovnarkom in protest at the Treaty of Brest-Litovsk. Russia thus became a one-party state and the Bolsheviks adopted the title 'The Communist Party'.

Ideology and the preservation of the Soviet State

Lenin's early actions to preserve the new State were often given an ideological justification. However they were also driven by the need to preserve Bolshevik (Communist) control.

Ideological justification	Actions to preserve Bolshevik control
To achieve the 'dictatorship of the proletariat', active repression of 'counter-revolutionaries' would be essential.	• Dec 1917 – Cheka created • Jan 1918 – Constituent Assembly dismissed • 1918–21 – repression and 'terror' imposed during the Civil War years.
A workers' state demanded the destruction of private enterprise and the capitalists.	• 1918–21 – Private enterprise and capitalism were replaced by central government control of industry and agriculture.

The importance of Marxist ideology for the new State was brought into question in 1921 when, faced by an economic downturn which provoked popular disturbances, Lenin appeared to 'change course' and launched his New Economic Policy (NEP). His decision to adopt a more capitalist economic policy suggests that pragmatism was more important to him than ideology, although it is not known whether he intended his new policy to be permanent.

New ideological principles also emerged in the years up to 1924:

- The Party could never be wrong. (This involved the destruction of all opposition voices; the Social Revolutionary Party was outlawed in 1922.)
- The Party always spoke with one voice (established by the 1921 ban on factions within the Party).

Stalin's rise; ideology and change

The power struggle and the emergence of Stalin

The power struggle which followed Lenin's death in 1924 was marked by arguments over ideology. The chief contenders for power were:

Stalin defeated these contenders in a series of manoeuvres during which the 'left' (represented by Trotsky, Zinoviev and Kamenev) argued for the abandonment of Lenin's NEP, while the 'right', led by Bukharin, Rykov and Tomsky, argued for its retention.

Leon Trotsky
Organised the October 1917 takeover; created the Red Army; hero of the Civil War; member of Sovnarkom; regarded by Lenin as the 'most able' man in the Central Committee; believed in permanent revolution; joined the Bolsheviks in summer of 1917; a Jew; bourgeois background

Grigorii Zinoviev
Founder member of Bolshevik party; close associate of Lenin 1903–17; joined Kamenev to oppose timing of October Revolution; not a member of Sovnarkom; powerbase in Leningrad; a Jew; bourgeois background

Joseph Stalin
Old Bolshevik but not senior member until 1912; member of Sovnarkom; General Secretary of Communist Party from 1922; positions in Orgburo and Secretariat; peasant background

The leadership candidates

Lev Kamenev
Old Bolshevik and close associate of Lenin; had opposed timing of October Revolution; not a member of Sovnarkom; powerbase in Moscow; a Jew; bourgeois background

Nikolai Bukharin
Joined Bolsheviks 1906; not a senior member until 1922; theorist; described by Lenin as the 'golden boy'; some support in Moscow and among youth; son of a schoolmaster

By December 1929 Stalin had emerged as the undisputed Soviet leader.

Stage 1, 1922–24	
Dec 1922	Stalin allied with Zinoviev and Kamenev (on the left) against Trotsky.
1923–24	Stalin built up support and manoeuvred against Trotsky.
Stage 2, 1924–27	
May 1924	Lenin's 'Testament' was released. It criticised Stalin (among others) but the Central Committee suppressed publication.
July 1926	14th Party Congress – Stalin supported Bukharin (on the right); Zinoviev and Kamenev attacked Stalin but lost every vote. A new Central Committee and Politburo were elected with a Stalinist-Bukharin majority.
Nov 1926	Zinoviev and Kamenev joined with Trotsky in the 'United Opposition'. Stalin accused them of 'factionalism' and defeated all three.
Stage 3, 1927–29	
Jan 1928	Stalin announced a new 'left-leaning' economic strategy, opposed by Bukharin.
Nov 1929	Bukharin and his supporters, Rykov and Tomsky, were removed from the Politburo.

The importance of ideology in the power struggle

As well as arguments over the NEP, the power struggle saw debate over two other ideological issues:

- **Permanent revolution versus 'socialism in one country'**

  - Trotsky believed the Russians should stir up revolution abroad and that there should be 'permanent revolution' until a truly socialist society was created.

  - Stalin preferred to focus on 'socialism in one country', aiming to create a 'workers' paradise' in the Soviet Union as an example to the rest of the world.

- **The nature of leadership**

  Marx had not seen a single leader as necessary in a socialist state. With the end of the Civil War, some Party members wanted to abandon strong central leadership and establish collective control. This was mainly because of fear of Trotsky, whose influence over the Red Army made him a potential 'strong man'.

SUMMARY

- Lenin's combination of ideology and pragmatism established many of the principles on which the Soviet State would be based.
- When Lenin died, in 1924, the State's future direction was still unclear and ideological divisions within the Communist Party continued.
- Stalin benefited from the principles established under Lenin, using the increase in central control and the ban on factions as the basis for his rise to power.
- Whether Stalin had genuine ideological convictions or used ideology to further his own ambitions is unclear. Regardless, by 1929 he had defeated his opponents on both left and right and emerged as the sole leader of the Soviet State.

 **APPLY**

APPLY YOUR KNOWLEDGE

To reinforce your understanding of the importance of ideology in Stalin's struggle for power, complete this flow chart showing the 3 key stages of that struggle. You can use this not only to record dates and events, but also to identify the ideological factors that influenced this struggle.

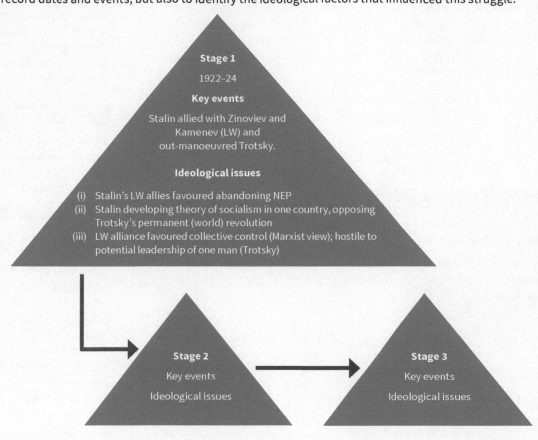

Stage 1

1922–24

Key events

Stalin allied with Zinoviev and Kamenev (LW) and out-manoeuvred Trotsky.

Ideological issues

(i) Stalin's LW allies favoured abandoning NEP
(ii) Stalin developing theory of socialism in one country, opposing Trotsky's permanent (world) revolution
(iii) LW alliance favoured collective control (Marxist view); hostile to potential leadership of one man (Trotsky)

Stage 2

Key events

Ideological issues

Stage 3

Key events

Ideological issues

TO WHAT EXTENT?

A LEVEL **To what extent, in the years 1903 to 1924, did Lenin abandon ideology in order to gain and consolidate power?**

Here are some of Lenin's key ideological aims:

- Seize power in the name of the workers.
- Establish a Marxist state and create a 'dictatorship of the proletariat'.
- Crush all opposition.
- Promote socialist thinking.
- Destroy capitalism.
- Achieve state ownership of the means of production.
- Spread the socialist revolution worldwide.

a For each, identify the ways in which Lenin *succeeded* in carrying out his aim, *partially succeeded* in carrying out his aim, and *largely failed in or ignored* achieving his aim.

b Now plan and write an answer to the question above.

EXAMINER TIP

In an essay, you might be asked to evaluate the importance of ideas and ideology on historical events and developments, such as Stalin's rise to power. To prepare for this, you might like to compile a list of 'other factors' affecting the power struggle.

REVIEW

Chapters 14 and 15 will provide a little more detail on the political and economic situation in the 1920s, which provided the backdrop to the power struggle.

REVIEW

You will need to look back to Chapter 12 for details on how Lenin gained and consolidated power in the early months.

EXAMINER TIP

This information in part **a** should help you to plan your essay. Remember, however, that the question dates are important here and a review of change and continuity over time would require a broadly chronological examination of the importance of ideology at the various critical stages of Lenin's leadership.

REVISION SKILLS

Sections 3 and 4 of this Revision Guide trace developments in Communist Russia between 1917 and 1941. To support your revision of this period, create a 24-year timeline and record specific events on it as you meet them. Colour code your entries: red: political/government, green: repression/opposition, light blue: economic, dark blue: social, purple: other. 1917 and 1918 have been started for you.

1917	Bolshevik takeover and establishment of Sovnarkom; decrees on peace and land (Oct); nationality decree (Nov); military and Church decrees (Dec); LW SRs joined coalition (Dec); Workers' control decree (Nov); nationalisation of Banks (Dec); creation of Cheka (Dec)
1918	Dismissal of Constituent Assembly (Jan) SRs left coalition (March); Treaty of Brest-Litovsk (March); beginning of Civil War and repression; state control of industry and agriculture imposed

EXAMINER TIP

Your timeline will be an essential revision aid. Use it to check context for extract work and to ensure accurate chronology and an appreciation of change and continuity in essay answers.

REVIEW

Details of events after the Bolshevik takeover in October 1917 are given in Chapter 12.

KEY QUESTION

One of the Key Questions asks:
How important were ideas and ideology?

It is therefore important to understand Marxist–Leninist ideas and ideology: terminology established by Stalin in the 1920s. With reference to Communist Russia from 1917, supply meanings for the following ideological terms:

- One-party state.

  _____

  _____

- Common ownership of the means of production.

  _____

  _____

- Socialism.

  _____

  _____

- Permanent revolution.

  _____

  _____

- Socialism in one country.

  _____

  _____

- Dictatorship of the proletariat.

  _____

  _____

- Democratic centralism.

  _____

  _____

EXAMINER TIP

Understanding ideological concepts will aid your appreciation of historical extracts and the use of appropriate ideological terminology will help to show conceptual awareness, adding depth to your essays.

REVIEW

You will need to look ahead to Chapter 14 in order to complete the final definition.

14 The Communist dictatorship

The consolidation of Bolshevik authority; political developments 1917–24

The early months, 1917–18

Shortly after coming to power in October 1917, Lenin had issued decrees on peace and on land. These were followed by a nationality decree (promising self-determination to ethnic peoples) in November and a decree to nationalise Church land and another to set up the Cheka (secret police) in December. In early 1918, further decrees clarified the separation of Church and State and the nationalisation of industry and socialisation of land. A permanent Red Army was also established.

The 1918 Constitution

In July 1918, the first Soviet Constitution for the 'Russian Soviet Federal Socialist Republic' (RSFSR) was proclaimed. It stated that:

- Supreme power rested with the All-Russian Congress of Soviets (made up of deputies from elected local soviets across Russia).
- The central executive committee of the Congress was to be the 'supreme organ of power'.
- The Congress would elect Sovnarkom.

Lenin claimed to have established '**democratic centralism**' with elections from the lowest level to the top, where the Congress could respond to needs and pass orders down the chain. However:

- The 'former people' (nobility and capitalists) were not allowed to vote or hold office.
- The workers' vote was weighted 5:1 against that of the peasants in the Congress elections.
- Sovnarkom was, in practice, chosen by the Communist (Bolshevik) Party's Central Committee; the Congress elections were only a formality.
- The real focus of power was the Party.

The Civil War, 1918–20

Following the Treaty of Brest-Litovsk,which ended Russia's part in the First World War in March 1918, political opposition groups joined to create a force of 'Whites'. These were supported by Britain, France and the USA. In March 1918, the Bolsheviks moved their capital to Moscow in view of the growing threat posed by a growing force of Whites in the South.

The Civil War cost around 10 million lives. However, the Bolshevik 'Reds' enjoyed geographical advantages, better communications and superior organisation (under Trotsky) than the Whites.

By the end of 1920 the Bolsheviks controlled most of the former Russian Empire.

The war continued into 1921 as a nationalist struggle against Polish armies. A Polish invasion of western Ukraine had been defeated at Kiev in May 1920; however a subsequent Polish victory led to the Treaty of Riga (March 1921). This granted self-rule to Poland and other nationalities.

The impact of the Civil War on government and Party

The Civil War brought even greater centralisation and Party control.

The parallel structure of Soviet government and Party

Soviet government	Party
Sovnarkom	Politburo
Central Committee	Central Committee
Congress of Soviets	Congress
Provincial and city soviets	Provincial and city parties
Local and district soviets	Local parties
a) Soviet government structure	b) Communist Party structure

- Policies and decisions were made by the Party and in 1919, a new Party 'Politburo' became the real centre for policy. The executive committee of the Congress of Soviets became simply a means of carrying out policies made by the Party and local soviets became the preserve of Party members only.
- The 1921 'ban on factions' made it difficult to criticise Party decisions: anyone who did not accept a Party decision could be expelled.
- In April 1922 the post of 'General Secretary' was created to coordinate the Party's workings. This post was filled by Stalin.
- From 1923, the *nomenklatura* system meant that appointments to key Party and government posts had to be agreed by the Party's Central Committee. This system created a loyal Party elite, who were given special privileges in return for ensuring obedience to central directives.

The impact of the Civil War on the national minorities; the 1922 Constitution

After the Civil War, the government ceased to support 'national self-determination'. Independence movements were denounced as 'counter-revolutionary'. In 1922, demands from Georgia for greater independence were brutally crushed on Stalin's orders (although Lenin condemned this).

In December 1922 the RSFSR was replaced by the Union of Soviet Socialist Republics (USSR). This was officially a federation of republics on a similar footing, but the states which made up the union were kept under firm control by Moscow.

The development of the Stalinist dictatorship

The political structure of the Communist State under Stalin

Stalin extended one-party rule and centralised control, using parallel government and Party structures and filling both with members of the *nomenklatura*. Party congresses were called less frequently (and never between 1939 and 1952) as Stalin grew more dominant.

As General Secretary, Stalin controlled appointments to all important positions in the Party and he developed a vast bureaucracy of loyal servants. Party membership increased massively as those who benefited from the Stalinist system signed up to it.

The 1936 Constitution

In 1936, a new constitution, drafted by Bukharin, was introduced.

- The USSR became a federation of eleven Soviet Republics (instead of seven).
- The All-Russian Congress of Soviets was replaced by a new 'Supreme Soviet'. This comprised the 'Soviet of the Union' and the 'Soviet of Nationalities'.
- Each republic was given its own supreme soviet and the right to leave the Union.
- There were to be four-yearly elections in which everyone over 18 (including the 'former people') could vote.
- Extensive civil rights and support for the ethnic minorities' position were promised.

However, in practice:

- The Supreme Soviet only met for a few days twice a year. It tended to communicate decisions rather than influence them.
- The republics were still tightly controlled, and when Party leaders in Georgia allegedly planned to leave the Union in 1951, they were purged.
- Elections were not contested.
- Civil rights and the ethnic minorities' position were largely ignored.

'Stalinism' and the Stalinist dictatorship – the cult of personality

From December 1929, Stalin developed his own cult. This promoted an image of himself that helped to inspire confidence during a period of rapid change. Stalin was universally portrayed as Lenin's true disciple and successor. Paintings, poems, posters and sculptures glorified him as the 'mighty leader' and 'father of the nation'. Photographs were doctored to remove his enemies.

Adulation for Stalin reflected traditional Russian loyalty to their leader. Like the tsars, he was seen as a God-like father figure.

Government by 1941

The political structures laid down under Lenin developed throughout the 1920s and early 1930s into a highly centralised form of government, dominated by one-party rule. Stalin took this authoritarian government to new lengths. In the early 1930s, he maintained his authority through his position as leader of the Communist Party. By 1941, he could act directly on his personal authority. He was above the party and no longer dependent on it.

The atmosphere of 'crisis' brought about by his economic policies helped to increase Stalin's power, as did the propaganda that celebrated his image, his purge of the old elites and his personal patronage over new, younger officials. Although he could be limited by the inefficiency of the bureaucracy, or occasionally hampered by opposition, from 1936 Stalin's rule was effectively a personal dictatorship.

SUMMARY

- In their first months of power, the Bolsheviks retained power through concessions and repression.
- The Civil War led to greater centralisation and Party control.
- Stalin extended one-party rule and central control, despite the seemingly democratic Constitution of 1936.
- By 1941 Russia was effectively subject to a personal dictatorship.

 **APPLY**

APPLY YOUR KNOWLEDGE

Draw a mind-map to illustrate the political impact of the 1918–21 Civil War on Russia.

REVIEW

When writing about Leninist Russia, it is important to be aware of the changes that occurred as a result of the Civil War. You might like to contrast the Leninist State of 1923–24 with that of October–December 1917 by looking back at Chapter 12.

ASSESS THE VALIDITY OF THIS VIEW

 A LEVEL **'There was more continuity than change between the type of state established by Lenin in the 1920s and that of Stalin in the 1930s.'** Assess the validity of this view.

In order to plan this essay, you will need to identify the main features of the Leninist State of the 1920s and consider which remained the same and which changed (or developed further) under Stalin. You might use the following diagram to help you.

a Complete and add to the following planning chart:

Leninist State in 1920s	Stalinist State in 1930s – change or continuity?
Cult of the leader	
Constitution	
Government and Party structures	
Party membership	
Party congresses	
Centralised control	
One-party rule	
Nomenklatura	
Other features?	

EXAMINER TIP

A thematic plan works well for this essay which is comparing types of rule in different decades. Always study questions carefully to decide whether a thematic or chronological approach is best. If in doubt, the former is usually (although not always) preferable because it is more likely to produce argued analysis.

b Use this chart to identify the judgement that you would advance in your introduction.
c The themes of the chart could be evaluated in separate paragraphs. Bearing your judgement in mind, write one paragraph in full.

IMPROVE AN ANSWER

A **How significant was the cult of personality to the Stalinist dictatorship before 1941?**
LEVEL

In response to the question above, the following paragraph was written:

> Posters were very significant for the cult of personality. This was because they reflected Stalin almost as a god – usually a massive figure for everyone to see. The posters were very effective as they were displayed on the streets of the towns and cities, on factory walls and alongside major roads. No one could escape the towering figure of Stalin looking down on them. They came to worship this 'mighty leader' and some people say this was no different from the way the Russian people used to worship the Tsar, carrying his icon for good luck. Photographs were also significant in the personality cult. There were lots of photographs of the 'dictator' Stalin in the newspapers as well as in books. These were doctored to show Stalin in the best possible light and if any of his enemies appeared in the pictures, they were obliterated. Because there were posters and photographs everywhere and the ordinary people could not escape from them, this shows how significant the cult of personality was before 1941.

a This paragraph is responding to a slightly different question from that actually posed. Can you suggest the question that would match the paragraph and explain what has gone wrong?

b Improve on this paragraph by linking it directly to the given question. You should not add to the evidence, but rewrite and reorder the commentary – expanding it a little if necessary.

EXTRACT ANALYSIS

EXTRACT A

By 1941, the Soviet political system had been transformed. In 1934, Stalin's power derived from his position as head of the Party apparatus. Decisions flowed from the Politburo through the Party apparatus and then to the economic ministries, the secret police, the army and the various organs of government. By 1939, the Party apparatus could no longer control Stalin. Stalin had achieved a personal authority independent of any single institution. He had established his right to issue orders on his personal authority, using any bureaucratic channels he chose. In particular, he could act directly through the secret police against the Party, the army or the economic ministries. Yet there was nothing to stop him acting through other institutions against the secret police.

Adapted from David Christian, *Imperial and Soviet Russia*, 1997

a Underline the statements of opinion about Stalinist government in this extract and identify the main argument.

b For each statement of opinion, supply one or more pieces of contextual own knowledge, to support or criticise that opinion.

c What conclusion would you draw, as to 'how convincing' the argument is?

REVIEW

Before attempting to write a full essay in response to this question, you will need to have studied the whole of Section 3, Chapters 13–18.

EXAMINER TIP

Although it is important to reflect the words of the question in your answers, you need to do so in a 'thinking' manner, otherwise the meaning of the question can become lost.

15 Economic developments

The economy under Lenin

Lenin struggled to establish a '**socialist economy**'.

State Capitalism

Initially he allowed peasants to take over the land and gave workers 'control' over their factories. However it was soon clear that neither workers nor peasants were ready for this responsibility. Production decreased, leading peasants to hoard their produce since there were fewer goods to buy.

This encouraged Lenin to think of a longer transition to a truly socialist economy. He accepted the need for an interim stage – 'State Capitalism'. In this stage private ownership would still exist.

In December 1917, **Veshenkha** (the Council of the National Economy) was established to supervise economic development but there was no nationalisation of industry.

War Communism

The demands of feeding and supplying the Red Armies in the Civil War forced a new economic direction known as War Communism. Lenin introduced:

- **food requisitioning (May 1918)**
  - Grain and other produce were forcibly bought or confiscated from the peasants.
  - *Kulaks* (viewed by Bolsheviks as 'enemies of the people') had their stocks seized.
- **nationalisation of industry**
  - By November 1920 most factories and businesses had been nationalised.
  - The State employed professional managers to reimpose worker discipline and increase output.
  - Working hours were extended.
  - Private trade and manufacture were forbidden.

War Communism created many problems:

- Most peasants hid their crops, grew less and some even murdered members of the requisition squads; grain shortages worsened, culminating in widespread famine in 1921.
- Industrial production fell, as transport was disrupted and factories were inefficient; money was largely replaced by a system of barter.
- The urban population declined, as workers tried to flee to the countryside, or succumbed to the typhus epidemic of 1920.

Demands for economic change

The food crisis brought a new wave of peasant revolts and further strikes and riots in the cities. Red Army troops crushed the unrest in the countryside and in 1921 martial law was declared to deal with protest in the cities.

In March 1921 the sailors at the Kronstadt naval base demanded an end to one-party rule. The Red Army and Cheka suppressed the rebellion and its leaders were shot.

Even some Bolsheviks pressed for greater worker control and opposed those who wanted to intensify War Communism.

It was probably the combination of these factors that led to Lenin's change of economic direction in 1921.

The New Economic Policy

In February 1921, **Gosplan** was created to advise on a new economic policy. The New Economic Policy (NEP) was announced in August 1921. It was supported by Bukharin, Zinoviev and most of the leadership, but lower-ranking Bolsheviks saw it as an ideological betrayal.

- State control of transport, banking and heavy industry was retained, but private ownership of smaller businesses and private trade were permitted.
- Rationing was ended and industries made to be more efficient.
- Grain requisitioning was halted and peasants could sell any grain left over after supplying a proportion to the government.

The NEP restarted the economy. By 1926, the production levels of 1913 had been reached again. Living standards rose, revolts and disputes ended and favourable trade agreements were reached. A money economy and private wealth returned and the *kulak* class re-emerged.

The economy under Stalin

Industrial development

In December 1927 Stalin announced the end of NEP. This was known as the **Great Turn**.

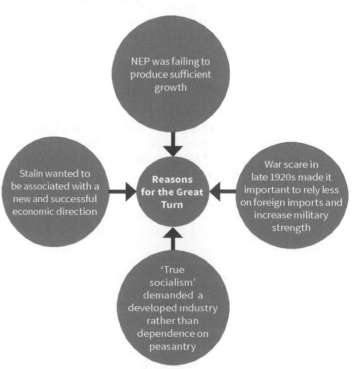

Economic plans	Aims	Results
First Five Year Plan 1928–32	• Increase production by 300%. • Develop heavy industry. • Boost light industry and electricity production.	Stalin claimed targets were met in four years. *But* • Shortage of skilled workers and poor central coordination. • No major targets achieved (although impressive growth).
Second Five Year Plan 1933–37	• Continued growth of heavy industry. • New emphasis on the light industries. • Concentration on engineering and tool-making. • Development of communications.	Rapid industrial growth (mainly in heavy industry); improvements to communications. *But* • Not all targets met. • Emphasis on quantity not quality.
Third Five Year Plan 1938–42	• Focus on heavy industry. • Promote rapid rearmament. • Complete transition to 'socialist economy' (Communism).	Heavy industry grew strongly. *But* • Lack of good managers, specialists and technicians following Stalin's purges. • Hard winter in 1938 and diversion of funds into rearmament and defence undermined plan. Plan finished early following 1941 German invasion.

Stalin's economic programme was to be implemented through a series of 'Five Year Plans'. These set challenging targets – to fail to achieve them was a criminal offence. This resulted in corruption and false reporting of statistics. The plans were accompanied by much propaganda.

Agricultural change

Changes in agricultural organisation were seen as necessary for rapid industrialisation. By 1927 the peasants were still not producing sufficient grain for export, which was necessary to feed and supply the industrial workforce. Also, there was pressure to create a more socialist system in the countryside.

The Great Turn therefore involved a move towards collective farming. This was announced in December 1927. It was intended to make farming more efficient, allow more mechanisation, facilitate grain collection and 'socialise' the peasants.

Collectivisation Stage 1 (1929–30)

In December 1929, Stalin announced forced collectivisation into state farms (***kolkhozes***) and the annihilation of the *kulak* class. In January 1930, collectivisation began using force and propaganda. Over half of households were collectivised by March. This created such hostility that the programme had to be slowed down.

Collectivisation Stage 2 (1930–41)

A new drive to collectivisation proceeded more slowly and involved the establishment of machine tractor stations (MTS). By 1941, all peasant households were collectivised.

The drive to collectivisation appeared successful but there were massive problems with its implementation:

- Dekulakisation removed millions of successful farmers.
- Grain and livestock was destroyed.
- The collectives were often poorly organised and lacked sufficient farming equipment.
- Peasants had little incentive to work hard for the collective. They were only interested in their small private plots from which they could sell any surplus at markets.
- 1932–33 brought a disastrous famine; millions of peasants starved.
- Grain output did not exceed pre-collectivisation levels until after 1935.

SUMMARY

- Under Lenin, the early Bolshevik policy of 'State Capitalism' gave way to a more centralised policy of 'War Communism' to meet the demands of the 1918–21 war.
- Unrest and protests led Lenin to relax central controls again in his New Economic Policy of 1921, and the economy revived.
- In 1927, the NEP was ended, as Stalin's Great Turn introduced a focus on rapid industrialisation, accompanied by a policy of collectivisation in the countryside.

 **APPLY**

APPLY YOUR KNOWLEDGE

It is important that you are able to condense information into 'helpful reminders' of each topic in your revision. Supply no more than 3 bullet points in each of the boxes below as key reminders of economic developments 1917–41.

Ruler	Key industrial developments	Key agricultural developments
Lenin 1917–24		
Stalin 1928–41		

EXAMINER TIP

For breadth essays, you will need to be able to select relevant material over a period of around 20 years to use as supporting evidence. Charts such as this will help you to think about the period and select the 'key' facts and developments before your exam.

REVISION SKILLS

You could create sets of flash cards for revision activities like this.

KEY QUESTION

The material in this chapter could be used to address the Key Question:

How important was the role of individuals?

Copy and complete the Venn diagram below to show the ways in which Lenin and Stalin steered economic development during their respective periods of power. The overlap should show the ways in which they adopted similar policies; other details within the circles should relate to the individual leader concerned, using dates where relevant.

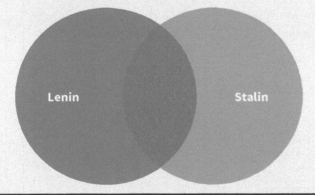

APPLY YOUR KNOWLEDGE

If you were required to write a breadth essay evaluating the success of economic development in the years 1917–41, you might include a paragraph assessing collectivisation under Stalin.

Look at the material given in this chapter, and:

a Write an opening sentence for the paragraph which gives an overall assessment of the success of collectivisation.

b Choose 4 pieces of relevant information which could be used to comment further on the detail of the policy and its success.

c Write this paragraph in full.

TO WHAT EXTENT?

A **To what extent were changes in economic policy in the years 1918 to 1941 merely a pragmatic response to changing circumstances?**
LEVEL

By breaking the given time-span down to identify key years when economic policy changed, you will be able to balance the effect of circumstances and other factors more easily.

a Suggest 4 key years when economic policies changed and write these in column 1. In columns 2 and 3, provide 2–3 bullet points of examples to justify your choices.

Economic change in years beginning:	Agriculture	Industry

b You then need to consider the influences on each 'turning point' year – noting the circumstances in which the change occurred and any other factors behind the changes.

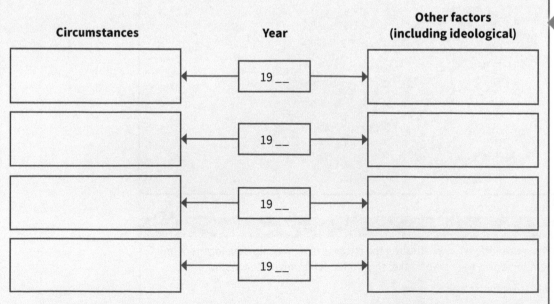

Circumstances   **Year**   **Other factors (including ideological)**

19 __

19 __

19 __

19 __

c Underline what you consider to have been the key reasons for the changes in the chosen years and give your judgement.

d Now plan and write your essay.

REVIEW

If you want to include 1941 (the outbreak of war between Germany and Russia), as a turning point, you will need to look ahead to Chapter 19.

EXAMINER TIP

This essay focuses on the popular topic of causation. For such essays, plans such as those suggested here can make an essay considerably more focused and effective.

REVIEW

It is important to be able to distinguish between breadth questions that require a primarily chronological approach and those that are best answered thematically. Look again at the activities in Chapter 13, page 73 (To What Extent activity) and Chapter 14, page 77 (Assess the Validity of This View activity) and ahead to Chapter 16, page 86 (Assess the Validity of This View activity) to remind yourself of these two different approaches to questions.

16 Leninist/Stalinist society

Class issues

The classless society

Following Marxist theory, the Bolshevik revolution campaigned against the 'class' enemies of the proletariat (the **burzhui**).

- Class titles were abolished.
- 'Former people' (nobles and bourgeoisie) were forced into menial tasks; their homes were turned into communal houses for workers (**komunalki**).
- During the Civil War, rations were allocated according to class (workers and soldiers received the most).
- Following some relaxation of policy during the years of the NEP, class-based attacks continued under Stalin.

The Communist aim was to create 'socialist man': a man or woman with a sense of social responsibility who would willingly serve the State.

The proletariat

'**Proletarianisation**' was an important step in creating 'socialist man'. Despite this, working life was harsh.

After the short 'workers' control' period of 1917–18, discipline in factories was restored. After 1918, workers could not leave their jobs and could be imprisoned or shot for missing targets. Unions became a means of controlling the workers. Living and working conditions remained grim throughout the NEP, and worsened because of collectivisation and the drive towards industrialisation.

From 1931, industrialisation created better opportunities for workers. Propaganda campaigns such as the Stakhanovite movement (named after Stakhanov, a miner whose inflated achievements were hailed as an example to others) increased 'socialist competition'. Education improved, the purges created vacancies at higher levels, and social mobility increased.

Nevertheless, living conditions still remained poor. Wages remained low and market prices high. From 1940, the prospect of war led to firmer discipline, and an end to many of the benefits of the 1930s.

Women

After 1917, the position of women changed significantly.

Early policies

Before the revolution, peasant women had been mainly expected to look after their households and children. They had no legal rights or privileges. In November 1917, the new government outlawed sex discrimination and gave women the right to own property. Further decrees:

- removed Church influence, facilitated divorce and legalised abortion
- gave women the right to work
- gave girls the same educational rights as boys.

This provided new opportunities for women, but also meant that they had to manage both work and home.

Stalinist policies

In the 1930s, Stalin revived traditional policies.

- The family was portrayed as all-important and women were encouraged to give up paid employment when they married.
- Marriage was encouraged; divorce and abortion were attacked, adultery became a criminal offence and contraception was banned.
- Financial incentives were offered for large families.

However, the numbers of women in work (in industry or on the collective farms) or education grew, helped by an increase in state nurseries and child-clinics. The divorce rate remained high, abortion continued, and although the majority of people married, the population growth-rate fell.

Young people

Education

Education was seen as essential to build a socialist society.

Under Lenin's leadership:

- Free education was provided at all levels in co-educational schools.
- New secondary schools combined general education with vocational training.
- Traditional learning was combined with physical work.
- Textbooks and exams were largely abolished.
- Some freedom, creativity and individualism were permitted.
- Physical punishment was banned.

Many policies were reversed under Stalin:

- Education for all was abandoned; some single-sex schools were reintroduced.
- Although 'practical' work' was encouraged for the less able, the emphasis was on former teaching to develop industrial skills.
- Collective farms or town enterprises were responsible for many schools.
- Universities were controlled by Veshenkha, the economic planning agency.
- A rigid traditional curriculum was enforced. Nationalism was promoted and military training introduced.
- Teachers were set high targets and closely supervised.

By 1941, there were marked educational improvements including a huge rise in literacy.

Youth organisations

In 1918 a young communist league was formed for youngsters aged from 14 to 21 years. A junior section (the Pioneers) followed in 1922. In 1926 the organisation was renamed '**Komsomol**' and the age-range was extended to between 10 and 28 years.

Under Stalin's rule, Komsomol grew in both membership and influence. It taught communist values through clubs, community centres and camps and had its own newspaper. It was closely linked to the Communist Party, to which it became directly affiliated in 1939. Members took an oath to live, study and fight for the Fatherland; they wore a uniform, helped carry out party campaigns and assisted the Red Army and police.

Religion

Marx saw religion as a means of justifying the power of the upper classes over the people. Lenin and Stalin adopted differing policies during their leaderships.

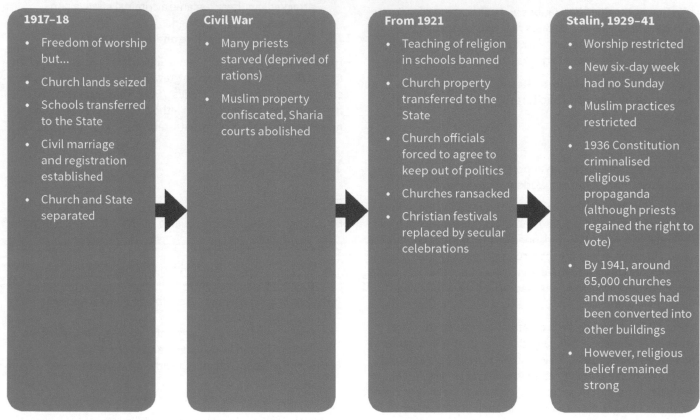

1917–18
- Freedom of worship but...
- Church lands seized
- Schools transferred to the State
- Civil marriage and registration established
- Church and State separated

Civil War
- Many priests starved (deprived of rations)
- Muslim property confiscated, Sharia courts abolished

From 1921
- Teaching of religion in schools banned
- Church property transferred to the State
- Church officials forced to agree to keep out of politics
- Churches ransacked
- Christian festivals replaced by secular celebrations

Stalin, 1929–41
- Worship restricted
- New six-day week had no Sunday
- Muslim practices restricted
- 1936 Constitution criminalised religious propaganda (although priests regained the right to vote)
- By 1941, around 65,000 churches and mosques had been converted into other buildings
- However, religious belief remained strong

Religious changes under Lenin and Stalin

National minorities

Lenin's nationality decree of 1917 fulfilled the Bolsheviks' promise of self-determination. However when this led to separatist movements, the Bolsheviks disagreed as to whether or not to impose integration on the nationalities. Stalin brutally suppressed moves towards independence in Georgia in 1922.

The Communists abolished anti-Semitic laws in 1917, encouraged national languages, and granted representation within the Party to the major nationalities. In 1926, Jews were given a 'national homeland' in the far eastern province.

In the 1930s Stalin's aim of creating a single 'Soviet identity' involved greater centralisation and less tolerance. Leaders of the republics had to follow the path set out in Moscow. Non-Russians were deported within the Soviet Union and anti-Semitic attitudes revived. From 1938, learning Russian was compulsory in schools, and Russian was the only language used in the Red Army.

Nevertheless, the Stalinist State remained officially opposed to racial discrimination. Most campaigns were politically rather than racially motivated.

Propaganda

Lenin used propaganda to convert people to socialism. Strong, visual messages were a powerful way of appealing to illiterate peasants.

Stalin exploited his own propaganda machine to gain support for collectivisation and industrialisation. The socialist message was reinforced by images of happy, productive workers, while heroes were praised as role models.

Stalin's propaganda also reinforced his own position, portraying him as a mighty, all-knowing leader, and a natural successor to Marx, Engels, Lenin and Stalin. Stalin encouraged cult status for Lenin after his death, and developed his own 'cult of personality'.

Cultural change

Greater freedom immediately after the revolution allowed culture to thrive. Freedom of expression was encouraged and the 1920s became the 'silver age' of Russian literature, poetry and music.

The Stalinist era reversed these developments. The visual and performing arts were seen as valuable only if they supported the creation of 'socialist man'. Creativity was replaced by conformity.

From 1932, writers, musicians, artists and film-makers had to belong to unions, which controlled their output. Writers and other artists were expected to depict 'social realism' – namely an uplifting vision of Soviet life in the socialist future. Literature and Art were to illustrate the inevitable 'march to Communism' and glorify the working man.

SUMMARY

- Under Bolshevik rule, the traditional classes such as the priests, nobles and bourgeoisie suffered. However, life for workers and peasants was also hard despite the emergence of new opportunities, for example for women or in education.
- Russian culture flourished in the 1920s but in the 1930s it declined as many earlier freedoms were curbed.
- The 1930s saw an extension of state control: the Church was further restricted and national minorities more tightly governed, while Stalinist propaganda promoted a return to 'traditional' Russian values.

 APPLY

APPLY YOUR KNOWLEDGE

a Look at the text and define or briefly explain the following terms (in relation to Stalinist Society):

Burzhui	
Proletariat	
Komsomol	
Socialist man (and woman)	
Social realism	
Stakhanovite	
Deportations	

b Write 2–3 sentences using these terms, to illustrate how each contributed to Soviet society in the 1920s and 1930s.

ASSESS THE VALIDITY OF THIS VIEW

A LEVEL **'Men benefited more than women from the social changes of the 1920s and 1930s in Russia.' Assess the validity of this view.**

Whilst it might be tempting to divide the answer into 2 parts, looking firstly at the degree to which men benefited from social changes and then evaluating the position of women, a better approach would be to select aspects of life to compare as in the given chart.

a To ensure your argument is supported by precise detail, complete each line of this chart with both a general comment and at least 1 piece of specific information with a date where possible.

	Men	Women
Ideology and attitudes		
Work opportunities		
Working conditions		
Living conditions		
Family		
Legal rights		

b Now plan and write your essay, using the thematic approach presented in this chart, addressing 1 theme per paragraph.

PLAN YOUR ESSAY

 How important was propaganda for the leaders of Russia in the years 1917 to 1941?

a Consider the ways in which propaganda would have been effective, and therefore important, and ways in which it would not. (In particular, reflect on which groups might have been less affected/ impressed by it or for whom its excesses might have encouraged feelings of hostility towards the regime.) Decide what judgement you would adopt.

b Write a conclusion for this essay which both conveys your judgement and summarises how you arrived at that judgement.

REVIEW

After studying Chapters 17 and 18 you could revisit this essay and create a plan which balances propaganda against other factors.

EXAMINER TIP

There are various ways of providing a balanced judgement. Looking at ways in which propaganda was effective (important) and ways in which it was not would be one. You could also weigh up the importance of propaganda against other factors, such as popular policies and fear.

KEY QUESTION

To consider the Key Question:

What was the extent of social and cultural change?

in Russia in the years 1917–41, create a set of 9 cards with the headings:

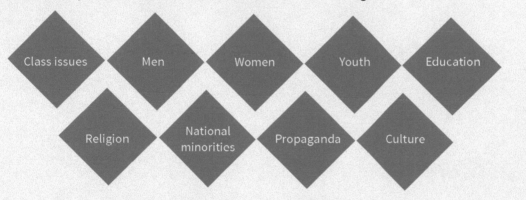

Class issues | Men | Women | Youth | Education

Religion | National minorities | Propaganda | Culture

a Provide a summary of key developments and issues on each card.

b Sort these cards into a 'diamond 9', ranked by the degree of change that occurred.

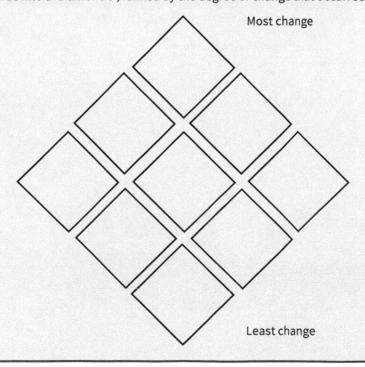

Most change

Least change

EXAMINER TIP

This activity will help you to prioritise relevant information when responding to exam questions.

17 Communist control and terror

Faction and opposition in the 1920s

Opposition, factions and the consolidation of power

On taking power, the Bolsheviks were not fully united in themselves. They also faced opposition from:

- other political parties
- those with alternative interests (from tsarists to peasants)
- ideologically opposed social groups – upper classes and bourgeoisie.

The Menshevik and SR walk-out from the Soviet Congress of October 1917 left the Bolsheviks in sole power. Kadet, Menshevik and SR leaders were arrested, other opponents were locked up and opposition newspapers were banned.

'Class warfare' was waged against the middle and upper classes. The *burzhui* were labelled 'former people'; their privileges were ended and they suffered heavy discrimination.

Factions and disagreements within the Party were ended by Lenin's 'ban on factions' of 1921. All Party members had to accept the decisions of the Central Committee or face expulsion from the Party. This eliminated any opportunity for debate or challenge.

The Red Terror

The outbreak of the Civil War, coupled with an attempt to assassinate Lenin in August 1918, led to a new wave of persecution against real and perceived enemies. This was known as the 'Red Terror'.

The Cheka (established in December 1917 under Dzerzhinsky) tracked down and destroyed the families of suspected traitors. Confessions and names of 'accomplices' were obtained by torture. Local Cheka agents sought out and 'discovered' opposition. Up to a million people were executed between 1918 and 1921; others were sent to Siberian labour camps (**gulags**), where many died. Even after 1921, when the worst of the Terror had passed, *kulaks* and Nepmen profiting from the NEP were subject to random persecution.

Opposition to Stalin and the purges

Stalin and opposition to 1932

Stalin extended the use of terror and class warfare to enforce collectivisation and industrialisation. In a series of 'show trials' between 1928 and 1932, 'bourgeois' managers, specialists and engineers were accused of sabotage or counter-revolutionary activities. Those escaping execution went to labour camps established by Yagoda from 1929 to boost economic growth while correcting prisoners.

The crisis of 1932

In 1932, at a time of strikes and famine, voices of opposition were heard within the Party elite. Ryutin even organised a petition for Stalin's removal. Stung by the 'Ryutin Affair', Stalin expelled many leading Communists from the Party and exiled them from Moscow. From 1933 to 1935 he conducted a general purge of the Party.

The Kirov Affair, 1934

At the 17th Party Congress in 1934, a show of unity masked underlying divisions. Some Politburo members wanted to maintain the pace of industrialisation, while others, including Kirov, the Leningrad (formerly Petrograd) Party Secretary, suggested stopping forcible grain seizures and increasing workers' rations; Kirov's approach appeared to enjoy more support.

Kirov was murdered in December 1934 and, despite a cover-up, Stalin was probably implicated. This provided an excuse for a decree allowing the NKVD (successor to the Cheka and headed from 1934 to 1936 by Yagoda) to arrest and execute anyone

The Great Purges

KEY CHRONOLOGY

1936 Aug	Show trial of Zinoviev, Kamenev and 14 others. All were found guilty of plotting to murder Stalin and other Politburo members and were executed
1937 Jan	At a show trial 13 prominent Communists were sentenced to death. Bukharin was expelled from the party and arrested
May/June	Eight senior military commanders, all Civil War heroes (including Marshal Tukhachevsky), were convicted of espionage and shot. A further purge of military personnel followed
1938 March	Bukharin and 15 others were shot for espionage and sabotage

found guilty of 'terrorist plotting'. In 1935, Zinoviev, Kamenev and 17 others were imprisoned. Around 11,000 'former people' were arrested, exiled or placed in camps and 250,000 Party members were expelled.

The Yezhovshchina, 1937–38

In 1937–38, the Great Purges merged with the Yezhovshchina (named after Yezhov, head of the NKVD). Terror was spread downwards into every town and village and increasingly hit ordinary citizens.

Everyone was watched, both by the NKVD and by friends and neighbours and each region was given a quota of 'enemies' to find. Many were executed and many died in prison. Yagoda, the former head of the NKVD, was shot in 1937.

The end of the purges

There were fewer purges after 1938, when it became clear that they were damaging industry and administration and threatening to destabilise the state.

In December 1938 Yezhov was replaced by Beria. 'Mass cleansings' were declared no longer necessary and hundreds of thousands were set free.

The execution of Yezhov and the assassination of Trotsky in Mexico in 1940 meant that almost everyone who might have rivalled Stalin for the leadership had been eliminated. Yezhov was generally blamed for the Terror, and popular faith in Stalin remained high.

SUMMARY

- The destruction of opposition escalated sharply from 1918 to 1921, as the Red Terror led to arrests and executions throughout the country.
- In the new highly centralised, one-party State, opposition became virtually impossible.
- Stalin's purges took repression and violence to new levels, affecting every section of society.
- By the end of the purges, Stalin was in a position of supreme power.

 **APPLY**

APPLY YOUR KNOWLEDGE

Look back through this chapter and create a timeline/flow chart to record the development of Communist control and terror from 1917 to 1941. For example:

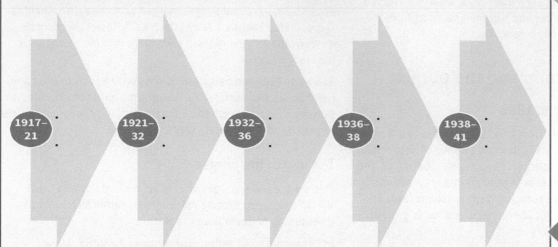

ASSESS THE VALIDITY OF THIS VIEW

It is important to break essay questions down, so that you examine all aspects. For example, you might be asked:

> **'The Stalinist purges were a necessary response to a genuine threat.' Assess the validity of this view.**

To answer this question, you would need to think about:

- The purges (dates and details of those purged).
- The reasons given for these purges, i.e. the 'threats' they were supposed to counter.
- The genuineness of the threats.
- The 'necessity' of the actions (and remember 'necessity' could be assessed from various angles, e.g. necessity for Stalin; necessity for the stability of the State).

a Breaking down the question should help you to formulate a response to it. Which of the following first sentences would you use in your introduction? (If you are not happy with any of them, provide your own.)

- 'The Stalinist purges were certainly a necessary response to a genuine threat.'
- 'The Stalinist purges were neither necessary, nor a response to a genuine threat.'
- 'The Stalinist purges were not necessary, but they were a response to a genuine threat.'
- 'The Stalinist purges may have been necessary for Stalinist authority, but they were certainly not a response to a genuine threat.'

b Now write an introduction to this essay, building on your chosen opening sentence to explain your choice of view with reference to the words of the question.

c When you have studied Chapter 20, you might like to attempt a full answer to this question. You might wish to argue that a 'threat' was stronger in one period than another.

KEY QUESTION

One of the Key Questions asks:

Why did opposition develop and how effective was it?

The following groups all opposed the leadership of the Soviet State in the years 1917–41:

- Supporters of other non-Bolshevik/Communist political parties.
- Those with alternative interests (from tsarists to peasants).
- Ideologically opposed social groups – upper classes and bourgeoisie.
- Leading Party members who disagreed with the official line.
- Minority nationality groups.

For each group, give examples of why they opposed, how they opposed and the degree of success/failure they met with.

KEY QUESTION

One of the Key Questions asks:

How important was the role of individuals and groups and how were they affected by developments?

A number of important individuals are mentioned in this chapter. Order the following chronologically and sort them by type – red for oppressors and blue for victims, with double shading for those who were both. Provide 1–2 bullet points on each, to show his part in Communist control and terror.

Lavrenty Beria
Leon Trotsky
Genrikh Yagoda
Nikolai Bukharin
Grigorii Zinoviev
Felix Dzerzhinsky
Mikhail Tukhachevsky
Sergei Kirov
Nikolai Yezhov
Lev Kamenev

EXAMINER TIP

Although some of these names may be difficult to remember (and spell), it is always worth learning them, so that you can write with precision in your essays. Appreciation of chronology is also important, so add specific dates wherever possible.

Victims and oppressors in Communist control and terror 1917–41

Oppressors (red) and victims (blue)	Part in Communist control and terror, with date(s)

18 The Soviet Union by 1941

RECAP

The political condition of the Soviet Union

One-party centralisation

Stalin had extended Lenin's single-party rule and Communist Party dominance so that by 1941 he led a highly centralised and authoritarian one-party state.

From the mid 1930s, Stalin was effectively a personal dictator. Despite this, he relied on a highly developed bureacracy which was subject to corruption. Moreover, some of his own policies (most notably the purges) actually weakened his control.

Attacks on opposition

Lenin had created the Cheka and developed a prison camp system to deal with his ideological and political enemies. He had carried out non-violent purges and introduced a ban on factions in 1921.

Stalin extended and intensified intolerance. During the Stalinist purges millions of ordinary citizens were arrested and 600,000 Party members were executed. The 'correction camps' developed into gulags providing slave labour. Nevertheless, he did not exert perfect control throughout the Soviet Union.

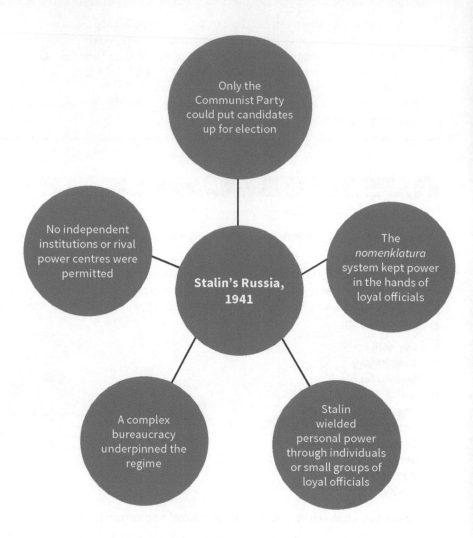

Only the Communist Party could put candidates up for election

No independent institutions or rival power centres were permitted

Stalin's Russia, 1941

The *nomenklatura* system kept power in the hands of loyal officials

A complex bureaucracy underpinned the regime

Stalin wielded personal power through individuals or small groups of loyal officials

Economic and social position

The Stalinist economy

By 1941, Stalin's Five Year Plans had transformed Russia into a highly industrialised and urbanised nation, while all Russian farms had been collectivised and the free market ended.

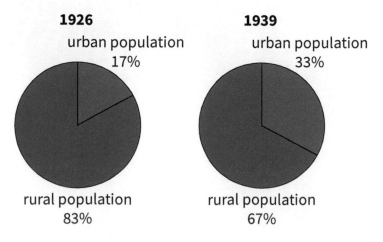

1926
urban population
17%

rural population
83%

1939
urban population
33%

rural population
67%

Rise in urban population, 1926–39

By 1940, the USSR had overtaken Britain in iron and steel production and was not far behind Germany. Moreover, Stalin's success in developing heavy industry, transport and power resources, and his huge investment in rearmament, were critical to the eventual Soviet victory in the Second World War.

However, there were economic weaknesses:

- Economic development was uneven – consumer goods were scarcer in 1941 than under the NEP.
- The quality of goods was poor, thanks to over-ambitious targets.
- The central planning system was inefficient and local organisation was sometimes chaotic.
- Grain production was lower in 1941 than under the NEP.

Stalinist society

Communist control in the countryside had been strengthened: peasants were living and working in the *kolkhozes*, supervised by Party officials and by NKVD units stationed at each Motor Tractor Station. In the cities, increased urbanisation had created a far stronger 'proletariat'. Socialist values were promoted through education, propaganda, the leadership cult, public celebrations, arts, culture and the show trials.

However, the quality of life did not improve significantly under Stalin:

- Living standards remained low.
- Freedom of movement was restricted.
- Censorship and propaganda dominated.
- Mass organisations manipulated the people.

For the working classes, capitalist exploitation had been replaced by Soviet oppression.

The Soviet Union by June 1941

The German invasion of June 1941 took Stalin by surprise. The USSR was not ready for war:

- The purges of the Red Army had weakened the army.
- Training was inadequate and military initiative had declined.
- Equipment and weapons were deficient.
- Increased military spending had reduced investment in the farm system, meaning that there was insufficient grain to feed the population.

Stalin's failure to prepare Russia for war allowed the German forces to overrun large amounts of Soviet territory in the first months of war.

KEY CHRONOLOGY

Political events

1918	Constituent Assembly dissolved
	Treaty of Brest-Litovsk
	Civil War begins
1921	Ban on factions
	Treaty of Riga; Civil War ends
1922	Constitution of USSR adopted
1924	Lenin dies
1926	United Opposition formed
1927	Defeat of left opposition
1929	Defeat of right opposition; Stalin undisputed leader
1934	Assassination of Kirov
1936	New Soviet constitution
1936–38	Stalin's purges
1941	Nazi invasion of USSR

KEY CHRONOLOGY

Economic and social events

1921–22	Great Famine
1928–32	First Five Year Plan
1929	Call for collectivisation and dekulakisation
1932–33	Famine in Ukraine and elsewhere
1933–37	Second Five Year Plan
1937–38	Height of Great Terror
1938–42	Third Five Year Plan

SUMMARY

- By 1941, Stalin led a centralised, authoritarian State, characterised by its intolerance of opposition and brutal persecution of its so-called enemies.
- Russia had been transformed into an industrialised and urbanised nation, with an economy that was strong enough to compete with the West.
- Instead of the classless society envisaged before the October Revolution, Russia had become a hierarchical society dominated by a privileged elite. Instead of 'withering away' the State had become more formidable, extensive and brutal.

 **APPLY**

APPLY YOUR KNOWLEDGE

Look at the information given on the diagram of Stalin's Russia in 1941 in Chapter 18, page 92.

If, as part of an essay, you were required to assess the political condition of the USSR in 1941, you would need to order these points logically and explain their significance.

a List the points in order of importance.

b Add a comment to explain the point and its significance fully.

c Write a paragraph encompassing this information, ensuring that one point leads smoothly into the next in a logical and coherent way.

 EXAMINER TIP

Prioritising and showing the interrelationship of ideas are important historical skills. Try to avoid turning your essays into lists and think instead about how one point relates to the next.

ASSESS THE VALIDITY OF THIS VIEW

> **A LEVEL** **'Purges and attacks on opposition had considerably weakened the USSR by 1941.' Assess the validity of this view.**

In consequence essays of this type, it is important that you focus on the 'impact' of events rather than on details of the events themselves. It is helpful, however, to break down consequences into different types. You might, for example consider the following:

- economic weakness
- military weakness
- political weakness
- psychological weakness.

a Find 1–2 pieces of evidence for each area to illustrate the ways in which the purges weakened the USSR.

 EXAMINER TIP

A Level essays fall into various types: causation, change and continuity, significance and consequence. Identifying the type should help your planning.

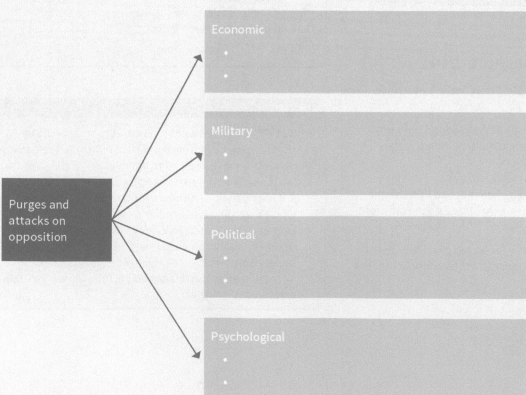

Weakness

Purges and attacks on opposition

Economic

Military

Political

Psychological

 REVIEW

For Lenin's early attacks on opposition, look back to Chapters 12 and 14.

b Find some counter-arguments, supported by evidence, suggesting the purges either made little difference or even strengthened the USSR.

c Decide your judgement and plan your essay thematically.

EXTRACT ANALYSIS

EXTRACT A

Stalinism was not simply nationalism, bureaucratisation, absence of democracy, censorship, police repression and the rest. These phenomena have appeared in many societies and are rather easily explained. Instead, Stalinism was excess and extraordinary extremism in each. It was not, for example, merely coercive peasant policies, but a virtual civil war against the peasantry, not merely police repression, or even civil war-style terror, but a holocaust by terror that victimised tens of millions of people for 25 years; not merely a revival of nationalist tradition, but an almost fascist-like aggressive patriotism, not merely a leader-cult, but deification of a despot. Excesses were the essence of historical Stalinism and they are what really require explanation.

Adapted from Stephen E. Cohen, *Bolshevism and Stalinism*, 1977

EXTRACT B

The State which set out to abolish the State failed to produce a society capable of constructing an economy which was able to satisfy the aspirations of its members.

The Communist Party mobilised the resources of the country during the 1930s in the pursuit of rapid growth of heavy industry, energy and transport. Success was such that its military potential made it possible to defeat Germany. Stalin can be forgiven for believing that he had found the key to political and economic success. Ironically, at its apogee, the Stalinist system was revealing the cracks which were later to undermine the foundations of the USSR. The very success of industrial expansion rendered it more and more difficult to manage the system from the centre. An army of bureaucrats had been brought into existence to run the State in the interests of the leader. However, this nomenklatura, once freed from the murderous arbitrariness of the Stalin era, became an interest group which gradually ran the USSR in its own way.

Adapted from Martin McCauley, *The Soviet Union 1917–1991*, 1993

EXTRACT C

Stalin's most important contribution to communist theory was in his advocacy and adoption of the notion of 'Socialism in One Country'. This was not a particularly insightful concept, since it represented little more than a theoretical justification of actual developments in the USSR. Nor was it Stalin who originally devised the concept. The policy basically justified attempts to build socialism in a country that Lenin had admitted was not, in itself, ready for socialism. The policy thus contradicted classical Marxism. But it appealed to Soviet citizens. Most were tired of wars and revolution and wanted stability. Socialism in one country was also used to justify the introduction of other key features of Stalin's approach. These were industrialisation, via a centrally planned economy, and collectivisation of agriculture. Although it would be stretching a point to argue that two further features of Stalinism – high levels of state terror and a personality cult – were part of communist theory, they did become salient features of communist practice.

Adapted from Leslie Holmes, *Communism, A Very Short Introduction*, 2009

REVIEW

The contextual own knowledge needed to evaluate the views in the extracts about the meaning of Stalinism will need to be drawn from the whole of Section 3 of this book, so you should look back over Chapters 13 to 18.

A **LEVEL** **Using your understanding of the historical context, assess how convincing the arguments in Extracts A, B and C are in relation to what is meant by 'Stalinism' in the USSR.**

a   Read each extract in turn and:

  - Underline the parts which offer an opinion/argument on the topic in the question.

  - Write a one-sentence summary of the overall argument.

  - Note any sub-arguments relating to Stalinism.

  - Make brief notes on key contextual own knowledge which could be used to corroborate the argument.

  _____

  _____

  _____

  _____

  _____

  _____

  _____

  _____

  - Make brief notes on key contextual own knowledge which could be used to criticise the argument.

  _____

  _____

  _____

  _____

  _____

  _____

  _____

  _____

b   You should now be in a position to write a full exam-style answer in response to the question. Remember you should be evaluating these extracts **'in relation to what is meant by Stalinism in the USSR'**. You should spend approximately 15 minutes on each extract.

EXAMINER TIP

You should always present the overall argument of each extract first in your evaluation. This should be developed and evaluated with reference to the text and your own contextual knowledge.

A Level extracts sample answer

REVIEW

On these Exam Practice pages, you will find a sample student answer for an A Level extracts question. What are the strengths and weaknesses of the answer? Read the answer and the corresponding Examiner Tips carefully. Think about how you could apply this advice in order to improve your own answers to questions like this one.

 Using your understanding of the historical context, assess how convincing the arguments in these three extracts are in relation to popular support for Stalinism.

30 marks

REVISION SKILLS

The A Level exam paper will have one extracts question which is compulsory; the question will be linked to three historical interpretations with different views. Read page 6 of this Revision Guide for details on how to master the extracts question.

EXTRACT A

The Soviet industrialisation drive was managed by one of the most powerful, coercive and centralised state systems of the twentieth century. In the mid 1930s, Stalin's authority grew to the point where he no longer depended on the Party, but established a uniquely personal form of rule. The atmosphere of crisis created by collectivisation, the purges, and fears of foreign attack, generated a paranoid mood which strengthened the leadership by making any form of opposition look like treachery. But despite its harshness, the Stalinist government enjoyed much popular support. Many people did well during the purge era, particularly those who rose rapidly through the Party's ranks. At the same time, many ordinary Soviet citizens seem to have accepted the patriotic promises of Stalinist propaganda. The huge mobilisational effort of the 1930s turned the Soviet Union into a great military and industrial power and generated a surprising amount of popular support.

Adapted from David Christian, *Imperial and Soviet Russia,* 1986

EXTRACT B

By greatly increasing the numbers of people who could read, the Communist Party ensured that there was a wider audience for its written propaganda. A fundamental part of Stalinist propaganda was the virtual deification of Stalin through the cult of personality. It had a number of purposes, including linking Stalin to the country's achievements and portraying him as Lenin's heir. This personalisation of power coincided with the process by which the dictatorship of the proletariat became the dictatorship of Stalin. During collectivisation and industrialisation millions suffered greatly at the hands of the Stalinist State. However, Soviet propaganda presented a picture which had some grains of truth in it, and while remembering the horrors that Stalinism brought to many, it must also be acknowledged that some people benefited from the system. Many thousands of workers and Communists were pulled up into the system, creating a huge cohort of beneficiaries.

Adapted from Jonathan Davis, *Stalin from Grey Blur to Great Terror,* 2008

EXTRACT C

Possibly the outstanding feature of the Stalinist system in the 1930s was its arbitrariness. No official, no specialist, no policeman could ever feel absolutely safe in his position. Since there was no personal security, there was no institutional security. No group or institution was ever permitted to congeal into a potential opposition. But not all the coercion in the world would have driven the Soviet Union forward had the population not been in sympathy with the goals of the Five Year Plans. There was enormous suffering, but Stalin was able to detach himself, in the common mind, from this to become the beloved leader of the nation. Many went to their deaths believing that had Comrade Stalin only known what was going on, he would have saved them from injustice. Stalinism flowered in the 1930s in responsive soil. It owed more to Russian political culture than to the westernising tradition of social democracy.

Adapted from Martin MacCauley, *The Soviet Union, 1917–1991,* 1981

Sample student answer

Extract A argues that Stalinism had an unexpectedly high degree of popular support. It points out that Stalin's regime was centralised and authoritarian, and maintained through an 'atmosphere of crisis'. It also suggests that some people benefited from the regime and that ordinary citizens believed the Stalinist propaganda. These factors and military and industrial successes meant that Stalin was generally supported.

The evidence largely appears to support this view. There was certainly an atmosphere of fear and repression ('a paranoid mood') under Stalin. This was caused by his collectivisation and industrialisation policies which often involved unrealistic targets and harsh punishments. Stalin's purges of Party members and senior military commanders such as Marshal Tukhachevsky and the Yezhovshchina spread terror. But despite this, there seems to have been little opposition to Stalin's regime and any perceived opposition was soon stamped out. The extract is correct to argue that many people benefited from Stalin's regime – the purges created new jobs in the bureaucracy and elsewhere, and Stalin created a new elite of loyal younger Party members with special privileges.

On the other hand, not all of Stalin's policies were popular. The first stage of his collectivisation policy had to be abandoned because of hostility in the countryside. Also, just because people were too afraid to protest does not mean they all supported Stalin. Propaganda increased the loyalty of the ordinary Russians and Russian peasants were traditionally devoted to whoever was their leader.

The argument in this extract is convincing because it explains the high degree of popular support for the regime with reference to Stalinist policies. It is also a balanced argument because it suggests this was achieved despite the harsh central authority and Stalinist repression. However, its view that 'many' people did well during the purge era could be challenged, particularly given the numbers persecuted in the Red Terror.

Extract B argues that increasing educational opportunities so that more people could read meant that Stalin could be portrayed as a god-like figure through the use of propaganda; this meant that Stalin could become a personal dictator.

The extract refers to 'greatly increasing the numbers of people who could read' and this is valid. Under Stalin, education grew although it became more traditional and concentrated on

EXAMINER TIP

The introductory sentence is strong, because it clearly sets out the overall argument, referring back directly to the words in the question. The rest of the paragraph makes a good attempt to summarise the sub-arguments.

EXAMINER TIP

This paragraph provides detail to support the overall argument, both by referencing the text and by providing detailed own knowledge to substantiate the comments. The use of words such as 'largely' can be helpful when you are providing a judgement that something is not entirely the case. The word 'perceived' shows conceptual awareness, making this a high-quality paragraph.

EXAMINER TIP

Again, there is good use of own knowledge to challenge the argument. The comment that 'just because people were too afraid to protest does not mean they all supported Stalin' is excellent and shows conceptual depth. The statement that 'Propaganda increased the loyalty of ordinary Russians' is not supported – it simply assumes that propaganda was successful. However, the final sentence shows good awareness that peasants had transferred their devotion to their tsar to Stalin.

EXAMINER TIP

This assessment is well-focused and reinforces the understanding of the overall argument as given in the introduction. It reaches a judgement on how convincing the argument is and comments on a possible limitation which, although undeveloped, shows awareness of an alternative side.

EXAMINER TIP

The answer has made the mistake of equating the first sentence with the overall argument, forgetting that the argument needs to be identified in relation to the question (in this case, popular support for Stalinism). In fact, the main argument is that popular support for Stalinism was achieved through propaganda which portrayed him as a god-like figure, alongside a political transformation that allowed him to become a dictator by allowing some people to benefit from his regime.

industrial skills. It goes on to talk of 'the virtual deification of Stalin through the cult of personality'. This is also true, as giant posters of Stalin were placed on the streets, in factories and even on collective farms. It also states that 'millions suffered greatly' from starvation during the famines, the strict discipline in factories and the persecutions during the purges. However, like Extract A, it points out that there were people who benefited from the system, which is also true, as seen above.

The argument is convincing in that it tries to give a balanced view of how some people suffered and others benefited from the regime. However it does not really give specific examples of who these were or why they benefited, which weakens it.

Extract C puts forward the view that Stalin was popular because he was able to separate himself in the people's mind from some of the less pleasant things in the 1930s. Although the regime was 'arbitrary' the extract suggests that the USSR would not have developed as it did if the people had not had 'sympathy with the goals of the Five Year Plans'. It argues that the regime enjoyed a high level of popular support because the ordinary people ('the common mind') still saw Stalin as their 'beloved leader'.

There is some evidence to support this view. For example, the Five Year Plans were so successful that Germany declared war on Russia in 1941 (earlier than planned) in order to prevent industrial expansion. This would have been difficult if the workers and managers had not supported the programme – even if extreme examples like that of Stakhanov were exaggerated. All peasant households had been collectivised in 1941, suggesting that the peasants were won over. The absence of any form of opposition, even cultural dissent, under Stalin, also suggests that people were generally supportive of the regime despite the Terror and the purges.

However, the argument is not entirely convincing. Not all targets were met in the Five Year Plans, and even after collectivisation, most peasants preferred to work on their private plots than for the kolkhozes. This suggests that there was not full popular support of Stalin's policies. There would not have been much popular support from the kulaks, who lost their land in dekulakisation, or from the peasants who lost grain and livestock under requisitioning. The believers would not have been happy about the restrictions on the Church either (including closing church buildings and replacing Sunday with a six-day week). Ethnic minorities would also have resented policies to strengthen

EXAMINER TIP

This paragraph fails to identify the overall argument, which has led to some irrelevant detail on education. It shows the application of own knowledge to support the detail of the extract, rather than support (and criticise) its views.

Comparison between extracts is not required at A Level and an answer on one extract should never rely on a cross-reference to information about another.

EXAMINER TIP

The answer attempts a judgement but unfortunately does not address the question. Instead it focuses on Extract B's last three sentences. By failing to identify the overall argument in the extract correctly, the answer has lost its way.

EXAMINER TIP

This first sentence of this paragraph identifies the main argument well, referring back to the question. It goes on to give a clear account of the sub-arguments, referring closely to the extract. The quotations chosen are short and appropriate.

EXAMINER TIP

This paragraph demonstrates good use of detailed and precise evidence to support the argument in the extract.

EXAMINER TIP

This paragraph demonstrates excellent use of detailed historical knowledge, which is effectively used to challenge the argument for popular support put forward in the extract. Notice the close adherence to the topic of the question which keeps the detail focused.

central control and reduce the nationalities' rights. This suggests that popular support for the Stalinist regime was actually more limited than the extract suggests.

The extract is not entirely convincing. It gives good examples of where there seemed to be popular support, which can be substantiated by other evidence, but it ignores a large number of groups, such as the kulaks and cultural dissidents, who did not support Stalinism.

EXAMINER TIP

A strong conclusion, giving a direct judgement. It is not expansive but it is clear and in accordance with what has gone before.

OVERALL COMMENT

Had this student sustained the quality seen in the answers to Extracts A and C across Extract B, this would have been worthy of the top level. However, the weaker answer to Extract B detracts from the overall mark, which would therefore be in Level 4. For two extracts, this student combines understanding with a strong appreciation of context to give an effective evaluation of the argument. In the other, there is some supported comment on the views in the extract, showing an understanding of context and a broad focus on the question, but the overall argument has not been identified and there is limited evaluation.

OVER TO YOU

Give yourself 60 minutes to answer this question on your own. Consider this checklist when reviewing your answer. Have you:

☐ Identified the overall argument of each extract?

☐ Shown the strengths **and** limitations of each extract?

☐ Referred to the detail of the extracts and your own knowledge to support your comments?

Go back and look at pages 71–96 to help review you refresh your knowledge of popular support for Stalin.

19 Stalinism in wartime

 **RECAP**

Russia at war: political authority and opposition

In 1939, Stalin had signed the Nazi–Soviet Pact with Germany. Although neither side had expected this alliance to last indefinitely, the German invasion of the USSR in June 1941 found Russia unprepared for war.

Stalin was stunned into inaction for a week. He left Molotov to make the announcement of war public and the Politburo to organise new governmental and military structures, including the creation of a civilian State Defence Committee (GKO).

Stalin's resumption of authority as Head of Government (a position created in May), and leader of Stavka (the Supreme Military Command) in July, placed all authority in his hands. Although he largely left the running of the war to his military commanders, Stalin used his position to bolster morale, build up patriotism and unite the nation.

Stalin's authority thus met with no outright opposition during the war period. However, not all Russians supported him. Many national minorities even welcomed the invading Germans as liberators from the Stalinist regime.

The political, economic and social impact of the war

Political impact

- The war saw the deportation of whole nations and ethnic groups away from their homelands, in an effort to counter potential threats to state security. (This was brutally implemented and many died.)

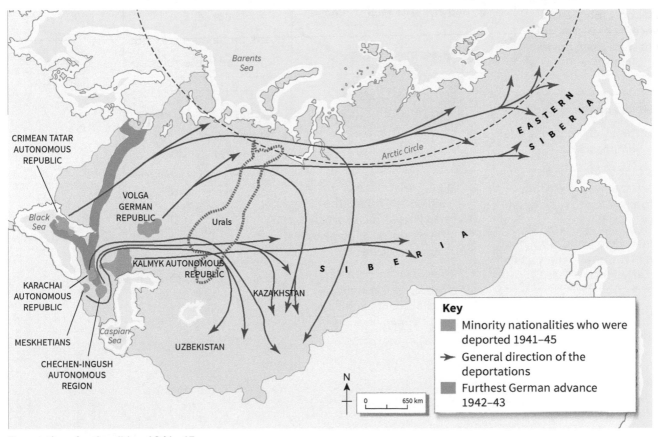

Deportation of nationalities, 1941–45

- The Communist Party grew and changed in composition, as millions of army and navy members joined as a result of the intense political propaganda meted out to the troops.
- Victory in war strengthened belief in the communist system. Stalin could portray the war as a victory of communism (i.e. Stalinism) over fascism.

Economic impact

The economy had to be reorganised to ensure economic survival:

- Farmland was destroyed to make it useless to the invading Germans.
- Factories and their workers were transferred from western Russia to an area east of the Ural mountains.
- Wartime production was quickly established, thanks to the USSR's centralised, planned economy.
- Most national expenditure was diverted to military requirements, with focus on building giant heavy industrial complexes to manufacture munitions. By mid 1943 the USSR's industrial output outperformed that of Germany.
- Food shortages were addressed by rationing and quotas from the *kolkhozes*.

Social impact

The panic caused by the invasion helped to reunite society, as men rushed to sign up for military service. Stalin referred to the 'Great Patriotic War' to strengthen a spirit of sacrifice for the Motherland, but physical conditions were very hard.

Soldiers and workers

All sections of society were recruited and centrally deployed for war work.

Working hours were increased.

Discipline (in both factories and army) was tightened.

Living conditions

Food shortages led to the deaths of millions.

Many had to flee the German advance or relocate to factories in the east.

Housing and fuel shortages were acute.

Health problems increased.

Many died in the gulags.

Churches

Persecution was temporarily halted.

The Churches were used to boost morale and encourage patriotism (but were given no real autonomy).

Social impact of war

Women and the family

The importance of the family was emphasised.

Women's burdens increased – they were essential wartime workers but also expected to raise large families.

Women worked in industry, on farms or in the armed forces, but received little reward.

Partisans

Many Soviet citizens and soldiers left behind the German lines formed partisan groups, using sabotage against the enemy.

They risked terrible Nazi reprisals, as did innocent civilians caught behind the German lines.

Propaganda and culture

Intense propaganda was used to promote unity.

Posters and the press encouraged heroism and self-sacrifice.

Artists and musicians enjoyed more freedom, to encourage an atmosphere of national reconciliation.

The effect of war on Stalin, government and the people

Stalin

The war turned Stalin into a hero. Yet, after 1945, his anxiety about real or imagined enemies grew stronger. Returning prisoners-of-war were frequently transferred to labour camps; collaborators who had fought for Germany against the USSR were executed, with reprisals against their communities; other returning servicemen were interrogated by the NKVD, and either rewarded with promotions or sent to the gulags.

Government

The war appeared to vindicate Stalin's belief in his system. The war established the USSR's reputation as a great military power and not only were all the regions occupied under the Nazi–Soviet pact retained, the USSR also acquired a band of satellite states in eastern Europe. Stalin thus continued as Head of Government and Party Secretary and the Politburo continued to operate as in the 1930s.

People

The Russian people endured terrible wartime suffering. Nearly 30 million civilian and soldiers were killed and 25 million people in the west lost their homes.

Despite this, the war brought hope for the future.

- The sense of collective endeavour revived hopes of change.
- Comradeship among soldiers helped spread new liberal thinking.
- Greater exposure to Western influence led to hope that post-war society might be more open.

Such hopes were not to be realised. In reality, the years between 1945 and 1953 were among the most bleak of the entire Stalinist period.

SUMMARY

- The Second World War, beginning for the USSR in 1941, had immense political, economic and social consequences.
- The Soviet armed forces rallied and the Soviet economy was restructured and survived. Government became even more personal and autocratic and Stalin emerged as a super-hero.
- For the Soviet people, the war brought extreme hardship and control. Used to suffering in the 1930s, the people of the Soviet Union fought for sheer survival, but as the promise of victory grew closer, so too did their hopes of change in the future.

 **APPLY**

APPLY YOUR KNOWLEDGE

Look carefully at the diagram on the social impact of war, on page 102. In an exam, you could be asked to evaluate the social impact of the war. To help in this:

a Organise the detail in a hierarchy. Select what you feel to have been the harshest impact, affecting the most people, to place at the top and work down to the least severe, affecting fewest people, at the bottom.

b Justify your choice.

_____

_____

_____

EXAMINER TIP

In an essay requiring an evaluation of the social impact of war, the ordering of factors in a logical way (from the most to the least harsh) would show that you had thought about the issues and were able to prioritise.

TO WHAT EXTENT?

A LEVEL **With reference to the years 1928 to 1945, to what extent was Stalin's political authority changed by the Great Patriotic War?**

a To answer this question, you will need to select relevant evidence from this chapter about the effect of war on Stalin's political authority. Looking at this thematically will enable you to make comparisons with the pre-war years. Find 2–3 bullet points of evidence for the following themes:

- Stalin's position at the head of government.

  _____

  _____

- Degree of delegation.

  _____

  _____

- Dealing with opposition (real and imagined).

  _____

  _____

- The Party.

  _____

  _____

- Propaganda.

  _____

  _____

- Personal prestige.

  _____

  _____

b Now plan and write an answer to the question. By comparing the wartime situation with what went before through each of these themes in turn, you should be able to write a well-focused, coherent and balanced essay.

REVIEW

For detail on Stalin's political authority in the years 1928–41, revisit Chapters 13, 14, 17 and 18.

EXAMINER TIP

Comparative essays always require careful planning. By avoiding a chronological run-through of Stalin's political authority in wartime, it becomes much easier to make meaningful comparisons across the period of this question.

IMPROVE AN ANSWER

An essay evaluating the success of economic change in the years 1928–45 would require a paragraph on the years of war. Here is a sample paragraph:

> In 1941 the Nazis invaded the USSR in a three-pronged attack. Once Stalin had recovered from the shock, which left him inactive for a week, he took steps to organise the Soviet economy to resist the attack. His military commanders followed a scorched earth policy so that farmland was left useless for the Germans. This did not help the Russian peasants, but many were, in any case, conscripted into wartime industry. Whole factories were dismantled and transferred east of the Ural mountains so that production could continue and there was a huge effort to step up armaments manufacture and the output of other heavy goods needed for the Russian armies. Even though the Germans penetrated deep into Russia, the Soviets drove them back from Stalingrad in 1943, scoring a moral victory. Despite all the upheaval, the Russian people survived by sheer hard work and extreme rationing which made the most of the little food there was and by 1945, the Red Army had forced the Nazis back to Berlin, where they were destroyed. This shows that, during the war years, the Russian economy was a success.

a Sections of this paragraph are irrelevant; score them out.

b The paragraph is poorly ordered with the comment on economic success coming last instead of first. Rewrite the first sentence.

c The information in this paragraph is presented very descriptively. Rewrite this paragraph to improve the answer and make the given information more relevant to the question.

EXAMINER TIP

The order and way in which you present your material within a paragraph is very important. Facts followed by a concluding sentence will never provide as convincing an argument as an opinion supported by facts.

KEY QUESTION

In order to add to your understanding of the Key Question:

What was the extent of social and cultural change?

it would be helpful to complete the change and continuity chart below:

Area	Key developments 1941–45	Change from 1930s	Continuity from 1930s
Women			
Working men			
Churches			
National minorities			
Cultural environment			

EXAMINER TIP

By drawing up charts of this type, you will be able to assess breadth developments, as required in essays, more easily.

REVIEW

For detail of society in the 1930s, look back at Chapter 16.

20 Political authority, 1945–53

 RECAP

Political authority and government to 1953 – High Stalinism

In the years 1945–53 (often known as 'High Stalinism'), Stalin's authority over State and Party reached new heights. As the hero of the war and the head of a new world superpower, no one would dare challenge his leadership.

Political High Stalinism

Stalin's post-war policies re-established the regime of the 1930s and assured his personal dominance.

- Wartime institutions were dismantled.
- The military hierarchy was downgraded – Stalin became Minister of Defence and senior officers were moved to inferior posts.
- Although a new Politburo and Secretariat were elected in 1946, Stalin remained Head of Government and Head of the Party.
- The Politburo became an advisory body with decisions made by Stalin and his inner circle.
- The Party lost its autonomy and became a bureaucratic structure, with members recruited from 'administrative' ranks; the 'old guard' of members committed to Marxist ideals disappeared.

Cultural High Stalinism

New controls over intellectual life were introduced in the Zhdanovshchina (so-called after Zhdanov, who launched a cultural purge in 1946). The movement stressed conformity to socialist ideals and promoted the cult of Stalin. Everything Western was condemned as bourgeois and decadent; all things Russian were regarded as superior and uplifting.

- 'Anti-Soviet' authors (particularly those supportive of Western culture) were condemned and the publication of works forbidden.
- Social realism again became the norm in literature, art, music and film.
- Only pro-Soviet foreign writers and artists were allowed to visit the USSR and very few Soviet citizens were allowed to travel to the West.

The revival of terror and destruction of 'supposed opposition'

High Stalinism also saw a revival of terror. Stalin demanded an excessive isolationism from the non-Soviet world, partly out of concern for national security and partly from fear of ideological contamination.

As well as harshly treating returned prisoners-of-war and former army officers, the regime maintained constant vigilance over Soviet citizens. Any contact with foreigners could lead to imprisonment in a gulag.

Under Lavrenty Beria, the head of the security service, the gulag system was vastly expanded. The NKVD was itself strengthened and reorganised.

Between 1945 and 1953, around 12 million were sent to the labour camps, where they suffered appalling conditions.

Dealing with 'opposition'

All potential opposition was crushed.

'Doctoring' History

Those in disgrace (including the old Bolsheviks) were deleted from history books and airbrushed from photographs.

Anti-Semitism

Stalin feared Soviet Jews as potential enemies. The director of the Jewish theatre in Moscow was killed in a suspicious car accident, Jewish wives of Politburo members were arrested, and a new campaign against 'anti-patriotic groups' was launched.

The Leningrad Case, 1949

Leading officials in the 'Leningrad Party' were arrested on false evidence and some were executed.

Suppression of opposition

The Mingrelian Case (Georgian Purge) 1951–52

This purge in Georgia was directed against Beria's supporters, who were accused of collaboration with the West.

The Doctors' Plot, 1952

Stalin used an alleged doctors' conspiracy to accuse Jews in the medical profession of attempting to murder Soviet leaders. Many were tortured to extract confessions.

Stalin's cult of personality after 1945

From 1946, Stalin became increasingly reclusive and irrational. However public adulation remained undimmed and he was accorded a god-like status. He was portrayed as the world's greatest living person and a 'man of the people' even though he spent most of his later years in seclusion. Newspapers praised him, towns took on his name, 'Stalin' prizes were founded, ovations were given, and monuments to him, including giant statues, were set up through the USSR and its satellite states.

The power vacuum on Stalin's death

At a Party Congress in October 1952 (the first since 1939):

- Stalin suggested stepping down from his position as Party Secretary, but Stalin had done nothing to prepare a successor and the suggestion was rejected by delegates bewildered by his intentions.
- The Politburo was replaced by a **Presidium** with members nominated by Stalin; this seemed to suggest preparations for a new purge.

Stalin's death in March 1953 led to hysterical public displays of grief. It also triggered a political leadership struggle between the three most prominent Party leaders: Beria, Malenkov and Molotov. Khrushchev, although a prominent speaker at the Congress, was initially considered lower in the power rankings.

> **SUMMARY**
>
> - From 1945 to 1953 Stalin's authority was so high that this period is often known as 'High Stalinism'.
> - Although he was politically supreme, Stalin ruthlessly suppressed all opposition, through the 'Zhdanovshchina' and revived the Terror.
> - It was almost impossible to question Stalin, or for a potential successor to emerge.

APPLY

APPLY YOUR KNOWLEDGE

a Draw a mind-map, similar to the one below, to illustrate the different elements that went to make up 'High Stalinism'.

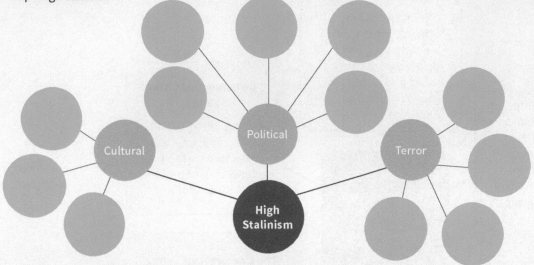

b Beneath your diagram, write a definition of the term, 'High Stalinism'.

EXAMINER TIP

It is often helpful to use historical terminology, such as 'High Stalinism' in essays, but you should never use terms that you have not properly understood.

REVIEW

To distinguish between 'High Stalinism' and the Stalinism of the 1930s, look back at Chapters 14–18.

ASSESS THE VALIDITY OF THIS VIEW

> **A LEVEL** 'The more power Stalin acquired, the more determined he became to persecute those whom he feared might oppose him.' Assess the validity of this view with reference to the years 1932 to 1953.

Since this essay addresses motivation over time, you should plan it along broadly chronological lines. To do so, it is helpful to think of key 'turning point' dates and to record the information in chart form. This will enable you to make a judgement.

a Complete the planning chart below.

Years beginning:	Stalin's power	Persecution of opposition	Does evidence support or contradict the view of the quotation?
1932			
1936			
1941			
1946			

b Decide on your judgement. You could then write the opening sentences of your paragraphs – or a full essay.

REVIEW

To remind yourself of Stalin's actions from 1932, look back at Chapter 17. Opposition in wartime is addressed in Chapter 19.

EXAMINER TIP

Remember that when you write your essay, your comment (Column 4) should come first in your paragraph and the evidence (Columns 2 and 3) should be used to support that.

EXTRACT ANALYSIS

EXTRACT A

Stalin and Zhdanov picked up where they had left off before the war, debating how to merge the patriotic Russianness of the war with the Bolshevism of the Revolution in order to eradicate foreign influence and restore morality, pride and discipline. Like two crabby professors, obsessed with the greatness of nineteenth-century culture and repulsed by the degeneracy of modern art and morals, the old seminarist and the scion of provincial intelligentsia reached back to their youths, devising a savage attack on modernism ('formalism') and foreign influence on Russian culture ('cosmopolitanism'). Poring over poetry and literary journals late into the night, these two meticulous, ever-tinkering 'intellectuals' who shared that ravenous Bolshevik appetite for education, cooked up the crackdown on the cultural freedom of wartime.

Steeped in the classics, despising new-fangled art, Zhdanov embarked on a policy that would have been familiar to Tsars Alexander I and Nicholas I. Victory had blessed the marriage of Russianness and Bolshevism: Stalin saw the Russians as the binding element of the USSR, the 'elder brother' of the Soviet peoples, his own new brand of Russian nationalism very different from its nineteenth-century ancestor. There would be no new freedoms, no foreign influences, but these impulses would be suppressed in an enforced celebration of Russianness.

Adapted from Simon Sebag Montefiore, *The Court of the Red Tsar*, 2003

a Comprehension

Read the extract carefully.

- Pick out two references that are factually correct.
- Pick out two references that show extreme opinion.
- Summarise the overall view of this extract.

b Evaluation

With reference to this extract and your understanding of the historical context, assess how convincing the argument is, in relation to the Zhdanovshchina.

APPLY YOUR KNOWLEDGE

Define the following words and terms, in relation to Stalin's political authority 1945–53, and write a sentence to show your understanding of each in context:

World superpower

_____

'Old Guard'

_____

Zhdanovshchina

_____

Ideological contamination

_____

NKVD

_____

Anti-Semitism

_____

Presidium

_____

EXAMINER TIP

Using these terms correctly in an exam question will help you to demonstrate your understanding of key concepts.

21 Khrushchev and reaction to Stalinism, 1953–64

 **RECAP**

Khrushchev's rise to power

As Stalin was dying, the newly created Presidium debated the succession.

Date	Key events in 1953
March	Malenkov was appointed Party Secretary and Chairman of the Council of Ministers. Within days, he was replaced as Party Secretary by Khrushchev. A collective leadership was established comprising Malenkov, Khrushchev, Molotov (Foreign Minister) and Beria (Head of NKVD). Khrushchev began appointing his protégés to important Party posts and quietly built up a strong support network in the Party's administration.
March–June	Beria proposed a departure from Stalinist policies, including the release of most political prisoners. The popularity of his proposals, combined with the power of his office, caused alarm among the Party elite.
June	Beria was arrested by the military, following a conspiracy involving Malenkov and Khrushchev.
Dec	Beria was executed after being secretly tried for 'criminal anti-party and anti-state activities'. His supporters were purged.

Policy differences caused further divisions in the leadership.

Malenkov (supported by Molotov)

Placed government before Party.

Wanted to launch a 'new course' (change collective farm policy, reduce peasant taxes, invest more in consumer goods).

Khrushchev

Placed Party before government.

Offered a less radical proposal (develop heavy and light industry, and implement Virgin Lands Scheme).

Leadership divisions, 1954

Khrushchev won Party support, thanks to the early successes of his Virgin Lands Scheme, and rose steadily to become the Party leader and head of government.

Date	Key events in 1955–58
Feb 1955	In February 1955 Malenkov was replaced as Chairman of the Council of Ministers by Khrushchev's protégé Bulganin. Khrushchev and Bulganin were to act as joint leaders until 1958.
June 1957	An attempt to have Khrushchev dismissed failed: Khrushchev brought supporters to Moscow to vote in the Central Committee, and enlisted the support of the Red Army, particularly the war hero Marshal Zhukov. Zhukov spoke out against Malenkov and Molotov. The plotters (labelled the 'anti-Party group') were outvoted, expelled from the Central Committee, and subsequently sent away from Moscow. Zhukov and other supporters were given seats in the Presidium.
Oct 1957	Zhukov was dismissed and a propaganda campaign launched against him.
March 1958	Bulganin was accused of encouraging the anti-Party group and forced to step down. Khrushchev took over as General Secretary of the Party. The two top jobs – in Party and government – were combined again.

Policies and ideology, and de-Stalinisation

By the beginning of 1956, Khrushchev had begun to reverse Stalinist policies, releasing prisoners and attacking the police and the gulag system.

At the 20th Party Congress in February 1956, he delivered a speech that was so sensitive that it was delivered in a secret 'closed session' (though its content soon spread). In it, Khrushchev:

- accused Stalin of responsibility for the purges, terror, torture, mass arrests, executions and the gulags
- blamed Stalin for betraying Leninist principles and for harming socialist progress
- questioned Stalin's war leadership.

However, Khrushchev's reformist principles were limited:

- His speech did not criticise economic controls, strong leadership, a single party or the elimination of factions.
- He brutally suppressed uprisings in Georgia, Poland and Hungary that were triggered by his speech.
- He refused to take action against those responsible for the crimes he had denounced.

Political and party change

The leadership struggle meant that both Party and government institutions became important again as centres for debate and decision-making. In contrast, the police became less influential: they returned to the control of the Party and government, the secret police were reduced in size and the independence of the judiciary was partly restored.

Khrushchev's use of traditional Party processes to further his aims in the power struggle (for example using the Central Committee against the Presidium) helped restore the Party's position to one similar to that of the 1920s.

Khrushchev also pursued the aims of:

- **democratisation:** weakening the bureaucracy and giving more responsibility to the people
- **decentralisation:** giving more initiative to the localities.

Measures included:

- Membership was expanded, bringing in more working-class members.
- Local soviets had their role expanded, and some power was moved from central ministries to provincial authorities.

SUMMARY

- A collective leadership established by the Presidium after Stalin's death was gradually dismantled as Khrushchev outmanoeuvred his rivals and rose to power.
- Khrushchev's 'Secret Speech' of 1956 marked an official move towards de-Stalinisation and a new regime.
- Under Khrushchev, Stalin's autocratic terror state was replaced by a central government system similar to that of the mid 1920s, dominated by the Communist Party. Nevertheless, Party influence was partly countered by policies of decentralisation.

APPLY

APPLY YOUR KNOWLEDGE

Look at the first section of this chapter on page 110, where two chronological charts have been supplied to enable you to chart Khrushchev's rise to power. Another way of accounting for Khrushchev's rise to power would be to look at the various factors that played a part, adopting a thematic approach.

a If you wanted to address factors, what themes would you choose? (You might find it helpful to look back at your work on Stalin's rise to power in undertaking this exercise.)

b Pick out the relevant detail from this section to create a mind-map showing the various factors that enabled Khrushchev to rise to power.

EXAMINER TIP

Questions sometimes require a chronological approach and sometimes a thematic approach. Consider both as you revise. Look back at the activities in Chapters 13, 14 and 16 to remind yourself of the two different approaches.

REVIEW

In order to compare Khrushchev's rise to power with Stalin's, look back to Chapter 13.

ASSESS THE VALIDITY OF THIS VIEW

 'Khrushchev was totally committed to dismantling Stalinism.' Assess the validity of this view.

The key word in this question is **'totally'**. Look through this chapter for evidence which shows a commitment to de-Stalinisation and evidence which counters this.

a Create a mind-map to help you to answer this question. Begin by identifying the key features of Stalinism – then look at whether Khrushchev accepted or changed each feature.

b When you have made your judgement, you will need to arrange your points in a logical way. Number them on your mind-map to help with this.

c Now plan and write a full answer to the exam question.

EXAMINER TIP

Always look out for 'absolute' words in exam questions. It is usually quite easy to challenge words such as 'totally', 'only' or 'solely'. Using a mind-map to think thematically should help you to find areas in which you might question the statement.

REVIEW

For detail on the key features of Stalinism look back to Chapters 13–18 and, in particular the extract analysis activity in Chapter 18.

KEY QUESTION

The ideas and ideology which shaped the years of Khrushchev's leadership can easily be overlooked.

To consider the Key Question:

How important were ideas and ideology?

it would be helpful to reflect on the material in this chapter and complete the following chart:

Khrushchev's leadership	Influence of ideas and ideology	Importance of other factors
Rise to power		
De-Stalinisation		
Political and party change		

EXAMINER TIP

When considering change in history, it is always useful to remember that the ideas/ideology of individuals and groups will play a varying part. Sometimes they are the prime movers of change, but at other times they are almost forgotten and more circumstantial factors predominate. Understanding the place of ideas and ideology can add weight to your arguments.

REVIEW

For further detail on Communist ideologies, look back at Chapter 13.

APPLY YOUR KNOWLEDGE

In order to appreciate continuity and change between the leadership of Stalin and that of Khrushchev, copy and complete this flow chart diagram, covering the years 1928–53. You will be able to complete the top 2 rows of each box here, and can add detail to the lower 2 rows after reading Chapter 22.

REVIEW

If you find you can't easily complete the boxes for 1928–41, then refresh your memory by revising Section 3.

REVISION SKILLS

You may find it useful to equip yourself with sheets of A3 paper and card, for producing large timelines and flow charts like this.

1928–32

Government and leadership:

Opposition:

Economy:

Society:

1932–41

Government and leadership:

Opposition:

Economy:

Society:

1941–53

Government and leadership:

Opposition:

Economy:

Society:

1953–64

Government and leadership:

Opposition:

Economy:

Society:

22 Economic and social developments

RECAP

Developments in industry

Industrial development under Stalin, 1945–53

The USSR faced a massive economic challenge after the Second World War.

- The war had destroyed 70% of the Soviet industrial capacity; western areas had been devastated.
- Foreign aid had ceased.
- Policing the USSR's new 'satellite states' in the Eastern bloc demanded a huge defence budget.

Stalin formed Comecon in 1949 to link the Eastern bloc countries economically, while Gosplan coordinated two more Five Year Plans.

Economic plans	Industrial aims	Industrial results
Fourth Five Year Plan 1946–50	• Rebuild heavy industry and transport (in an effort to catch up with the USA). • Revive Ukraine.	• Most heavy industry targets met (thanks to maintenance of wartime controls on labour). • The USSR stronger than before the war; second to the USA in industrial capacity.
Fifth Five Year Plan 1951–55	• Initially – focus on heavy industry and rearmament. • Under Malenkov – new emphasis on consumer goods, housing and services.	• Most targets met. • Some improvement in consumer supplies.

Industrial development under Khrushchev, 1953–64

In the economic debates that accompanied the leadership struggle, Khrushchev pushed for his own agricultural proposals and opposed Malenkov's proposal to move the economic focus away from heavy to light industry. Once in power, he moved away from Stalin's rigid planning system.

Decentralisation and industrial planning

By 1953, problems with Stalinist system were slowing economic growth.

- Central planning was too complex.
- Managers avoided improving output (to prevent a rise in targets the following year).
- Targets did not reflect consumer demand.
- Inefficient use of resources demanded increased investment.

Khrushchev drove a number of key changes which departed from previous policy:

Date	Key change
1956	Sixth Five Year Plan was launched (abandoned after two years).
1957	60 central ministries abolished and the USSR divided into economic regions, with local economic planning and supervision.
1959	Seven Year Plan announced. (This merged into a seventh 'Five Year Plan', 1961–65.)

Industrial change

The Seven Year Plan focused on improving living standards for ordinary people. Emphasis moved from the old heavy industries to the 'modern industries', such as chemicals, housing and consumer goods, and to the exploitation of natural resources (gas, oil and coal) and building of power stations. Communications, transport (rail and air) and technology, above all space science, were also promoted.

Statistically, Khrushchev seemed successful.

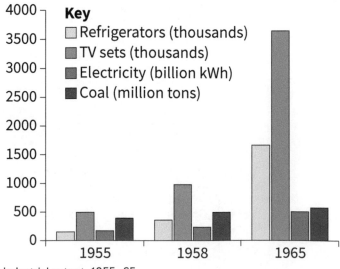

Key
- Refrigerators (thousands)
- TV sets (thousands)
- Electricity (billion kWh)
- Coal (million tons)

Industrial output, 1955–65

However:

- His decentralisation measures added another layer of bureaucracy. (His system would be abandoned in 1965.)
- Although living standards improved, quality of life remained poor.
- Heavy spending on armaments and the space race distorted the economy.
- The USSR failed to overtake the USA economically (although it narrowed the gap). The economic growth rate actually fell between 1958 and 1964.

Developments in agriculture

Agriculture under Stalin, 1945–53

The war left Soviet agriculture in a desperate position. The two post-war Five Year Plans therefore tried to rebuild the agricultural economy.

- **The Fourth Five Year Plan (1946–50):** aimed to force the *kolkhozes* to deliver agricultural products, revive the wheat fields of Ukraine and revitalise barren land.

It involved huge state direction, high quotas and low wages, and higher taxation on private plots. Output increased, but the peasants were left with little and farming practices were held back by inaccurate (ideological) scientific theories.

- **The Fifth Five Year Plan (1951–55):** continued the aims of its predecessor, but also included Khrushchev's initiative to develop 'virgin' lands and build huge agricultural farms or 'agrocities'. However production still lagged behind industry and by 1955 it was still lower than in 1940.

Agriculture under Khrushchev, 1953–64

Khrushchev declared that the Stalinist regime had concealed shortcomings in agriculture and that its policies had been counter-productive. He decided to decentralise agriculture, placing the implementation of his reforms in the hands of the local Party organisations.

The results of his reforms look impressive, but many of Khrushchev's aims were not fulfilled.

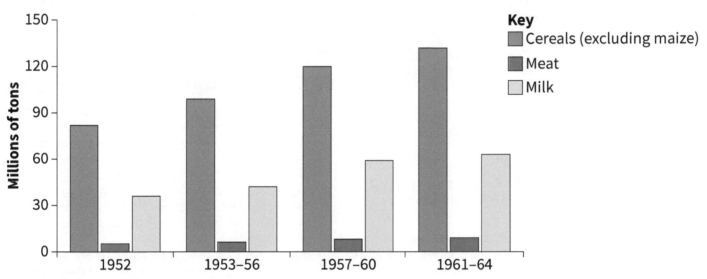

Average production, in millions of tons

Khrushchev's aims for agriculture	Problems with fulfilment
Incentivise peasants by raising prices, reducing quotas and taxes and allowing collectives to set their own targets.	Constant changes in the prices offered made it difficult for farmers to plan ahead. Peasants still preferred to work on their private plots rather than for the collectives. Constant interference in farm management, by Party officials, bred frustration.
Increase production through more widespread provision of electricity, fertiliser and machinery, and by combining collectives into larger farms.	Problems of distribution in remote areas. Maintenance of machinery and tractors cost money and the required skills were not always available.
Cultivate lands in regions of western Siberia and northern Kazakhstan that had not previously been farmed (the Virgin Lands Scheme).	After initial success, the lands became overworked and infertile and grain had to be imported.
Address the USSR's food shortages by growing new crops such as maize.	New crops were not always suitable for the land, and sometimes detracted from the growth of much-needed wheat.
Create huge, collective farm/towns ('agrocities') that were subject to urban working conditions.	This aim was never implemented.

Social developments

Social change under Stalin, 1945–53

Standards of living for ordinary Russian people did not improve. Peasants' income remained low, while in the towns living and working conditions were still harsh, workers could still be relocated, Party officials received higher rations, women were expected to work as well as run the household and look after their families, and there was a shortage of consumer goods.

Social change under Khrushchev, 1953–64

Khrushchev was committed to improving the living standards of the Soviet people. Through his de-Stalinisation policies and economic reforms:

- Consumer goods became more widely available.
- Housing initiatives helped alleviate overcrowding.
- Taxation was lowered and pensions improved.
- Working hours were reduced and there was a move towards equal wages.
- Trade unions were given more responsibilities and greater influence in employment negotiations.
- Educational provision, medicine and welfare services and transport were improved.

However, high-ranking Party officials retained privileges, and living standards were still significantly lower than in Western industrialised states.

The quality of life and cultural change

Social life and cultural change

After the repression and fear of the 'Zhdanovshchina', Khrushchev's de-Stalinisation policies brought greater personal freedom for Soviet citizens.

Restrictions on contact with Western culture were relaxed. Reading of foreign literature and listening to foreign broadcasts was permitted, while some travel to and from the USSR was allowed. Such exposure to Western influences brought discontent with the rigidity of Soviet life, especially among young people, which led to increased hooliganism and student protests against controls.

Writers and musicians who had been persecuted under Stalin were rehabilitated and permitted to work again, even if their work criticised the Stalinist regime.

However artistic works were still judged by their commitment to 'social responsibility', and any that challenged the basis of Communism or the Soviet State (such as *Dr Zhivago* by Pasternak) were still outlawed.

The Churches

Khrushchev revived the socialist campaign against the Churches.

- The school curriculum was atheistic and children were not allowed to attend Church services or be taught religion by their parents.
- Thousands of monasteries, convents, Orthodox churches and seminaries were closed (many were converted to museums or community centres, with an emphasis on socialist values).
- Pilgrimages were banned and church services strictly regulated.
- Excess religious devotion could lead to imprisonment; clergymen could be sent to labour camps.

Ethnic minorities

Khrushchev did not encourage greater independence for the nationalities. The Party taught that ethnic distinctions would ultimately disappear and that a single common language would eventually be adopted by all nationalities in the USSR. Restrictions on Jews were maintained.

SUMMARY

- The destruction caused by the Second World War posed immense challenges for the Soviet economy, which Stalin addressed with renewed emphasis on industrial growth.
- A relaxation of rigid centralised planning and organisation under Malenkov was followed by more systematic decentralisation of industry and agriculture under Khrushchev – although Khrushchev's economic changes had mixed results.
- Khrushchev's economic reforms and de-Stalinisation campaigns improved living standards for the Soviet people, and allowed greater freedom in terms of Soviet culture.
- Such liberalisation was not felt everywhere; the Churches were strongly curbed and the nationalities encouraged to conform to 'Russian unity'.

APPLY

APPLY YOUR KNOWLEDGE

Summarise the results of economic change in the years 1945–64 using the following table.

| | Stalin, 1945–53 | | Khrushchev, 1953–64 | |
	Industry	Agriculture	Industry	Agriculture
Successes and achievements				
Failures and limitations				

EXAMINER TIP

This chart would be useful for an essay addressing consequence and demanding an evaluation of the success of economic policies. It is important that you can follow developments from one leader to the next for breadth essays.

ASSESS THE VALIDITY OF THIS VIEW

A LEVEL | **'No communist leader was ever able to solve USSR's agricultural problems.' Assess the validity of this view with reference to the years 1921 to 1964.**

a Obviously, the main problem faced by the Communist leaders was how to increase production. In order to answer this question, you will need to break this problem down further, thinking about the peasants/labourers, agriculture organisation and equipment/techniques. When you have devised a list of problems, consider the success/failure of Lenin, Stalin and Khrushchev in addressing each one.

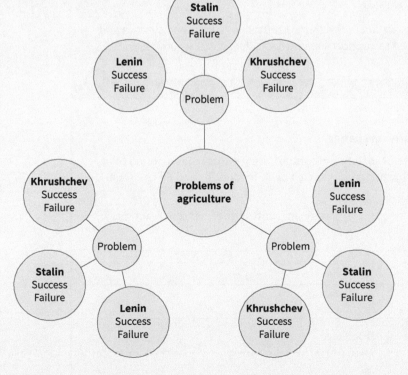

EXAMINER TIP

The broader your essay (in terms of chronological span) the more selective you will need to be in choosing relevant evidence to support your arguments.

REVIEW

You will need to look back at Chapters 15 and 19 in order to consider the full question.

b Choose one of the problems on your list and write a paragraph for this essay. Remember to begin with a reference to the question so it is clear what you are trying to argue.

EXTRACT ANALYSIS

EXTRACT A

Khrushchev was no ideologist, but a pragmatic activist who took his Marxism largely for granted – and dug industriously in Lenin's collective works whenever he felt the traditional need for theoretical justification. His over-riding passions were agricultural improvement and commitment to industrial growth. It was in these terms that he saw socialist competition with the capitalist world and the triumph of communism. At the 21st Party Congress in January 1959, he made extravagant promises about the economic future, both in terms of consumption and in the context of comparison with the United States. At the 22nd Party Congress, the new programme of the Communist Party, which had not been touched since 1919, provided a cautious, but nonetheless determined projection into a fully communist future. In 1964, he was speaking openly of making consumer goods and agricultural investment the top priority. He was willing to pin his reputation on the success of these policies. But the facts were against him.

Adapted from John Peter Nettl, *The Soviet Achievement*, 1967

Read the extract.

a Here is a list of statements; does this extract support or oppose each of them?

	Support	Oppose
• Khrushchev was a committed Marxist.	☐	☐
• Khrushchev acted in response to circumstances.	☐	☐
• Agricultural improvement was more important to Khrushchev than industrial growth.	☐	☐
• Khrushchev did not believe in competing with the capitalist world.	☐	☐
• Khrushchev made lavish promises about future economic growth in 1959.	☐	☐
• In 1964, Khrushchev promised that consumer goods and agricultural investment would be prioritised.	☐	☐
• Khrushchev produced economic success.	☐	☐

b Explain the overall argument of the extract in relation to Khrushchev's aims and success and find one piece of contextual evidence to support and one to challenge this argument.

KEY QUESTION

One of the Key Questions asks:

What was the extent of social and cultural change?

a Create a mind-map to show the state of society and culture during Khrushchev's period of power. Colour code this to indicate (i) change with more liberal tendencies and (ii) continuation or a return to conditions in the past.

b Use your diagram to assess the extent of social change and write a three-sentence summary.

_____

_____

_____

_____

_____

23 Opposition and the fall of Khrushchev

 RECAP

Opposition from cultural dissidents

Under Khrushchev, greater intellectual and artistic freedom allowed a new group of 'cultural dissidents' to emerge. They were committed to greater democracy, toleration, and civil rights and used the arts to convey political messages.

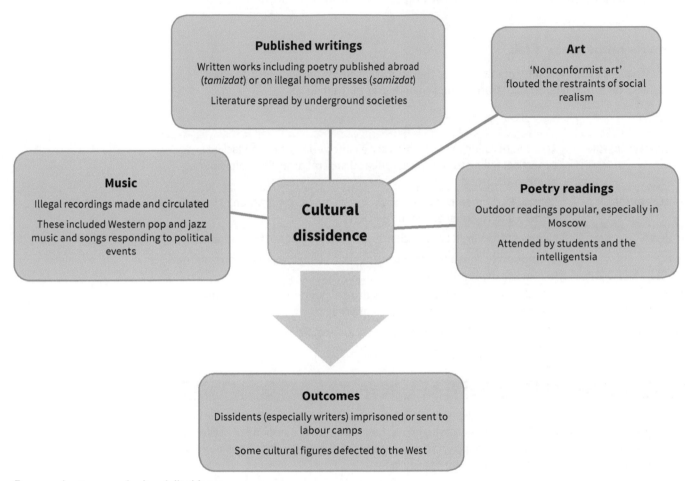

Published writings

Written works including poetry published abroad (*tamizdat*) or on illegal home presses (*samizdat*)

Literature spread by underground societies

Art

'Nonconformist art' flouted the restraints of social realism

Music

Illegal recordings made and circulated

These included Western pop and jazz music and songs responding to political events

Cultural dissidence

Poetry readings

Outdoor readings popular, especially in Moscow

Attended by students and the intelligentsia

Outcomes

Dissidents (especially writers) imprisoned or sent to labour camps

Some cultural figures defected to the West

Forms and outcomes of cultural dissidence

Opposition from within the Party

There was some political opposition. Khrushchev's rise to power had involved a struggle between reformers, such as Bulganin, and pro-Stalinists, such as Molotov and Malenkov (who was essentially a Stalinist supporter, despite some reforming tendencies). Khrushchev's victory over the 'anti-Party' group that tried to oust him in 1957 was a victory for the reformers over those who wanted to restore 'Stalinism' and police rule.

Treatment of political opposition was less harsh than under Stalin.

- Political opponents were demoted and often sent far from Moscow, but generally not shot.
- Millions of political prisoners were rehabilitated (declared not guilty), and those still alive were released from prisons and labour camps.

Outright opposition among ordinary Soviet citizens remained minimal, although in Georgia, Stalin's birthplace, there were violent nationalist demonstrations in Tblisi on 4–10 March 1956 in protest against Khrushchev's de-Stalinisation speech.

Khrushchev's fall from power

In April 1964, Khrushchev's protegé, Brezhnev, gave Khrushchev's 70th birthday speech, praising his various achievements. Khrushchev was presented with honours, including the 'Hero of the Soviet Union' gold medal.

However, in October 1964, Khrushchev was recalled from holiday and summoned to an emergency meeting of the Presidium, where he was criticised by several of his former supporters, including Brezhnev. He was forced to resign and Brezhnev became First Secretary while Kosygin became Premier.

Pravda announced that Khrushchev had resigned because of age and ill-health but within weeks, a damning list of criticisms of Khrushchev and his policies had been published. Nevertheless, Khrushchev was granted a personal pension and allowed to live in obscurity, outside Moscow, until his death in 1971.

Reasons for Khrushchev's fall

Khrushchev had gained the enmity of many influential people including hardline (pro-Stalinist) conservatives, Party officials, administrators and senior figures in the military.

Focus of criticism	Detail
Personal/style of rule	Accused of ruling in a 'one-man style'; interfering where he lacked expertise; failing to take advice; nepotism; embarrassing behaviour at home and abroad.
Decentralisation	Central Party members were upset by the autonomy granted to local Party leaders and regional economic councils.
Agriculture	Failure of the Virgin Lands Scheme and the shortage of food supplies.
Industry	Promotion of consumer goods production alienated those who preferred to focus on heavy industry.
Military	Offended the military by drive to reduce expenditure on conventional weapons and concentrate on nuclear arms.
Foreign policy	Handling of the Cuban Missile Crisis criticised. Personally blamed for the USSR's poor relations with Communist China.

SUMMARY

- Khrushchev faced opposition from cultural dissidents who wanted to see further change and from hardline Communist Party members who hoped for a return to the stability of Stalinism.
- Although Khrushchev was generally supported by reformers, some believed he had not gone far enough, or weakened his own reforms with rash initiatives.
- By 1964 he had alienated a wide variety of different interest groups who combined to force him from power.

 APPLY

APPLY YOUR KNOWLEDGE

a Which of the following are valid reasons for Khrushchev's fall from power in 1964?

> Khrushchev's decentralisation policies were disliked by Central Party officials.

> Khrushchev launched the Virgin Lands Scheme to try to improve the USSR's agricultural output.

> Khrushchev was blamed for the handling of the Cuban missile crisis.

> There were violent nationalist demonstrations in Tblisi in protest against Khrushchev's de-Stalinisation speech.

> Khrushchev represented the reformers and angered those who wanted to restore 'Stalinism' and police rule.

> Khrushchev was opposed by senior military figures.

> Cultural dissidents were committed to greater democracy, toleration, and civil rights.

> Khrushchev liked to 'meddle' in areas where he had limited expertise.

Valid

Not valid

EXAMINER TIP

Distinguishing between policies and personality is an important aspect of the Key Question: **How important was the role of individuals?**

REVIEW

You might also like to reflect on the relative importance of policies and personality in Khrushchev's rise to power, details of which are in Chapter 21.

b With reference to your selected reasons and others given in this chapter; which do you judge to have been the more important – Khrushchev's policies or personality? Explain your answer.

ASSESS THE VALIDITY OF THIS VIEW

> **A LEVEL** 'Opposition from within the Party was more dangerous to the leader than the opposition of cultural dissidents in the years 1945 to 1964.' Assess the validity of this view.

a Underline the key words and dates in this question. Which word will require clarification?

This essay lends itself to a two-column plan, divided between the last years of Stalin's rule and Khrushchev's leadership, as follows:

	Opposition of cultural dissidents	Opposition from within the Party
1945–53		
1953–64		

b Record the ways in which the opposition was dangerous to the leader in the appropriate places.

c Make a judgement and write an introduction to this essay, setting out your view and clarifying what you understand as 'dangerous to the leader'.

EXAMINER TIP

Never assume the reader shares your understanding of key words in essay questions. In this essay you would need to clarify how you will judge whether actions/ behaviour is '**dangerous**', before you begin.

REVIEW

Look back to Chapter 20 in order to complete the first row of the plan.

PLAN YOUR ESSAY

A LEVEL **'Opposition to the Soviet leader was totally ineffective in the years 1941 to 1964.' Assess the validity of this view.**

Whatever judgement you choose to adopt in response to an essay question, you will always need to show 'substantiated' argument in your essay. 'Substantiation' is the supporting of comment with relevant, precise and specific evidence.

a Provide two pieces of evidence to substantiate each of the following judgements:

Opposition from cultural dissidents was ineffective.	
Opposition from Party members was effective.	

b Write a substantiated conclusion to this essay based on one of these two judgements. You could argue either way, but your conclusion should summarise the arguments you would have made in your essay.

KEY QUESTION

Why did opposition develop and how effective was it?

is a Key Question which you should now be in a position to trace through the Communist era, in the years 1917–64.

Complete the grid below by selecting relevant detail from the material you have studied.

	Lenin	Stalin pre 1941	Stalin post 1941	Khrushchev
Why?				
How effective?				

REVIEW

You will need to look back to Chapters 12, 13, 14, 17, 18, 19, 20 and 21 in addition to the material in this chapter.

EXAMINER TIP

A chart such as this will be a useful revision aid for breadth questions which address opposition. In particular, it should enable you to address change and continuity.

24 The Soviet Union by 1964

The years 1941–64 were a period of instability and change. After the tough Stalinist post-war period, reforming governments:

- dismantled parts of the 'Stalinist system'
- began to redistribute some of the wealth generated by Soviet industrialisation to the ordinary Soviet citizens.

The political condition of the Soviet Union

Stalin had made himself central to the Soviet political system, especially in the post-war era when he was portrayed as a god-like figure, without whom no decision could be made.

His death in 1953 left both a political vacuum and an expectation of change.

The years 1953–64:

- established a new-style leadership backed by the authority of the Party rather than resting on the force of the individual
- saw some moves away from the autocratic and coercive practices of the Stalinist era.

However, the power and privileges of the Party elite depended on the Party's control over the State and its resources. This made it essential for them to preserve the one-party State and centralised economy. Consequently, many of the reforms were half-hearted and erratic.

The economic condition of the Soviet Union

The industrial base created under Stalin meant that by 1953 the economy had recovered from the destruction of the Second World War. Khrushchev was therefore able to redirect some resources away from heavy industry and armaments towards consumer goods, housing and agriculture. Technology also developed, and nuclear weapons, along with advances in rocketry, perpetuated the USSR's reputation as a great military power.

After 1953, the challenge in both industry and agriculture was how to stimulate greater productivity without relying on increased labour or new materials. Khrushchev attempted a limited degree of decentralisation in an attempt to incentivise workers and peasants. He was particularly keen to increase agricultural productivity.

However:

- Changing the workings of the centralised command economy created new problems for the planners and led to an expanded bureaucracy.
- Khrushchev's campaigns were sometimes ill-thought-through.
- Increases in yields were more the result of the cultivation of new land than of technical improvements.
- There was no significant increase in the output from either factories or farms.

By 1964 no solution to the major issue of how to sustain economic growth had been found.

The social condition of the Soviet Union

Soviet living standards began to rise rapidly in the 1950s and Soviet consumers began to benefit from Soviet industrialisation. The improvements generated a mood of optimism and it seemed that the USSR might be really building a 'better' society. However, beneath the surface there were still massive problems that had not been solved.

SUMMARY

- There were a number of positive changes in the years up to 1964.
- Major political, economic and social weaknesses remained.
- Some attempts at reform created new problems.

KEY CHRONOLOGY

Political developments	
1941	Nazi invasion of USSR
1945	End of Second World War
1953	Death of Stalin
	Malenkov becomes Head of State
	Khrushchev becomes First Secretary of the Communist Party
1955	Bulganin replaces Malenkov as Head of State
1956	Khrushchev's Secret Speech
1957	'Anti-Party' group defeated
1964	Removal of Khrushchev

Economic and social developments	
1946	Beginning of Zhdanovshchina
1946–50	Fourth Five Year Plan
1951–55	Fifth Five Year Plan
1954	Virgin Lands Scheme adopted
1956	Sixth Five Year Plan (abandoned 1958)
1957	Economic decentralisation adopted
1959	Seven Year Plan adopted
1961–65	Seventh Five Year Plan

APPLY

APPLY YOUR KNOWLEDGE

To consider the success of Khrushchev as leader of the USSR:

Look at the Key Chronology of political developments given on page 123. Write 1 development on each of 9 diamond-shaped cards. Write the date on the back of the card. Beneath each heading:

a Provide 1–3 bullet points to explain the issue on the card and 3–4 to explain the significance of the issue.

b Sort these cards into a 'diamond 9', ranked by importance for the development of the USSR.

c Re-sort the cards in chronological order to test your understanding. (You will be able to check this by turning them over.)

EXAMINER TIP

This activity will help you to prioritise relevant information and ensure chronological understanding. Both skills are essential for exam essays.

REVISION SKILLS

The 'diamond 9' is a useful way of prioritising detail. Look back to Chapter 16, page 87 to remind yourself of how it works.

ASSESS THE VALIDITY OF THIS VIEW

A **LEVEL** **'The economy of the USSR was in a much stronger position in 1964 than it had been in the 1930s.' Assess the validity of this view.**

a A change and continuity chart, as given below, will help you to assess the degree to which the economy was strengthened (or otherwise) between these dates.

	Situation in 1930s	Situation in 1964	
Industry			**Positive changes**
Agriculture			

	Continuity		
Industry			
Agriculture			

Industry			**Negative changes**
Agriculture			

EXAMINER TIP

Ensure you substantiate your argument with some precise examples to support your comments. In a question like this, it is important to compare directly between the dates given, and to distinguish between industry and agriculture.

REVIEW

To remind yourself of the economic situation in the 1930s, look back to Chapter 15. Chapter 18 summarises the position in 1941, Chapter 19 looks at the effect of war, and Chapter 22 examines post-war developments.

b Use your diagram to help you to decide whether the economy got stronger, stayed the same, or worsened.

c Write a conclusion to this essay, offering a judgement on the view given.

EXTRACT ANALYSIS

EXTRACT A

Khrushchev's achievements were undeniable, especially in the ending of the Terror and the raising of the general standard of living. But further improvement was not forthcoming and Khrushchev's futurological boasts, his idiosyncratic bossiness and his obsessive reorganisations had taken their toll on the patience of practically everyone. He was a complex leader. At once he was a Stalinist and anti-Stalinist, a communist believer and cynic. Yet it must be remembered that his eccentricities in high office also resulted from the immense, conflicting pressures upon him. Unlike his successors, he was willing to try to respond to them by seeking long-term solutions. But the attempted solutions were insufficient to effect the renovation of the kind of state and society he espoused. Reforms were long overdue. His political, economic and cultural accomplishments were a great improvement over Stalin. But they fell greatly short of the country's needs.

Adapted from Robert Service, *Russia*, 1997

a This extract states at the beginning, '*Khrushchev's achievements were undeniable*'.

- What phrases in the extract support this statement?
- Provide 3–4 pieces of contextual evidence to support this statement.

_____

_____

_____

_____

b This extract states at the end, '*(His) reforms fell greatly short of the country's needs.*'

- What phrases in the extract support this statement?
- Provide 3–4 pieces of contextual evidence to support this statement.

_____

_____

_____

_____

c Summarise the overall argument in this extract, then attempt an answer to the following question: 'Using your understanding of the historical context, assess how convincing Extract A is in relation to Khrushchev's leadership between 1953 and 1964.'

REVIEW

To remind yourself of the context of Khrushchev's leadership, look again at Chapters 21–23.

EXAMINER TIP

You should spend around 15 minutes on this exercise. As always, begin your answer with a summary of the overall argument and then look at any sub-arguments. All should be supported and criticised with reference to the text and your own contextual knowledge and you should arrive at a substantiated judgement.

REVISION SKILLS

Now that you have completed your revision of Tsarist and Communist Russia 1855–1964, you should extend the revision activities suggested in this Revision Guide to encompass the whole of the content. These are:

- Key Question cards (Chapter 1).
- 6-section poster reminders of the key topic areas with one poster per book section (Chapter 11).
- Colour-coded thematic timeline (Chapter 13).

EXAMINER TIP

These 3 activities will ensure your awareness of all the major elements of the Component 1 (breadth) exam: appreciation of the Key Questions; appreciation of key topic areas; specific understanding of chronology linked to the major themes.

A Level essay sample answer

REVISION PROGRESS

 REVIEW

On these Exam Practice pages you will find a sample student answer for an A Level essay question. What are the strengths and weaknesses of the answer? Read the answer and the corresponding Examiner Tips carefully. Think about how you could apply this advice in order to improve your own answers to questions like this one.

> **A LEVEL** 'Despite his policy of de-Stalinisation, the main features of Stalinism still remained in the USSR at the time of Khrushchev's fall from power in 1964.' Assess the validity of this view.
>
> 25 marks

Sample student answer

When Khrushchev came to power in 1955, it was already clear that he would want to make some changes, due partly to his action against Beria, followed by the release of political prisoners and reforms to the gulag system. However, his 'secret' de-Stalinisation speech in 1956 took most Party members by surprise. In it, Khrushchev accused Stalin of responsibility for the purges, terror, torture, mass arrests, executions and the gulags. He blamed Stalin for betraying Leninist principles and harming socialist progress and even questioned Stalin's war leadership. It might have seemed that he was attacking the whole concept of 'Stalinism'. However, his speech did not attack the core principles of the Stalinist period. There was no criticism of economic controls, strong leadership, a single party or the elimination of factions.

To some extent Khrushchev succeeded in changing the Stalinist system which he inherited. Firstly, he changed matters politically. The dual institutions of the Party and government again became important centres for debate and decision-making, while the police became less influential and the size of the secret police force was reduced. The independence of the judiciary was also partly restored. Khrushchev's de-Stalinisation speech heralded a 'thaw' which permitted political freedoms that had been unheard of under Stalin. For example, the Soviet population was given access to foreign media and political writings, which had been censored under Stalin, could be published. Additionally, foreigners were encouraged to visit the USSR for the first time. Such measures were clearly a rejection of the Stalinist method, and they helped to make the country more open than ever before. Additionally, by

REVISION SKILLS

A Level essay questions may contain a quotation advancing a judgement, in which case the quotation will be followed by 'Assess the validity of this view'. Read page 7 of this Revision Guide for details on how to master the essay question.

EXAMINER TIP

This is a very strong introduction in many respects, with good detail and an explanation of what is meant by Stalinism at the end of the paragraph. However it is entirely contextual, and falls short of stating a view (judgement) in relation to the question.

EXAMINER TIP

It is better to avoid 'firstly', 'secondly' and so on, which produces a list; it is a good idea, however, to look at the question thematically, as is done here. There is a good range of specific examples to support the opening comment.

destroying Stalin's reputation as an infallible leader, he permitted a new questioning which reduced the power of Stalinism and was clearly the key factor undermining the Stalininst method of control.

Furthermore, some of the actual political methods changed under Khrushchev. He ran the State in a more humane way. For example, rivals such as Malenkov were neither executed nor imprisoned. This helped to relieve fear within the country. He also released thousands of intellectuals who had been imprisoned under Stalin. Additionally, and perhaps more significantly, Khrushchev helped restore the Party's position to one similar to that of the 1920s, weakening the bureaucracy and giving more initiative to the localities. Party membership grew as more working class members were brought in and power was moved from central ministries to provincial authorities. All of these points cumulatively show that the political system was being steered away from the Stalinist reliance on fear to a new relationship founded on popular consent.

Decentralisation did not only feature politically, but also economically, with Gosplan's controls passed to economic ministers. This was a complete change from the way all economic decisions had always come from Moscow. There were other economic initiatives, too. Although Khrushchev continued to use the Five Year Plan system, a greater emphasis was placed on consumer goods. This was a move away from the Stalinist focus on heavy industry and thus a definite signal of change from Stalinism. Additionally, Khrushchev encouraged the exploitation of new resources in western Siberia which was another part of his attempt to make the economic system more efficient.

De-Stalinisation occurred in agriculture as well as industry. Agriculture had always been a problem under Stalin due to a lack of investment and expansion. Khrushchev set about making changes. For example, the Virgin Lands Scheme attempted to use previously unfarmed areas for food production and this was undoubtedly successful in raising maize production by 10%. Peasants were more humanely treated under Khrushchev, and the number of compulsory deliveries they had to make was reduced. All of these economic changes show that Khrushchev was arguably attempting to move away from a Stalinist method of running things.

However, to a lesser extent, Khrushchev was not successful in removing the main features of Stalinism, and this can be seen through the limitations of the Secret Speech and the de-Stalinisation campaign. Although the Secret Speech blamed Stalin for past excesses, it did not lay any blame on the Party itself, instead portraying it as a 'victim'. Khrushchev refused to take action against those responsible for the crimes he had denounced. Consequently, the one-party State remained dominant and opposition, termed 'faction', was still seen as suspect. Additionally, the main policies of Stalin – state control of agriculture and industry through collectivisation and industrialisation – were intentionally overlooked and thus continued to be generally accepted. The policy of de-Stalinisation was also inconsistent. For example, Khrushchev's own conservative views saw the closing down of the first exhibitions of abstract art. This again demonstrates that although Khrushchev wanted more popular consent, his essential conservatism prevented de-Stalinisation from having a greater effect.

EXAMINER TIP

'Additionally' is overused in this essay. Look out for examples – there are two in the paragraph above. Like 'also' it can make an essay too list-like and its overuse should be avoided. Picking out a development that is 'more significant', however, is very good – provided the view is upheld.

EXAMINER TIP

This paragraph introduces the next theme, but could have begun with a clearer link to the question.

EXAMINER TIP

This paragraph is more descriptive than analytical. Adding a comment at the end shows an attempt to link to the question but a stronger link should have been given in the first sentence.

EXAMINER TIP

This paragraph offers balance to the argument, identifying areas where de-Stalinisation did not take place or was limited.

De-Stalinisation, in fact, had a bigger impact on the satellite states with the Polish and Hungarian leaders feeling it gave them permission to reform and start their own 'thaw'. Khrushchev imitated Stalin in his ruthless reaction to these developments, especially in Hungary where the reform movement was crushed by Soviet tanks. This demonstrates that Khrushchev still had some of the same intentions as Stalin, including maintaining the USSR's role as the leader of the Communist bloc in Eastern Europe.

As well as many Stalinist policies, other Stalinist political features also remained. Khrushchev consolidated his power by promoting his own supporters, using the same methods of patronage and control as Stalin. He also attempted to create his own cult of personality, copying one of Stalin's key methods of control. This ensured that a state of corruption remained in the USSR. All of these actions demonstrate that many similarities remained between Khrushchev and Stalin in their running of the Soviet Union.

Arguably, the most important argument is that Khrushchev's policies failed to improve or change the economy. In industry, decentralisation was not accompanied by any proper direction, which resulted in a state of confusion. Under the five-year planning system, government priorities still took precedence over the needs of the consumer and the focus remained on growth as opposed to quality. This meant that economic growth continued its patterns much as it had under Stalin. Finally, in addition to this, the arms race continued and thus the taxes required were heavy. Khrushchev supported the build up of the arms race through his tough foreign policy, which nearly led to nuclear war with the Cuban Missile Crisis.

There were, finally, flaws with agriculture. Many of Khrushchev's policies failed, for example, the Virgin Lands scheme, partly through insufficient foresight and partly through a predominance of central planning. Khrushchev's reforms were not enough to change the Stalinist methods of running the country.

In conclusion, Khrushchev clearly attempted to make some change to Stalinism, but he did not challenge the essence of Stalinism. The USSR remained a one-party state with a centrally planned economy and with policy direction in the hands of a strong leader. Since Khrushchev was a communist and enjoyed the privileges of a Stalinist-type leadership, he did not see any need for fundamental reform. Therefore, despite de-Stalinisation, any reform was superficial. In 1964, the USSR still retained the main features of Stalinism.

OVERALL COMMENT

This essay might be awarded a low Level 5. It shows a very good understanding of the demands of the question and is analytical, well-organised and effectively delivered. There is a good deal of well-selected and precise supporting information, even if there is a little irrelevance and occasional slips of style. The biggest criticism would be the failure to set out a judgement at the beginning which can then be sustained through the essay, but the balance and final conclusion would certainly suggest that the essay should reach the top level.

OVER TO YOU

Give yourself 45 minutes to answer this question on your own. Consider this checklist when reviewing your answer:

☐ Have you explained the 'main features' of Stalinism clearly?

☐ Did you address the question in the first sentence of each paragraph?

Go back and look at Chapters 21–23 (pages 110–111, 114–116 and 119–120) to help refresh your knowledge.

Activity answers guidance

The answers provided here are examples, based on the information provided in the Recap sections of this Revision Guide. There may be other factors which are relevant to each question, and you should draw on as much own knowledge as possible to give detailed and precise answers. There are also many ways of answering exam questions (for example, of structuring an essay). However, these exemplar answers should provide a good starting point.

Chapter 1

⚙ Apply Your Knowledge

a **Autocracy:** State ruled by Tsar, with unlimited powers.

Russian Orthodox Church: Official (Christian) Church in Russia, closely linked to Tsar and State.

Bureaucracy: Paid noble officials, through whom orders passed from central government to rest of Russia.

Conscript army: Army of soldiers forced to serve for 25 years.

Police state: State with little freedom and much censorship. Police (and secret police) could arrest anyone suspected of anti-tsarist behaviour.

Serfdom: System in which over 50% of Russian population were 'property' of their owners. Just over half privately owned (by nobles); remainder were 'state serfs'. Most worked on the land in village communes.

Liberal intellectuals: Educated Russians influenced by Western liberal ideas, they argued for a civil society based on the rule of law.

Productive and non-productive classes: Productive: urban artisans, manufacturers and merchants, and (predominantly) peasant serfs; provided around 90% of country's finance through taxes (and serfs paid feudal dues). **Non-productive:** royal court, clergy, nobility, civil and military officials and army and navy officers; around 10% of the population but owned 75% of the land and paid no taxes.

b They illustrate and explain:
   i) political weaknesses (autocracy; bureaucracy; liberal intellectuals; police state)
   ii) economic and social weaknesses (serfdom; productive and non-productive classes; Russian Orthodox Church)
   iii) military (conscript army) weaknesses.

⚖ 🅐 To What Extent?

Economic factors weakening the State
- Economy mainly rural.
- Some areas suffered from poor territory and climate.
- Economy based on serfdom.
- Serfs poor, with little opportunity to earn wages or to buy and sell.
- Little incentive for landowners to make money except by exploiting their serfs.

Other factors weakening the State
- Politically and socially Russia was backward. Society remained feudal.
- Serfs' living conditions primitive and backward.
- Small non-productive classes owned most of the land; no middle class.
- Serfs illiterate, superstitious and hostile to change.
- Bureaucracy corrupt and incompetent.
- Liberal demands for reform repressed.
- Army relied on conscript (forced) labour.
- Defeats in Crimean War revealed Russia's weaknesses and caused both loss of morale and demand for change.

Ways in which the State remained strong
- Tsar had unlimited powers.
- State strongly supported by the Orthodox Church.
- State's powers enforced by the police.
- Large army.

💡 Key Question

The Russian economy in 1855:
- Mainly rural.
- Europe's main exporter of agricultural produce.
- Serf-based (serfs were poor).
- Little internal market demand.
- Few incentives to make money.
- Backward compared to the industrialised West.

Chapter 2

⚙ Apply Your Knowledge

Example answer in relation to the emancipation reform:

Ideas/motives behind the reform
- Need to maintain agricultural production.
- Need to produce surplus grain for export, to fund investment in industry.
- Desire to reduce social unrest.
- Influence of Western liberal ideas.

Beliefs or ideas that limited the reform
- Conservative nature of Russian government.
- Need to preserve autocracy.
- Nobles' desire to ensure that their status was not eroded.
- Complexity of emancipation process.
- Peasants' resistance to change.

Group or groups that benefited most
- Serfs.
- Intelligentsia (through the *zemstva*).

Group that lost power
- Nobles.

Your evaluation of the other reforms should follow a similar pattern.

⚖ 🅐 Assess the Validity of This View

a **Education**
   - **Liberal:** Universities could govern themselves and appoint staff; responsibility for schools moved from Church to *zemstva*; primary and secondary education extended and open to boys and girls of all classes.
   - **Non-liberal:** After 1866, government control reasserted.

Serfs
   - **Liberal:** Serfs were granted freedom and a land allotment.
   - **Non-liberal:** Freed serfs had to pay 'redemption payments' and remain within their *mir* until these had been paid.

Local government
   - **Liberal:** Elected local councils (*zemstva*) replaced rights and obligations of serf-owning gentry; some peasant representation; *zemstva* had power to improve public services; elected town councils (*dumas*) were established in towns.
   - **Non-liberal:** *Zemstva*'s powers strictly limited; voting procedure favoured nobility; provincial governors could overturn *zemstvo* decisions.

Military
   - **Liberal:** Length of service reduced; punishments less severe; military colonies stopped; better provisioning, medical care and education; modern weaponry introduced; new command structure created; Military Colleges set up; conscription for all (not just peasants).
   - **Non-liberal:** Conscription remained and military service still demanding.

Judiciary
   - **Liberal:** New 'Western' system with a single system of courts; accused presumed innocent until proven guilty with right to a lawyer; criminal cases heard before barristers and jury; elected JPs independent from political control; court proceedings became public.
   - **Non-liberal:** Limitations and exclusions; new decree allowed for political crimes to be tried by special procedures.

Others
   - **Liberal:** Political prisoners released; censorship and restrictions on foreign travel and university entrance relaxed; tax debts cancelled; some freedoms initially granted to Poland; reduced corruption in Church; reforms for Jews and ethnic minorities; some economic liberalisation.
   - **Non-liberal:** Concessions to Poles and Jews reversed after 1863 Polish rebellion; censorship tightened again in 1870s and Church reform stopped.

b - Include assessment of both ways in which and the degree to which reforms helped extend 'liberalism' in each area.
   - Introduction should set out your view and define what is meant by a 'liberal' state.
   - Paragraph on each set of reforms, discussing the ways in which they helped to create a liberal state and the ways they did not.
   - Overall conclusion should draw together all points made, to confirm and repeat your overall view.

⬆ 🅐🅢 Improve an Answer

Answer 2 is the better example because:
- It avoids narrative description.
- It begins with a clear comment on the question.
- It contains clear and wide-ranging information with further analytical comment.

📝 🅐🅢 Plan Your Essay

Statements could include:

Agree
- Defeats in Crimean War (e.g. Inkerman, Balaclava, Sebastopol) had revealed Russia's military inadequacies (e.g. outdated technology, poor transport, inadequate leadership, problems of conscripted army). Dmitry Milyutin argued only a 'free' population would provide necessary labour to improve army.
- Wider consequences of war (e.g. damage to trade or increase in peasant uprisings) had proved reform was needed.
- War had brought renewed calls for reform from the intelligentsia.

Disagree

- Other factors also contributed to Alexander's decision to implement reform.
- Intelligentsia called for reform even before the Crimean War.
- Economic motives – emancipating serfs would provide incentives for peasants to work; and would ultimately provide money and labour to invest in industry, leading to greater prosperity.
- Social unrest in Russia was not new.

Chapter 3

🌐 Apply Your Knowledge

Reactionary changes 1861–81

- Educational reforms were partly reversed (*zemstva*'s powers reduced, Church authority restored, traditional curriculum prioritised, universities tightly controlled).
- Ethnic minorities were persecuted.
- The police were strengthened.
- Judicial system allowed political agitators to be prosecuted, tried (in show trials) and exiled.

Reactionary changes from 1881

- Reforming ministers replaced by conservatives.
- Nobles reinstated to positions of authority and state authority increased.
- Police system further strengthened – the Okhrana was permitted to arrest, imprison or exile anyone suspected of criminal activity.
- Alexander II's judicial reforms were partly reversed.
- Alexander II's educational reforms were further eroded.
- Censorship increased.

Reforming signs and changes 1866–81

- More state teacher-training colleges set up (though mainly to increase tsarist authority).
- Military reforms made the army more efficient.

Reforming signs and changes from 1881

- Redemption fees reduced and arrears cancelled in central provinces.
- Poll tax abolished and inheritance tax introduced, making taxation fairer.
- Right of appeal to higher courts allowed.
- Peasants' Land Bank established in 1883.
- Some reformist factory legislation introduced.

⬆ Improve an Answer

Strengths

- There is comparison throughout the paragraph.
- There is evidence of useful knowledge (e.g. Manifesto of Unshakeable Autocracy').

Weaknesses

- First sentence is descriptive, and does not contribute to an analysis of the question. Several statements are without explanation or support (e.g. 'Alexander had been planning to provide some democracy in Russia').
- The word 'liberal' is used inappropriately, and extreme terms such as 'total', 'complete contrast' and disaster' are given with no explanation.

Are the allegations fair?

- The allegations have some truth but are overstated.

🔵 Ⓐ Assess the Validity of This View

a An example of Alexander II's conservatism and reaction would be increased censorship and Church control of education. You should complete the rest of the mind-map in a similar way.

b Your answer should include examples of both reaction/conservatism and non-conservatism. These could include:

Conservatism:

- Nobles reinstated to positions of authority in local government.
- State authority increased.
- Alexander II's educational reforms partially reversed.
- Alexander II's judicial reforms similarly watered down.

Non-conservatism:

- Redemption fees reduced and arrears cancelled (1881).
- Peasants' Land Bank established (1883).
- Some reformist factory legislation introduced.

Your judgement is likely to be that the years 1881–94 were not exclusively reactionary but that conservatism and reaction dominated over any reforming impulses, whilst in some areas conditions did not change.

💡 Key Question

Your answer might include the following:

- His firm belief in absolutism led him to choose conservative ministers and made him determined to prevent opposition.
- His fear of revolutionary activity made him reactionary and repressive.
- His belief in nationalism led him to firmly repress the nationalities.
- His personal anti-Semitism led to his persecution of the Jews.

Chapter 4

🌐 Ⓐ Apply Your Knowledge

a and **b** (red is repression, blue is concession)

- Permission to have own parliament – Finns.
- Repression of native language – Finns, Poles, Baltic Germans, Ukrainians.
- Closure of national bank – Poles.
- Permission to re-adopt Lutheranism instead of Orthodoxy – Latvians, Estonians.
- Restrictions on living locations – Jews.
- Adherence to Russian Orthodox faith – everyone.
- Ban on participating in local elections – Jews.

c Your essay might conclude that although Russification may have strengthened the Empire in some ways (improving its administration and allowing modernisation), overall it seems to have weakened it, by increasing national feeling among the ethnic nationalities and fuelling political opposition.

🌐 Apply Your Knowledge

Russification policies

- **Finland**
  - Weakened the parliament.
  - Imposed the Russian language.
  - Abolished the Finnish postal service.
  - Replaced the coinage.
- **Poland**
  - Changed the administration.
  - Closed the National Bank.
  - Imposed the Russian language.
  - Insisted that Polish literature was only studied in Russian translation.
- **The Baltic provinces**
  - Imposed the Russian language.
- **Ukraine**
  - Limited the use of the Ukrainian language. Closed all theatres.
  - Extended military conscription throughout the Empire.

- Mixed ethnic groups in the army.
- Crushed ethnic uprisings.
- Encouraged adherence to the Russian Orthodox Church, restricting other faiths.

Anti-Semitic policies

- 1881–84 – Allowed anti-Jewish pogroms in Ukraine and beyond. (Destruction of property, rape and murder.)
- 1882–94 – Series of laws passed that curtailed rights of Jews, e.g.
  - 1882 – May Laws restricted rights of Jews (e.g. confined them to living in ghettoes in towns and cities).
  - 1886 – Decree prevented Jews from running inns.
  - 1892 – Jews were forbidden from participation in local elections.

✏️ Ⓐ Plan Your Essay

A good introduction might look as follows:

The policies of Alexander III affected individuals and groups in all sections of Russian society. The reactionary nature of these policies meant that many groups suffered; the peasantry and local government officials were affected by the part-reversal of Alexander II's reforms of local government; intellectuals and reformers felt the impact of his ruthless suppression of dissent, including the clampdown on education and the increase in censorship; and the population as a whole suffered from the increasing use of the police to crush any form of opposition. However, the ethnic nationalities of the Russian Empire, each of which had its own culture, traditions, language and sometimes religion, suffered particularly badly. The systematic imposition of 'cultural Russification' in, for example, Poland, Finland, the Baltic and Ukraine, as well as legislation that restricted the rights of the Jews throughout the Empire, meant that the ethnic minorities experienced the worst repression of all the groups in the Empire.

Chapter 5

🌐 Apply Your Knowledge

a and **b** **The Organisation (1863):** a student organisation at Moscow University that pressed for radical reform.

Tchaikovsky Circle (1868–89): primarily a literary society; organised production and distribution of scientific and revolutionary literature; wanted to bring about social (but not political) revolution.

Narodniks (established 1874): believed in peasant-led demand for change and socialisation of the land; mostly students who 'went to the people' and tried unsuccessfully to stir up peasant discontent.

Land and Liberty (1877–89): similar to the earlier Narodniks, tried to work among the peasantry to stir up opposition and pressed for constitutional reform; some members used violent methods.

Black Partition (1879–81): an offshoot of Land and Liberty; worked peacefully towards sharing the land among the peasantry.

People's Will (established 1879): another offshoot of Land and Liberty; used violent methods, aiming to undermine government through political assassinations (e.g. of Alexander II in 1881).

Emancipation of Labour (1883): the first Marxist group, founded by Plekhanov and others in Switzerland; arranged for Marxist tracts to be translated and smuggled into Russia.

🔵 Ⓐ To What Extent?

You should produce your own mind-map for this activity. For an example of how to start a mind-map see page 22.

🔍 🅰 Extract Analysis

a **Extract A**

- Repressive reigns of Alexander III and Nicholas II did not eliminate opposition to tsarist regime. Discontent about oppression and incompetence was growing among numerous political and national groups. Unemployment was causing anger among new industrial workers, making them highly likely to cause trouble.

  - o Calls for reform from moderate liberals grew during the reigns of both tsars; in particular, the *zemstva* increased demands for national representation.

  - o In late 19th century, radical groups were established who spread Marxist and socialist ideas; these included the Narodniks and Land and Liberty.

  - o Nicholas II's reign saw the establishment of the Social Democratic Workers' Party and the Social Revolutionary Party among others.

  - o From 1900, discontent among industrial workers grew; trade unions were formed (though illegal until 1905 and strongly restricted after 1906), and strike activity became a threat to the government, especially in 1905 and 1912.

Extract B

- Individuals and groups who opposed the tsarist regime were mainly from same social class as those who were a part of that very regime. The 'common people' and working class scarcely contributed to Russian politics.

  - o Reformers (both moderate liberals and radical reformers) were usually members of the intelligentsia, from wealthy upper classes, educated and had money and leisure to travel and compare Russia with other countries.

  - o Majority of Russian peasants were illiterate, uneducated, religious and deeply loyal to the Tsar.

Extract C

- Very optimistic to believe economic moves towards capitalism, which involved huge social issues, could be achieved with little change to existing social and political system (based largely on an agricultural society), particularly if Tsar did not believe that change was necessary.

  - o Industrialisation involved increasing urbanisation as peasants migrated to towns and cities.

  - o This caused social problems as working and living conditions in towns were poor.

  - o However in 19th century, economic growth progressed well, while agriculture and the countryside changed little.

b A good answer will identify the overall argument of each extract clearly and will both support and criticise this argument using relevant contextual own knowledge. It is also likely to look at sub-arguments and interpretations within the extract to provide a rounded and convincing judgement on 'how convincing' the extract is.

🆎

a See answers for the A Level question, above.

b A good answer will evaluate each source in the way suggested for A Level. However, an essay answer also needs a clear judgement as to which extract is the more convincing. This should be substantiated with reference to the detail of the extracts and contextual own knowledge. In this case, Extract A addresses a wider range of groups with clearer explanation while Extract B focuses exclusively

on the importance of the middle and upper class intelligentsia in opposition. it contradicts Extract A in suggesting that the ordinary people played little part – and own knowledge might suggest this is a less convincing interpretation, particularly given the 'people's' involvement in 1905 and 1917.

Chapter 6

⚙ Apply Your Knowledge

Successes

- Grain exports increased by 18% (1881–91), as a percentage of total Russian exports.

- By 1892, Russian budget was in surplus.

- By 1897 Russia was world's fourth-largest industrial economy.

- Exports and foreign trade increased.

- The railway network was vastly expanded.

Failures

- Peasants suffered badly – after paying taxes and giving their grain to the State, many had nothing left for the winter.

- Thousands died in the famine of 1891–92.

- Grain production remained low compared to Western Europe.

- Lands Banks established to help both peasants and nobles purchase land did not produce many benefits.

⚖ 🅰 Assess the Validity of This View

a **Examples of progress**

- Economic reforms encouraged investment and enterprise.

- Industry expanded (helped by foreign capital and investment).

- New industrial developments included coal and oil extraction, iron mining/working.

- The railway network expanded.

- Grain exports increased by 18%, 1881–91 as a percentage of total Russian exports.

- By 1892, Russian budget was in surplus.

- By 1897 Russia was world's fourth-largest industrial economy.

- Some peasants (*kulaks*) prospered.

- A new middle class began to emerge.

No progress

- Russia's economy remained comparatively weak.

- The peasantry was still poor.

- The domestic market remained small.

- Russia still exported mainly grain rather than industrial goods.

- Society was still strongly divided.

- Living conditions for the peasants remained poor.

Examples where matters got worse

- Most peasants suffered from economic reforms, which meant they had to pay the taxes and give their grain to the State; thousands died in the famine of 1891–92.

- New urban workers suffered poor living and working conditions.

b A good introduction will:

- Make clear that there was some progress and that this progress was in many ways impressive.

  - o This might be linked to the degree of industrial development as an example that will be developed in the essay.

- Mention areas where matters got worse:

  - o This could be supported by mention of the social conditions and living standards of both peasants and urban workers.

- Emphasise that, in broad terms, much remained much the same.

  - o This could be linked to the structure of society and the nature of the economy.

The introduction will need to convey a judgement. This is likely to state that the progress was outweighed by more negative factors and that the premise of the quotation is therefore incorrect.

💡 Key Question

a

The landed elite

Change

- Their personal landholdings had declined since emancipation.

- They might be employed in professions, business or state positions.

Continuity

- They often retained much of their previous wealth.

- They often retained their former status and authority.

The middle class

Change

- This class emerged from the upwardly mobile working class and the 'downward' trend when nobles' sons became entrepreneurs.

- Opportunities included building railways, starting factories or becoming managers.

Continuity

- The 'professional' class of lawyers, doctors and teachers continued (although it expanded in number). This group remained very small in relation to the other groups (only around 2% of the population in the 1890s).

The urban working class

Change

- This class was growing.

- Many peasants moved to the towns and settled, bringing up families there permanently.

Continuity

- Some peasants worked only temporarily in the towns, returning to the country at peak farming periods.

- Poor living and working conditions in the city did not improve.

The peasantry

Change

- Richer peasants (*kulaks*) prospered following emancipation.

- It was possible for them to buy up land, employ labour and buy and sell grain at a profit.

Continuity

- Poorer peasants' lives did not improve (and sometimes got worse).

- Living standards generally remained poor.

b You might argue that the position of the peasants changed the most (emancipation) and the position of the landed nobility changed the least (continuing political importance).

📝 Revision Skills

You should produce your own revision chart for this activity.

Chapter 7

⚙️ Ⓐ Apply Your Knowledge

a   You should produce your own timeline for this activity. For an example of a good timeline see page 9.

b   As well as considering repression and concessions, you would also need to examine broader reasons for the survival of tsardom, including:
  - power of Church/ Divine Right
  - traditional social structure
  - loyalty of peasants
  - political apathy
  - the problems of organised opposition.

🕐 Ⓐ How Successful?

a   **Aims**
  - **Moderate liberal opposition:** a sharing of authority, reducing tsarist power; representative assemblies; civil liberties.
  - **Radical socialist opposition (SRs):** land redistribution (left of Party favoured terrorism/ assassination to achieve aims).
  - **Radical Marxist opposition (SDs):** the overthrow of the autocracy/capitalism in a revolution led by the working classes.
  - **Other opposition:** ethnic minority groups hoped for greater independence; labour groups such as Trudoviks wanted democratic representation and improved working conditions.

b   **Successes**

  Little overall success before 1905 – some progress for the moderate liberals when *zemstvo* representatives invited for discussions in St Petersburg in 1904; after this, *zemstva*'s rights expanded; radical groups succeeded in stirring up unrest in countryside and towns from 1902. SRs carried out political assassinations.

  Some success in the 1905 revolution – moderate liberals achieved aim of national representation when October Manifesto established State Duma; radicals achieved wave of strikes in towns, St Petersburg Soviet established in October 1905 and trade unions legalised.

  Limitations to success 1905–14 – as dumas were constantly undermined, trade unions were restricted; working conditions poor and strikes repressed. Stolypin's land redistribution did not meet SR expectations. No workers' revolution; capitalism continued to flourish; ethnic minorities suppressed.

c   **Sentence starters** could include the following:

  Neither radicals nor liberals enjoyed much success in their opposition to tsardom before 1905...

  The revolution of 1905 gave the opposition an opportunity to show their power but it was really only the moderate liberals that gained anything from the events of that year...

  The radical socialist opposition made some progress towards their aims, but their overall successes remained few...

  Many of the issues which fuelled the opposition movements were ignored...

  From 1905 to 1914, many of the achievements of the 1905 Revolution were eroded...

🔍 Extract Analysis

a   Overall argument highlighted in yellow.
b   Useful references highlighted in pink.

  Nicholas had been blessed with neither his father's strength of character, nor his intelligence. That was Nicholas' tragedy. With his limitations, he could only play at the part of an autocrat, meddling in (and in

the process, disrupting) the work of government, without bringing to it any leadership. He was far too mild-mannered and shy to command any real authority among his subordinates. Being only five feet seven inches tall and feminine in stature, he didn't even look the part of an autocrat. Yet it would be a mistake to assume that Nicholas' failure stemmed from a fundamental 'weakness of will'. Beneath his docile exterior, Nicholas had a strong sense of his duty to uphold the principles of autocracy. He stubbornly defended his autocratic rights against the encroachments of his ambitious ministers and even his own wife. It was not a 'weakness of will' that was the undoing of the last Tsar but, on the contrary, a wilful determination to rule from the throne, despite the fact that he clearly lacked the necessary qualifications to do so.

c   You should use the points you have identified in the earlier parts of this activity to help you plan your answer.

📝 Revision Skills

You should produce your own revision chart for this activity.

Chapter 8

⚙️ Apply Your Knowledge

a   You should produce your own mind-map for this activity. For an example of how to start a mind-map see page 22.

b   🅰🅢 A good essay would:
  - Provide a focused introduction making the agreement/disagreement or compromise view clear and indicating factors to be discussed in answer.
  - Examine impact of expansion of Russian railway network on economy, in relation to promotion of industry and mining/ improvement in communications/ development of financial sector/ employment/society.
  - Examine importance of other factors that helped promote economic growth between 1894 and 1914.
  - Provide a conclusion which repeats view of introduction and summarises why that view is convincing.

b   Ⓐ A good essay would:
  - Provide a focused introduction setting out argument and showing an understanding both of 'economic growth' overall and of 'significant' factors in this. Introduction should make clear what 'investment in railway construction' refers to.
  - Examine significance of investment in railway construction (who? where? with what results?) in relation to economic change and growth.
  - Examine significance of other factors promoting economic change and growth.
  - Provide conclusion which upholds argument set out in introduction and shows effective judgement of 'significance' (i.e. relative importance).

🕐 Ⓐ Assess the Validity of This View

a   **1894**

  Land ownership
  - Land still held in common by the *mir* while peasants paid redemption dues to acquire their own plots (49 years if dues from 1861).
  - Estates subdivided by the *mir* as sons inherited; increasingly less land for each peasant to farm.

  Land use
  - Farming in scattered strips; planting and use controlled by *mir*.
  - Agricultural practices and tools traditional.

  1914

  Positive changes
  Land ownership
  - Peasants' Land Banks (1883 and 1906) helped peasants buy land.
  - Stolypin's land reforms (1906) made more land available for peasants to buy; allowed peasants to leave *mir*; made land the property of individual; allowed for strips to be consolidated into a compact farm; redemption payments abolished (1907).
  - Some peasants (*kulaks*) prospered by buying up land and hereditary ownership of land by peasants increased.
  - Over-population of countryside eased by emigration of 3.5 million peasants to Siberia.

  Land use
  - *Kulaks* farmed larger holdings more efficiently, e.g. use of fertilisers.
  - Grain production rose; Russia was world's leading cereal exporter by 1909.
  - Siberia developed into a major agricultural region.

  Continuity
  Land ownership
  - Most farms continued in traditional way under *mir*; Stolypin's reforms slow to take effect; applications left unprocessed; only around 10% of land was in private ownership.
  - 90% of peasant holdings were still in traditional strips.
  - Noble landowners still dominant.

  Land use
  - Traditional agricultural practices continued; strip farming inefficient.

  Negative changes
  Land ownership
  - Emergence of *kulaks* resented by the (majority) poorer peasants; unrest in countryside.
  - Dispossessed peasants abandoned *mir* and became migrant labourers.
  - Emigration failed to solve problem of increasing rural poverty as population grew.
  - Famine and starvation more frequent.

  Land use
  - Demand for export left land increasingly exhausted.

b   You might decide that, although there was limited change to agricultural practices overall, the problems of land ownership got better, but more slowly than intended.

c   Your conclusion should:
  - Draw together the strands of your argument.
  - Summarise the extent of continuity and change in both land ownership and land use.
  - Conclude with a clear statement, supported by the evidence you have given, that directly answers the question posed.

🔼 Ⓐ Improve an Answer

a   **Weaknesses**
  - Some dates and detail (1855, Crimean War) are irrelevant.
  - The meaning of some sentences is unclear (e.g. 'This all changed in the 1890s...' is ambiguous).
  - The state of the economy in 1890 is not made clear.
  - There is no direct judgement on the question, although this is implied.

Strengths

- There is contrast between the period pre-1890 and 1914.
- The final two sentences suggest the argument that the essay will make (with good supporting detail in the sentence 'By 1914...', and some detail in the last sentence).

b A good introduction would:

- Set out the argument of the essay.
- Clearly explain the economic situation in 1890 and the extent of change by 1914.
- Consider what is meant by the terms '**economic backwardness**' and '**a strong and prosperous country**'.

💡 Key Question

Change

Industry

- Increasing government involvement – protective tariffs and foreign loans and expertise.
- Growth of railways improving infrastructure.
- Growth of heavy industry and opening up of Baku area.
- Relative decline of traditional industry e.g. textiles – particularly towards the end of the period.

Agriculture

- Growth in grain exports (used to finance industry).
- Neglect of agricultural modernisation or diversification as emphasis was on industry.

Results

Industry

- Russia became the world's fourth-largest industrial economy by c1900 and fifth largest by 1914.
- State controlled 70% of Russia's railways and large amounts of heavy industry by c1900.
- Russia had the second largest railway network in the world by 1914.
- Russia was the world's fourth-largest producer of coal, pig-iron and steel by 1914.
- Russia became the world's second-biggest oil producer and fourth in gold mining by 1914.
- Russia's oil production trebled 1885–1914.
- Russia's annual growth rate was more than 8% per annum 1894–1914.
- Russia became internally self-sufficient.

Agriculture

- Poor living standards for peasants who were pressurised into growing grain to support State.
- Under-funding and limited diversification for agriculture.
- Recurrent famine in countryside.
- Harsh agricultural policies made land-holding a major cause of disturbances and promoted Stolypin's attempt at reform.

Chapter 9

⚙ Apply Your Knowledge

Urban workers' standard of living

- Rents high, some could not afford accommodation.
- Wages generally failed to keep up with inflation.
- Women were especially poorly paid.

Peasants' standard of living

- Heavily taxed; redemption payments; control of *mir*.
- Subsistence farmers – some helped by seasonal work in towns.
- Subject to weather conditions/famine.

Urban workers' quality of life

- Living conditions basic; accommodation (both factory-owned and privately rented) over-crowded and lacked sanitation.
- Some legislation offered improvement – reduction in working hours; use of contracts; employment of children under 12 banned; sickness and accident insurance; increased educational provision (but not all enforced or practical).

Peasants' quality of life

- Living conditions basic (except for the *kulaks*).
- Poor health (although *zemstva* offered increasing social/health care); many classed unfit for military service; few doctors; high mortality rates.
- Little educational provision; too few teachers; around 60% illiteracy in 1914.

⚖ 🅰 Assess the Validity of This View

a You might choose to prioritise the statements like this:

1 Half the population of St Petersburg arrived in the 20 years up to 1914. (Major change as peasants moved to the towns and cities.)

2 Many nobles turned to industrial enterprises and financial speculation. (Provided new opportunities for both nobles and peasants.)

3 Many peasants' sons rose to become factory managers. (New development, allowing new social mobility for peasants.)

4 Substantial amounts of nobles' land transferred to townsmen or peasants. (Some peasants prospered, but for many, conditions changed little.)

5 The *kulak* class prospered in the countryside. (Less than 1% of the population).

6 Many peasant farmers migrated to Siberia. (Only a relatively small number (3.5 million) did this.)

7 The *zemstva* provided increased amounts of health care. (The peasants' general health remained poor.)

8 There were new opportunities for women. (This made little difference to the peasantry, where women had always worked alongside men.)

b Based on the prioritisation above, you might conclude that the key social change was indeed in the position of the peasants, and that this was to a great extent because increasing industrialisation meant that many peasants moved to the towns and cities to become urban workers.

c One way of structuring your essay might be:

- To begin with the key changes affecting the peasants, i.e. points 1–3 above. These would need explaining with reference to economic change and legislation, such as Stolypin's agricultural reforms and would probably deserve a short paragraph each.
- To explain 'lesser' changes affecting the peasantry, i.e. points 6–9 above. These might be combined into 2–3 paragraphs and explained.
- A 'balancing' paragraph explaining the limitations to social change for the peasantry.
- Further 'balance' on other important social changes.

🔍 🅰 Extract Analysis

Between 1850 and 1914, Russian society saw both the creative and the destructive sides of modernisation. Slowly, Russia's social structures were assuming the familiar features of capitalism and the traditional social and economic structures of Russian society lost vitality. By 1900 many peasants and many nobles had abandoned their traditional way of life. It is no coincidence that in 1905, the Tsarist government came close to collapse. Did this mean that the government had failed to solve the dilemma of modernisation? Not necessarily. To survive it

had to preserve the traditional bases of its support. Yet to modernise, it had to allow the emergence of new social and economic forces. Eventually the government would have to start looking for support amongst these new groups without alienating its traditional supporters. This was a delicate political manoeuvre. The crises of the first decade of the twentieth century suggest that the Russian government lacked the insight or the skills needed to initiate success. The Russian government was drifting in very dangerous waters.

a Yellow highlighter marks the distinctive view on social change and the tsarist autocracy: Russian social structures changed and the tsarist government proved unable to both retain its traditional basis of support and win over the support of the new social groups.

Pink highlighter represents the sub-arguments and views: social change was brought about by the growth of capitalism; government failure to adapt brought it close to collapse in 1905; the situation had become acute by 1914.

b
- **Evidence to support the author's argument:** detail on effect of emancipation, emergence of *kulaks* and take-off of economy; troubles of 1905; state of country in 1914.
- **Evidence that would contradict it:** stability and loyalty to tsardom; Stolypin's reforms and Duma system showing adaption to change.
- **Evidence to support other views/ arguments:** years of Red Cockerel; strike activity; opposition movements.
- **Evidence that would contradict them:** limitations to opposition; tercentenary celebrations; patriotic response to war, 1914.

c Your answer should show your understanding of **a**, supported and criticised by the evidence collated in **b** above.

⬆ 🅰🅢 Improve an Answer

a First sentence simply repeats the sentence in the extract. Final sentence reaches a judgement, concluding that the extract does clearly show impact of economic factors on economic change; however it does not explain why the extract is convincing.

b **Strengths:**

- Plenty of references to the detail in the extract.
- Shows overall understanding of content.
- Provides a judgement at the end.

Weaknesses:

- Identifies interpretation with first sentence rather than looking at source holistically.
- Goes through source repeating what is said and using words such as 'this shows' rather than commenting on interpretations and then supporting these views.

Chapter 10

⚙ Apply Your Knowledge

- **Lenin:** Social Democratic Workers' Party. After Party split in 1903, he led the Bolsheviks, campaigning for total dedication to revolution by centralised organisation of professional revolutionaries, uncompromised by political alliances.
- **Chernov:** Social Revolutionary Party. Party's most influential theorist and editor of party journal; became leader of the SRs in the Second Duma of 1907.
- **Trotsky:** Social Democratic Workers' Party. After 1903 split, he supported Martov and the Mensheviks (although he later joined the Bolsheviks in 1917).
- **Struve:** Moderate liberal opposition. In 1903 he founded Union of Liberation, which pushed for constitutional system through which urban workers could campaign legally to improve their conditions.

- **Martov:** Social Democratic Workers' Party. He led the Mensheviks after 1903 split in Party, supporting a broad party with a mass working-class membership that co-operated with liberal parties.

How Important?

You should produce your own diagram for this activity.

Key Question

a and **b**

1894–1900

- **Political:** Accession of Nicholas II.
- **Economic and social:** Railways expanded, industrial growth; increasing urbanisation.
- **Intellectual ideas:** Moderate liberals called for a reform of tsardom and national representation; growth of Marxism/socialism.
- **Opposition movements:** 1898 Social Democratic Workers Party founded; 1899 Social Revolutionary Party established.

1900–05

- **Political:** 1904–05 Russo-Japanese War; 1905 (July) Bloody Sunday; 1905 (Oct) October Manifesto.
- **Economic and social:** Continued industrial growth and urbanisation; living and working conditions poor; numerous strikes in 1905; censorship relaxed.
- **Intellectual ideas:** Moderate liberals increased calls for national representation; further growth in Marxism/ socialism; trade unions formed (legalised 1905).
- **Opposition movements:** 1903 Union of Liberation founded; 1903 SDs split into Bolsheviks and Mensheviks.

1906–14

- **Political:** 1906–07 First Duma; 1907 Second Duma; 1907–12 Third Duma; 1912–17 Fourth Duma; radical opposition leaders exiled or imprisoned; 1914 Germany declares war on Russia.
- **Economic and social:** Agricultural reform; strikes in cities (from 1912).
- **Intellectual ideas:** Trade unions restricted.
- **Opposition movements:** Less opposition – moderate liberals tried to cooperate with the Duma system; radical opposition parties weakened and divided.

c Your answer might refer to the following:

- **1894–1900:** modernisation, industrialisation and urbanisation drove intellectuals to push for reform; moderate liberals called for reform of tsardom and national representation, while other intellectuals adopted more radical Marxist and social ideas.
- **1900–05:** further industrialisation and urbanisation led to greater support for reform, as opposition movements were able to exploit discontent at poor living and working conditions. Russia's defeat in Russo-Japanese War further fuelled calls for reform.
- **1906–14:** Following 1905 Revolution, establishment of State Duma meant that moderate liberals provided little further opposition; clampdown on trade unions and the imprisonment or exile of radical opposition leaders, coupled with the fact that the radical parties were divided as to how to react to the events of 1905, meant that radical opposition also decreased.

Plan Your Essay

You should produce your own mind-map for this activity. For an example of how to start a mind-map see page 22.

d Using your plan:

- Address the factor in the question – lack of unity – first, giving plenty of examples in support.
- Evaluate the other types of factors and comment on their importance.

- Ensure you make your overall view clear in the introduction, substantiate it in the essay and repeat it in the conclusion. In this way you should show sustained judgement.

Chapter 11

Apply Your Knowledge

You should create your own flow chart for this activity.

Assess the Validity of This View

a **Factors linked to the Tsar himself**

- **1894–1904:** Personality; lack of interest in politics; determination to uphold autocracy.
- **1905–14:** Determination to undermine the Duma (Fundamental Rights).
- **1914–March 1917:** Poor judgement (self-appointment as Commander-in-Chief of the army, dependence on Rasputin, refusal to listen to advice).

Factors linked to the growth of opposition

- **1894–1904:** Peasant unrest in countryside following 1891–92 famine; establishment of opposition parties; formation of trade unions (e.g. Father Gapon's, 1904).
- **1905–14:** Workers' discontent stemming from increasing urbanisation and industrialisation (strikes of 1912 onwards); legalisation (despite repression) of trade unions from 1905; *but* establishment of State Duma and weakening of opposition parties contributed to a reduction in opposition.
- **1914–March 1917:** discontent arising from impact of First World War (loss of morale among soldiers and civilians, impact on living conditions).
- **Other factors – e.g. economic; social; military**
- **1894–1904:** Impact of 1891–91 famine; erosion of traditional land-based economy; early urbanisation and industrialisation; peasant unrest from 1902; impact of Russo-Japanese War.
- **1905–14:** Relaxation of censorship; spread of education; continued growth of cities.
- **1914–March 1917:** Impact of First World War (cost of war, impact on trade and industry, slump in grain production, loss of land); wartime defeats and humiliation; the Tsar's self-appointment as Commander-in-Chief; influence of Rasputin.

b You should highlight your own key points for this activity.

c Your introduction should:

- Set out the key factors which contributed to the collapse of tsarist authority in 1917 for detailed examination in the body of the essay.
- Focus on factors highlighted as the most important; you can discuss less important factors in later paragraphs.
- Make it clear what line of argument you will put forward – of all the factors that you will examine, was the impact of the First World War the most important?

Your essay might proceed with a paragraph on each factor, considering it across the whole period of the question, and assessing its relative importance in the collapse of tsardom. Your conclusion should both set out and explain your overall judgement.

Alternatively, you could structure your essay chronologically, examining factors that triggered the collapse of tsardom in 1917, and working backwards to consider to what extent tsarist authority had already been undermined before 1914.

Key Question

1914

- **Political:** Dissolution of the Duma.
- **Economic and social:** Mobilisation of 15 million men; loss of industrial capacity in Poland and western Russia following the German and Austro-Hungarian invasions.
- **Military:** Lack of clothing and weapons for soldiers; defeats at Tannenburg (Aug) and Masurian Lakes (Sept).

1915

- **Political:** Establishment of organisations such as the Union of Zemstva, Zemgor and the 'Progressive bloc' (which became a focus for discontent); Tsar's self-appointment as Commander-in-Chief of the army.
- **Economic and social:** Rising cost of war; falling production.
- **Military:** Loss of the majority of experienced officers; continued military defeat and humiliation.

1916

- **Political:** Growing influence of Rasputin.
- **Economic and social:** Rising cost of war; falling production.
- **Military:** Army morale low (15 million desertions).

1917

- **Political:** Establishment by the Duma of a provisional committee (Feb); creation of Petrograd Soviet (Feb).
- **Economic and social:** Escalating strikes in St Petersburg and Moscow.
- **Military:** military discipline had broken down; widespread mutiny.

Revision Skills

You should produce your own revision chart for this activity.

Chapter 12

Apply Your Knowledge

a and **b** Judgement of success is subjective, but measurements that might be included on the line include the following:

- **Control of industry:** Workers' control decree.
- **Land ownership:** Decree on land.
- **Opposition/co-operation from other socialist parties:** Gained the approval of 2nd 'All-Russian Congress of Soviets' for a socialist government; alienated the Mensheviks, leaving a Bolshevik and left-wing SR government coalition.
- **Opposition from liberals and the right:** Arrested members of Provisional Government (Kerensky left to try to gain support at the front).
- **Peace with Germany:** Decree on peace.
- **Establishing an effective government:** Set up all-Bolshevik Sovnarkom as new government.
- **Social issues:** Nationality decree; new legal system; sex discrimination outlawed; removal of titles/class privilege; persecution of *burzhui*.

 Assess the Validity of This View

a **Peasants**

- **Social discontent:** Land hunger in countryside grew steadily worse; little change despite Stolypin's reforms; peasant unrest in countryside; peasant seizures of land escalated after Feb 1917 and in war years.
- **Bolshevik ideology shown in:**

  Broad ideas: Land free for use of all; no private ownership.

  Lenin's advancement of ideas: April Theses promised 'Land'; belief in land distribution appealed to poor peasant majority; encouraged pacificism. *But* Lenin's main interest was in the cities (proletariat rather than peasants); peasants played no direct part in Bolshevik takeover.

Industrial workers

- **Social discontent:** Poor living and working conditions; food shortages exacerbated by First World War; discontent seen in strike activity (especially 1905, 1912 and during war years – peaked Feb 1917 but continued under Provisional Government).

- **Bolshevik ideology shown in:**

  Broad ideas: Nationalisation of industry; dictatorship of proletariat.

  Lenin's advancement of ideas: April Theses promised peace, bread and all power to the soviets; belief in control of industry appealed to workers suffering poor working conditions. *But* Lenin was not supportive of 'July Days' or appeals to work with others to improve the workers' lot (e.g. encouraged non-cooperation with Petrograd Soviet); Bolshevik takeover not dependent on workers.

b   You should choose your own judgement for this activity.

c   Your introduction might:

- Show (briefly) you understand why there was social discontent between 1894 and 1917 – and how this manifested itself.

- Show you understand both the broad theories of Marxism and Lenin's own ideology.

- Give your judgement in relation to the question.

🔍 Extract Analysis

a   The tsarist government's failings in the war and its weakness at home led to the self-destruction of the autocracy on a wave of discontent. Had the democratic February Revolution managed to hold, most likely, Russia today would be a great democratic state, rather than one that has disintegrated... Lenin embarked on a course of violent seizure of power. His slogans, primitive and rabble-rousing, worked without fail... The power of Kerensky's Provisional Government melted like ice in the spring thaw. Meanwhile, the Bolshevik demagogues promised the gullible and ignorant peasants-in-uniform prosperity, land, bread, hospitals and liberty.

b   Following the collapse of the autocracy through its own shortcomings, the February Revolution might have allowed Russia to become a powerful democratic nation. However, following Lenin's return in April 1917 the Bolsheviks' false promises deceived the Russian peasants and tricked the peasant-soldiers into deserting, allowing the Bolsheviks to defeat the Provisional Government and seize power.

c   • The statement that Russia 'would today be a great democratic state rather than one that has disintegrated' is subjective/biased.

- The extract is melodramatic. It conveys a totally one-sided and heavily negative opinion. (Examples of extreme/negative language include: 'primitive and rabble-rousing', 'war-weary, land-starved hungry people', 'melted like ice in the spring thaw', 'gullible and ignorant peasants-in-uniform', 'demagogues').

- Phrases such as 'worked without fail' are unsupported by any historical evidence and the whole extract lacks precision.

🗂 🅰🆂 Plan Your Essay

a   **Strengths of the Bolsheviks 1903–Oct 1917**

- Increasingly dominated the Party after the 1903 split and influential through 1905 Revolution; represented in Fourth Duma (1912).

- Strengthened by war and tsarist overthrow, and by Lenin's return (Apr 1917); armed after Kornilov coup (Aug 1917).

- Sept 1917 – majority in the Petrograd Soviet; Oct 1917 – huge membership, 41 newspapers and had 10,000 Red Guards in Petrograd factories (work of Trotsky).

Weaknesses of the Bolsheviks 1903–Oct 1917

- Were in minority among the socialists, and even in the SD Party after the 1903 split.

- Need for radical reform seemed less after the 1905 Revolution – membership declined.

- Organisational problems: lack of finance; shortage of secret printing presses; Lenin and others in exile; faced tsarist represssion to 1917.

- Jun 1917 – the All-Russian Congress of Soviets passed a vote of confidence in the Provisional Government; July 1917 – uncontrolled rioting (the 'July Days' was blamed on the Bolsheviks).

- No 'popular' revolution in October.

Other factors – e.g. the failures of the Provisional Government

- Lack of support for the Provisional Government: viewed as a 'committee of the wealthy' by working classes; lost support of upper classes following Kornilov coup (Aug 1917).

- Failure of Provisional Government policies: decision to continue war; no land redistribution.

- War brought deteriorating situation in cities, including worsening pay and conditions and food shortages.

- Failure of Provisional Government strategies in Oct 1917.

b   You should consider how you would approach your own essay for this activity.

c   • Paragraph 1 might address longer-term factors - looking at Bolshevik strengths 1903 – July 1917 and particularly how they increased after the February Revolution.

- Paragraph 2 might address the developments July–Oct 1917, looking at the short-term factors in the build-up to revolution.

- Although the chronological split is uneven, this approach would facilitate a good assessment of Bolshevik strengths in the collapse of the Provisional Government in Oct 1917.

Chapter 13

⚙ Apply Your Knowledge

Stage 2 (1924–27)

Key Events:

- Publication of Lenin's 'Testament' (released May 1924, criticising Stalin) suppressed.

- July 1926: 14th Party Congress – Stalin supported Bukharin (RW); Zinoviev and Kamenev attacked Stalin but lost every vote. A new Central Committee and Politburo elected with a Stalinist-Bukharin majority.

- Nov 1926: Zinoviev and Kamenev joined with Trotsky in the 'United Opposition'; Stalin accused them of 'factionalism' and defeated all three.

Ideological issues:

- Stalin appeared to favour continuance of the NEP (Bukharin's preference).

- Stalin upheld ideology that the Party can never be wrong and that opposition was 'factionalism'.

Stage 3 (1927–29)

Key events

- Jan 1928: Stalin began a new 'left-leaning' economic strategy, opposed by Bukharin.

- Nov 1929: Bukharin and his supporters, Rykov and Tomsky, removed from Politburo.

Ideological issues:

- Stalin veered back to support abandonment of the NEP.

- Stalin claimed that 'true socialism' demanded a developed industry rather than dependence on peasantry.

⚖ 🅰 To What Extent?

a   • **succeeded:** seize power in the name of the workers; crush all opposition.

- **partially succeeded:** promote socialist thinking; destroy capitalism; achieve state ownership of the means of production.

- **largely failed or ignored:** establish a Marxist state and create a dictatorship of the proletariat; spread the socialist revolution worldwide.

b   A good answer would:

- Consider Lenin's actions in 1903 when he 'used' ideology to gain leadership of the Bolsheviks, and in the years to 1914, when it could be argued that Bolshevik attempts to stir workers to action focused more on living/working conditions than on pure socialism.

- Examine importance of ideology after Lenin returned to Russia in April 1917 and in the takeover in October, when weaknesses of the Provisional Government and the military and organisational abilities of Trotsky were highly (and probably more) significant.

- Consider clash of ideology and pragmatism during Lenin's early months in power, during the Civil War and to 1924.

📋 Revision Skills

You should produce your own timeline for this activity. For an example of a good timeline, see page 9.

📍 Key Question

- **One-party State:** A state ruled by one political party in which the existence of any other parties is forbidden.

- **Common ownership of the means of production:** When the factories/farms that produce goods/food supplies are owned by all rather than private individuals.

- **Socialism:** The political and economic theory that the means of production, distribution and exchange should be owned by the community as a whole.

- **Permanent revolution:** Theory associated with Trotsky that revolution had to continue across different countries in order to establish communism.

- **Socialism in one country:** Theory that the USSR should focus on creating communism in Russia alone, rather than on spreading revolution to other countries.

- **Dictatorship of the proletariat:** A State in which the working class holds political power.

- **Democratic centralism:** A system in which all people can pass their views on to local officials, who, in turn, can pass them up to the central authority. This debates issues and passes down orders for the people to follow.

Chapter 14

⚙ Apply Your Knowledge

You should produce your own mind-map for this activity. For an example of how to start a mind-map see page 22.

⚖ 🅰 Assess the Validity of This View

a   **Stalinist State 1930s – continuity**

- One-party rule: continued and extended.

- Government and Party structures: continued and extended (parallel structures).

- Centralised control: continued and extended.

- *Nomenklatura:* continued.

Stalinist State 1930s – change

- Cult of the leader: developed (both for Lenin and, increasingly, for Stalin).
- Constitution: changed (1936 Constitution).
- Party membership: increased massively.
- Party congresses: called less frequently (never between 1939 and 1952).

b **Possible judgement:** The administrative workings of government remained much the same under Stalin, but the leader came to play a more important role – in particular, by-passing the Party congresses.

c You should produce your own written answer for this activity.

⬆ Improve an Answer

a The paragraph addresses the question: 'What forms of propaganda were significant for the cult of personality?' It looks at different forms of propaganda and relates them to the cult of personality. Instead it should have evaluated how important the cult of personality was to Stalin's rule before 1941.

b The cult of personality was significant to the Stalinist dictatorship before 1941 because it helped to strengthen Stalin's authority by portraying him almost as a god. Russian people were encouraged to worship this 'mighty leader', in the way that they had formerly worshipped the Tsar. Furthermore, the message was conveyed in a way that no-one could escape from. Towering figures of Stalin were displayed on posters on the streets of the towns and cities, on factory walls and alongside major roads. The cult was also reinforced by photographs of Stalin in books and newspapers, which were doctored to show him in the best possible light, with his enemies obliterated from the pictures. Such saturation helped Stalin maintain loyalty despite his dictatorship.

🔍 Extract Analysis

a **Statements of opinion about Stalin's government:**

'By 1941, the Soviet political system had been transformed. In 1934, Stalin's power derived from his position as head of the Party apparatus.'

'By 1939, the Party apparatus could no longer control Stalin. Stalin had achieved a personal authority independent of any single institution.'

Main argument: By 1941, the political system in the USSR had changed; instead of owing his power to his position as head of the Communist Party, Stalin had now gained personal power that did not rely on any political institution.

b **By 1941, the Soviet political system had been transformed:**

- The system established by Lenin in the 1920s had been dominated by the Communist Party.
- By 1941, Stalin was effectively a dictator, working predominantly through small groups of loyal supporters rather than through Party or government channels.

In 1934, Stalin's power derived from his position as head of the Party apparatus:

- In 1934, Stalin had extended the one-party rule and centralised control that had been established under Lenin, and was exercising power through the parallel structures of Party (headed by Sovnarkom) and government (headed by the Politburo).

By 1939, the Party apparatus could no longer control Stalin. Stalin had achieved a personal authority independent of any single institution:

- From 1939, Party Congresses were no longer called (until 1952).

- By 1941 Stalin controlled appointments to all important positions in the Party and had developed a vast bureaucracy of loyal servants through whom he worked.

c You should produce your own conclusion for this activity.

Chapter 15

⚙ Apply Your Knowledge

For Lenin, bullet points might include the following:

Key industrial developments

- Workers' control over factories under State Capitalism, 1917–18.
- Nationalisation of industry under War Communism, 1918–21.
- Some private ownership permitted under New Economic Policy, from 1921.

Key agricultural developments

- Peasants allowed to take over the land under State Capitalism, 1917–18.
- Food requisitioning (May 1918) under War Communism, 1918–21.
- Grain requisitioning halted under New Economic Policy, from 1921.

For Stalin, they might include:

Key industrial developments

- The Great Turn and development of heavy industry under First Five Year Plan, 1928–32.
- Continued development of heavy industry and new emphasis on light industry and communications under Second Five Year Plan, 1933–37.
- More development of heavy industry and focus on rearmament under Third Five Year Plan, 1938–42.

Key agricultural developments

- Great Turn, announced 1927.
- Forced collectivisation under Collectivisation Stage 1, 1929–30.
- Slower collectivisation and establishment of MTSs under Collectivisation Stage 2, 1930–41.

🏛 Ⓐ To What Extent?

You might choose to select 1918, 1921, 1928 and 1941 as your 4 key years. If so, your assessment might include the following:

a **1918 (War Communism replaced State Capitalism)**

- **Agriculture:** food requisitioning began; *kulaks* had their stocks seized.
- **Industry:** War Communism introduced; industry nationalised, managers employed again, working hours extended, private trade and manufacture forbidden.

1921 (NEP replaced War Communism)

- **Agriculture:** Grain requisitioning halted, peasants could sell any grain that was surplus after supplying a proportion to the government.
- **Industry:** State control of transport, banking and heavy industry retained but private ownership of smaller businesses and private trade permitted; rationing was ended; industries made to be more efficient.

1928 (the Great Turn, announced 1927)

- **Agriculture:** move towards co-operative farming began.
- **Industry:** First Five Year Plan announced, setting challenging targets in heavy and light industry (followed by Second, Third and Fourth Five Year Plans).

1941 (Germany declares war on Russia)

- **Agriculture:** Farmland destroyed to make it useless to the invading Germans; food

---

shortages were addressed by rationing and quotas from the *kolkhozes*.

- **Industry:** Factories and their workers transferred from western Russia to an area east of the Ural mountains; wartime production was quickly established, thanks to the USSR's centralised, planned economy; most national expenditure was diverted to military requirements, with focus on building giant heavy industrial complexes to manufacture munitions.

b **1918 (War Communism replaced State Capitalism)**

- **Circumstances:** Civil War (armies had to be supplied and fed).
- **Other factors:** Socialist ideology required the abolition of private enterprise.

1921 (NEP replaced War Communism)

- **Circumstances:** Problems created by War Communism, e.g. grain shortages worsened culminating in 1921 famine; industrial production fell; money largely replaced by barter; urban population declined; peasant revolts and strikes in the cities caused by food shortages; Kronstadt rebellion.
- **Other factors:** Some Bolsheviks were pressing for greater worker control and an end to War Communism.

1928 (the Great Turn)

- **Circumstances:** NEP failing to provide sufficient growth; war scare in late 1920s made it important to reduce dependency on foreign imports and increase military strength; peasants still not producing enough grain for export.
- **Other factors:** 'True socialism' required a developed industry rather than dependence on the peasantry; pressure to create a more socialist system in the countryside; Stalin wanted to be associated with a new and successful economic direction.

1941 (Germany declares war on Russia)

- **Circumstances:** Outbreak of war – economy had to be reorganised to ensure economic survival.
- **Other factors:** War was the overriding factor.

c and d You should produce your own judgement and use the points you have identified in the earlier parts of this activity to help you plan your essay.

💡 Key Question

Lenin only

- Allowed peasants to take over the land and gave workers control in the factories. (Initially – Oct–Dec 1917).
- Allowed some private ownership (State Capitalism early 1918, and NEP from 1921).

Stalin only

- Focus on development of heavy industry (Five Year Plans).
- Imposed collectivisation in agriculture.

Overlap (under Lenin's War Communism 1918–21 and under Stalin from 1927)

- Implemented food requisitioning and seizure of *kulaks'* stocks.
- Implemented nationalisation of industry; private enterprise forbidden.

⚙ Apply Your Knowledge

a Stalin's collectivisation policy, which took place between 1927 and 1941 and was intended to make farming more efficient, allow more mechanisation and facilitate grain collection, had mixed results.

b Your answer could include 4 pieces of information from the following:

i) Moves to encourage voluntary collectivisation between Dec 1927 and Dec 1929 had little success, forcing Stalin to announce a policy of forced collectivisation into state farms in December 1929.

ii) The first stage of forced collectivisation (1929–30) succeeded in collectivising over half of households, but the speed of implementation caused so much resentment that the programme was abandoned.

iii) By the end of the second stage (1930–41) all peasant households had been collectivised and machine tractor stations established.

iv) Despite the apparent success of the policy, there were problems with its implementation (including the loss of millions of successful *kulaks*, destruction of grain and livestock, poor organisation and lack of equipment in the collectives, little incentive for peasants to work hard for the collective).

v) Millions of peasants starved in the famine of 1932–33.

vi) Grain output did not exceed pre-collectivisation levels until after 1935.

c You should use the points you have identified in the earlier parts of this activity to help you plan your essay.

Chapter 16

🌐 Apply Your Knowledge

a *Burzhui* : The middle and upper classes, defined as the 'class' enemies of the proletariat.

Proletariat: The urban working class.

Komsomol: The Communist youth organisation.

Socialist man (and woman): A man or woman with a sense of social responsibility who would willingly serve the State.

Social realism: The form of art and literature demanded by Stalin's regime, in which artists and writers had to present an uplifting vision of Soviet life in the socialist future, glorifying the working man.

Stakhanovite: A worker like the miner Stakhanov, whose inflated achievements in productivity were publicised as an example for others to follow.

Deportations: Forced migrations of non-Russians to other parts of the Soviet Union.

b In Soviet society, there was no place for the **burzhui**, nor for non-Russians who faced **deportations**. Instead, society revolved around the **proletariat** who were encouraged, through organisations such as the **Komsomol**, to develop into true '**socialist men and women**'. For some this meant working as **Stakhanovites**; others were driven by a view of the future which was reinforced by the culture of **social realism**.

🎓 Assess the Validity of This View

a **Ideology and attitudes**
- **Men:** Proletariat 'backbone' of nation; equality; limited private life.
- **Women:** The equal of men; workers.

Work opportunities
- **Men:** State-allocated employment; work for all.
- **Women:** Until 1930s, expected to work; thereafter women encouraged to give up work upon marriage.

Working conditions
- **Men:** Harsh – low pay, strict labour discipline; strikes illegal; internal passports; had to meet targets (quotas); agricultural collectives; 7-day working week, long hours. In 1930s, Stakhanovite movement set hard targets but it became easier to change jobs and wage

differentials, bonuses and payment by the piece were introduced.
- **Women:** Same conditions as men, but pay was lower.

Living conditions
- **Men:** Poor – primitive in countryside; cramped communal apartments in towns (better housing given as reward in 1930s).
- **Women:** As for men; women often had to work and run the home.

Family
- **Men:** Limited private life; only civil marriage; in 1930s marriage and large families encouraged.
- **Women:** Many had to both work and look after family in 1920s. In 1930s, financial incentives to give up work and have many children; divorce and abortion attacked; state nurseries and child clinics increased.

Legal rights
- **Men:** Proletarians were citizens with right to work; *burzhui* were non-persons.
- **Women:** Sex discrimination outlawed, girls received the same educational rights as boys, and women could own property and work; divorce and abortion made easier in 1920s but discouraged in 1930s, when adultery became a criminal offence, contraception was banned and some single-sex schools were reintroduced.

b You should use the points you have identified in the earlier parts of this activity to help you plan your essay.

✏️ Plan Your Essay

a **Important**
- To address illiterate peasants, through strong visual messages (especially in the early years).
- To convert people to socialism in the early years and to reinforce the socialist message in the 1930s (indoctrination).
- To gain support for policies such as industrialisation and collectivisation.
- To create an atmosphere of unity and sense of patriotism among peasants and workers.
- To encourage hard work and increasing productivity among workers.
- To reinforce Lenin's and Stalin's personal authority.

Not important
- The regime relied on effective policing and 'fear' to control the population.
- Policies and new opportunities won over the people more than propaganda.
- Propaganda could be counter-productive, creating cynicism about the regime's successes and thereby about the country's leadership.

b A good conclusion will include:
- A clear judgement on the question, e.g. that propaganda played a major part in each leader's personal authority.
- A summary of the argument that has led to that judgement, e.g. that the immersive propaganda helped prevent people from thinking for themselves and made them more ready to accept the regime and its leader.
- Some reference to the alternative arguments, e.g. that fear alone would never have provided such a stable society and that when policies failed (as for example in some aspects of the Five Year Plans) it was propaganda that prevented the people turning against their leaders.

💡 Key Question

a and **b** You should produce your own 'diamond 9' of key developments and issues.

Chapter 17

🌐 Apply Your Knowledge

You should produce your own timeline/flow chart for this activity. For an example of a good timeline see page 9.

🎓 Assess the Validity of This View

a You should select or formulate your own introduction for this activity.

b Your introduction should start with the opening sentence that you chose in part **a** of this activity. It might show an awareness of the scope of the purges and the perceived 'threats' which they addressed.

The scope of the purges might include:
- The purge of the Communist Party, 1933–35.
- The murder of Kirov, 1934; imprisonment of Zinoviev and Kamenev, 1935.
- The Great Purges, 1936–38; the executions of Zinoviev, Kamenev and Bukharin.
- The Yezhovshchina, 1937–38.
- The murder of Trotsky, 1940.
- The purges of the 1940s.

Perceived threats might include: sabotage of policies; political opposition; personal ambition; individual power-bases; support for leader's enemies; spread of/ sympathy with subversive ideas.

c You should use the introduction that you wrote for part **b** as the basis for your essay.

💡 Key Question

Supporters of other non-Bolshevik/Communist political parties
- **Why:** Disagreed with Bolshevik/Communist aims and ideology; favoured different tactics and wanted to share power.
- **How:** Mensheviks and SRs walked out of Soviet Congress of Oct 1917; left-wing SRs walked out of Sovnarkom in March 1918.
- **Degree of success/failure:** Largely failed – after Oct 1917 walkout, the Bolsheviks ruled alone except for a few left-wing SRs in Sovnarkom (other party leaders were arrested and opposition newspapers were banned); after these departed in March 1918 the Bolshevik/Communist Party ruled entirely alone.

Those with alternative interests (from tsarists to peasants)
- **Why:** To prevent the spread of Bolshevism.
- **How:** Joined the 'White' forces and fought the Bolsheviks in the Civil War.
- **Degree of success/failure:** Failed – opponents of Bolsheviks were imprisoned.

Ideologically opposed social groups – upper classes and bourgeoisie
- **Why:** They were ostracised by Bolshevik ideology and their homes, wealth and way of life destroyed.
- **How:** Some participated in the Civil War.
- **Degree of success/failure:** Failed – the *burzhui* were labelled 'former people'; their privileges were ended and they suffered heavy discrimination; some fled the country.

Leading Party members who disagreed with the official line
- **Why:** Ideological and personal differences.
- **How:** Tried to win support from others within the Party to challenge the leader.
- **Degree of success/failure:** Failed – 1921 'ban on factions' ended disagreements. Eliminated in purges of 1930s.

Minority nationality groups
- **Why:** Hoped for greater independence.
- **How:** Some joined the Civil War on the side of the 'Whites'.

- **Degree of success/failure:** Treaty of Riga (March 1921) granted self-rule to Poland but Russification imposed on the majority of nationalities from 1922 and strengthened by Stalin. 1936 Constitution ambiguous – it promised autonomy to ethnic groups but Stalinist deportations and purge in Georgia 1951 suggested continued repression.

🔍 Key Question

Felix Dzerzhinsky
- Appointed Head of Cheka, 1917.
- Responsible for Red Terror under Lenin.

Leon Trotsky
- Led the Red Army in the Civil War, 1918–21.
- Exiled by Stalin and assassinated in 1940.

Genrikh Yagoda
- Established the gulag system from 1929 and Head of NKVD, 1934–36.
- Executed 1937.

Sergei Kirov
- Leningrad Party Secretary who wanted to slow pace of economic change, 1934.
- Assassinated 1934 in suspicious circumstances suggesting Stalin to blame.

Grigorii Zinoviev
- 'Old Bolshevik'; arrested and accused of inciting terrorism, 1935.
- Executed 1936 following a show trial.

Lev Kamenev
- Colleague of Zinoviev and 'Old Bolshevik', arrested 1935.
- Given show trial and executed in Great Purge, 1936.

Nikolai Bukharin
- 1937 – accused of knowing of a Trotsky-inspired conspiracy to murder Stalin and arrested.
- 1938 – shot after trying to defend himself of charges.

Mikhail Tukhachevsky
- Senior commander and 'hero' of the Civil War; arrested, tortured and made to confess, 1937.
- Convicted of espionage and shot, 1937.

Nikolai Yezhov
- Head of NKVD 1936–38 and responsible for Yezhovshchina.
- Used as scapegoat for excesses of Terror and removed, 1938; shot, 1940.

Lavrenty Beria
- Head of NKVD from 1938.
- Under him, pace of persecution slowed, although purges continued.

Chapter 18

⚙ Apply Your Knowledge

a and **b**

Stalin's Russia, 1941: one possible order of priority with comments:
- Stalin wielded personal power through individuals or small groups of loyal officials. This meant that his rule was effectively a personal dictatorship.
- No independent institutions or rival power centres were permitted. Stalin's regime was therefore able to stand unchallenged.
- Only the Communist Party could put candidates up for election. This prevented any form of political opposition.
- The *nomenklatura* system kept power in the hands of loyal officials. Through this system Stalin was able to control all appointments, and prevent opposition.

- A complex bureaucracy underpinned the regime. This meant that responsibility for government and administration shifted from the Communist Party to a new younger elite of officials who owed their privileges to Stalin and were strong supporters of him.

c You should use the points you have identified in the earlier parts of this activity to help you plan your paragraph.

🎓 Assess the Validity of This View

a **Economic weakness**
- Purge of skilled Russian managers, technicians, workers and foreigners led to skills shortages in industry.
- Fear of missing targets led to grain hoarding among peasantry; in industry it stifled creativity and encouraged false reporting.

Military weakness
- Stalin's purge of senior military commanders weakened the military (e.g. it left the USSR unprepared for war in 1941).

Political weakness
- Elimination of opposition prevented new ideas (e.g. no room for the educated moderate liberals or alternative paths to socialism) and stultified political life.

Psychological weakness
- Atmosphere of fear and terror created (the Red Terror, Stalin's purges).
- Lenin's ban on factions ended disagreements and allowed a strong Party to emerge.
- Lenin's purge of the *burzhui* boosted confidence among peasants and workers.

b
- Enforced support for Stalin's economic programme resulted in the USSR becoming a highly industrialised and urbanised nation; the labour camps contributed to economic growth.
- Stalin's purges of the Communist elite encouraged a younger generation with the prospect of new opportunities.
- The purges and attacks prepared the population for obedience and hardship and so made them more ready to fight the war.

c You should use the points you have identified in the earlier parts of this activity to help you plan your essay.

🔍 Extract Analysis

Extract A

a • **Opinion/argument:** Answers could include 'Stalinism was excess and extraordinary extremism'; 'a virtual civil war against the peasantry'; and 'a holocaust by terror that victimised tens of millions of people'.
- **Overall argument:** Stalinism was an extremist form of rule, resting on the deification of the leader and involving virtual civil war, terror and aggression.
- **Sub-arguments:** Stalin ...
  o waged virtual civil war on peasants
  o led a civil-war style terror
  o encouraged a fascist-like aggressive patriotism
  o sought deification.
- **Own knowledge:**
  o Stalinist collectivisation and enforcement of economic policies.
  o Stalinist terror.
  o Stalin's leadership in war.
  o The cult of the leader.

Extract B
- **Opinion/argument:** 'mobilised the resources of the country during the 1930s in the pursuit of rapid

growth of heavy industry, energy and transport' and 'industrial expansion'.
- **Overall argument:** Stalinism involved the mobilisation of all the resources of the country to create a strong economy, a process which rested on an army of bureaucrats – the *nomenklatura*.
- **Sub-arguments:** Stalin ...
  o pursued the rapid growth of heavy industry, energy and transport
  o strengthened the USSR militarily
  o held false assumptions about his achievements which contained the seeds of their own destruction in the creation of the *nomenklatura*.
- **Own knowledge:**
  o Stalin's Five Year Plans.
  o USSR military success in Second World War.
  o The *nomenklatura* and Stalinist bureaucracy.

Extract C
- **Opinion/argument:** '"Socialism in One Country"'; 'industrialisation, via a centrally planned economy and collectivisation of agriculture'; 'high levels of state terror and a personality cult'.
- **Overall argument:** Stalinism meant a drive towards 'socialism in one country', involving a centrally planned economy directing industrialisation and collectivisation, which was accompanied by state terror and a personality cult.
- **Sub-arguments:**
  o Socialism in one country appealed to Soviet citizens who wanted stability.
  o Stalinist policies contradicted Marxist theory.
- **Own knowledge:**
  o Socialism in one country.
  o The centrally planned economy.
  o Stalinist terror.
  o The Stalinist personality cult.
  o Marxist and Stalinist ideology.

b As well as drawing on the information that you have compiled in part **a**, try to follow the steps set out in the section 'How to master the extracts question' on page 6 of this guide.

Chapter 19

⚙ Apply Your Knowledge

a and **b**

You might choose to organise the detail and justify your priorities like this:
- **Living conditions:** whole population affected by food, housing and fuel shortages and health problems; millions died.
- **Soldiers and workers:** all sections of society forced into war work, in harsh conditions.
- **Women and the family:** women had to perform war work for low pay, while still expected to raise large families.
- **Partisans:** partisans and civilians behind German lines could face terrible reprisals from the German forces.
- **Propaganda and culture:** all sections of society affected, but artists and musicians actually enjoyed more freedom.
- **Churches:** Churches enjoyed a break from persecution.

🎓 To What Extent?

a **Stalin's position at the head of government**
- Temporarily weakened on outbreak of war – he withdrew from public and left the preparations for war to Molotov and the Politburo.

- Ultimately strengthened – he resumed political authority as Head of Government (May) and assumed military authority as Head of Stavka (July).
- He remained Supreme Leader, using his position to boost morale and patriotism.

Degree of delegation

- Initially delegated to Molotov and Politburo.
- Largely left the running of the war to his military commanders.

Dealing with opposition (real and imagined)

- During the war, brutally deported whole nations and ethnic groups to new homes far away in the Empire.
- In 1945, became increasingly paranoid about opposition; returning prisoners of war and many other returning servicemen sent to labour camps imprisoned, collaborators executed.

The Party

- Grew and changed in composition, as millions of soldiers/sailors joined following propaganda given to the troops.
- Enjoyed greater confidence and stronger belief in the communist system, thanks to victory in the war.

Propaganda

- Centred on promoting patriotism and unity, heroism and self-sacrifice.
- Propaganda used to encourage patriotism and an atmosphere of national unity under an unsurpassed leader.

Personal prestige

- Soared as a result of the war – Stalin could portray himself as a great war hero who had achieved victory and gained new satellite states for the USSR.
- Internationally, by end of war was recognised as a world leader.

b Your answer should:

- Offer a judgement on the extent of change to Stalin's political authority as a result of war. It doesn't matter whether you argue that the war only confirmed the authority he had acquired in 1930s or that it made a huge difference, but you should adopt a view.
- Proceed thematically looking at the various aspects of political authority before and after the war. Remember that each paragraph should begin with a comment linking to the question and the extent of change, e.g. 'Propaganda was used to enhanced the leader's authority both before and during the war; the change was in the type and extent rather than the method...'

⬆ Improve an Answer

a Irrelevant (for an essay on the success of the economy):

in a three-pronged attack ... Once Stalin had recovered from the shock, which left him inactive for a week ... Even though the Germans penetrated deep into Russia, the Soviets drove them back from Stalingrad in 1943, scoring a moral victory. ... by 1945, the Red Army had forced the Nazis back to Berlin, where they were destroyed.

b The war years, 1941–45, demonstrated how successfully Stalin's economic policies of the 1930s had strengthened the USSR's economy.

c You should use the points you have identified in the earlier parts of this activity to help you write your paragraph.

💡 Key Question

Your answer for women might include:

Key developments 1941–45

- Importance of family emphasised.
- Women's burdens increased (workers and homemakers).

- Women worked in industry, on farms or in the armed forces, but for little reward.

Changes from 1930s

- In the 1930s women were encouraged to give up paid employment when they married.

Continuity from 1930s

- Importance of family was emphasised in 1930s too.
- Despite encouragement for women to give up work, the numbers of women in work or education grew in the 1930s.

Other rows of the chart should be completed similarly.

Chapter 20

🎯 Apply Your Knowledge

a You should produce your own mind-map for this activity. For an example of how to start a mind-map, see page 22.

b 'High Stalinism' – refers to the period 1945–53, when Stalin's authority over State and Party was greater than at any time before.

⚖ Ⓐ Assess the Validity of This View

a **1932**

- **Stalin's power:** Had grown since 1929, with the defeat of both left and right opposition.
- **Persecution of opposition:** Terror used – dekulakisation; 'show trials' (1928–32); accusations of industrial sabotage or counter-revolutionary activities; Party members purged in Ryutin Affair (1932) and political purges (1933–35); Kirov murdered (1934).
- **Evidence:** The detail above suggests that Stalin became more determined to escalate terror in 1930s when his power was growing.

1936

- **Stalin's power:** Effectively a personal dictatorship.
- **Persecution of opposition:**
  - o Great Purges (1936–38) in which prominent Communists executed; military commanders purged; Yezhovshchina (1937–38) affected ordinary citizens.
  - o Fewer purges from 1938 – 'mass cleansings' declared no longer necessary; many set free.
  - o 1940 – Yezhov executed, Trotsky assassinated.
- **Evidence:** The detail above partly supports view of question; however, decreases in purges from 1938 may act as a balance to this view.

1941

- **Stalin's power:** Absolute and unchallenged supreme commander; war hero.
- **Persecution of opposition:** Opposition disappeared in wartime – so no evidence to support question.

1946

- **Stalin's power:** High Stalinism – god-like status, despite increasing reclusiveness and irrationality; Politburo became advisory, Party lost its autonomy; Stalin's request to resign in 1952 was refused.
- **Persecution of opposition:** 1952 replacement of Politburo by a Presidium.
- Terror revived; Former soldiers harshly treated, Soviet citizens under constant surveillance; contact with foreigners could lead to imprisonment in a gulag, NKVD strengthened, 12 million sent to labour camps 1945–53.
- Photos of perceived opponents airbrushed, Party officials executed in the Leningrad Case (1949), doctors arrested and tortured (Doctors' Plot, 1952), Beria's supporters purged in Mingrelian

Case (1951–52), 'anti-patriotic' campaign launched including anti-Semitic attacks.

- **Evidence:** Supports extreme paranoia when Stalin was at height of power.

b Based on the evidence above, you might conclude that the statement is broadly valid – i.e. that as Stalin's power increased he became more determined to persecute those whom he feared as potential opponents, although there were some periods (e.g. in the late 1930s and during the war years) when persecution declined.

🔍 Extract Analysis

a • **Factually correct:** Attack on modernism and foreign influence on Russian culture; crackdown on the cultural freedom of wartime; Stalin saw the Russians as the binding element of the USSR; enforced celebration of Russianness.

- **Extreme opinion:** Like two crabby professors; these two meticulous, ever-tinkering 'intellectuals'; that ravenous Bolshevik appetite; a policy that would have been familiar to nineteenth-century tsars; cooked up the crackdown.
- **Overall view:** After the war, Stalin and Zhdanov embarked on a rigorous crusade of cultural Russification, using victory to justify the repression of cultural freedom and foreign influences and the imposition of a strong sense of Russian identity.

b The argument is convincing in that it makes points which can be supported by contextual evidence, e.g.:

- The Zhdanovshchina, launched by Zhdanov in 1946, condemned everything Western as bourgeois and decadent and praised everything Russian as superior and uplifting.
- Post 1946, 'anti-Soviet' authors were condemned, little contact with the West was allowed, and social realism was reinstated as the norm in the arts.
- The parallel drawn with tsarist policies 'a policy that would have been familiar to nineteenth-century tsars' relates well to Alexander III's policies of cultural Russification.

  It is not convincing where it expresses views that cannot be supported by knowledge of the context e.g.

- 'Like two crabby professors, obsessed with the greatness of nineteenth-century culture ... they reached back to their youths', which suggests a reason for the Zhdanovshchina which cannot be verified.
- 'Poring over poetry and literary journals late into the night ...' (although we know Stalin was often up late, he preferred watching films and talking to cronies over deciding policy).
- 'cooked up the crackdown' – which suggests a conspiratorial approach not in keeping with the facts.

🎯 Apply Your Knowledge

- **World superpower:** An extremely strong nation with influence beyond its national borders. Superpower status after 1945 enhanced Stalin's political authority.
- **'Old Guard':** The original Bolsheviks, who were committed to Marxist ideals and whom Stalin destroyed in the purges of the 1930s.
- **Zhdanovshchina:** The cultural purge initiated by Zhdanov in 1946 to impose 'Russian' and socialist ideas in the arts and eliminate foreign influence, so supporting the culture of High Stalinism.
- **Ideological contamination:** The undermining of socialist/Stalinist ideology by other influences, which Stalin sought to prevent, particularly after 1945 when soldiers returned from the West.

- **NKVD:** The secret police under Stalin (successor to the Cheka), used to reinforce Stalinist authority.
- **Anti-Semitism:** Discrimination against Jews (seen as potential enemies by the Stalinist regime and persecuted).
- **Presidium:** The organisation that replaced the Politburo in 1952, comprising members nominated by Stalin and used as Stalin's personal tool.

Chapter 21

🌐 Apply Your Knowledge

a Themes could include:
- **Individuals:** Rivalry among the Party leaders; elimination of opponents.
- **Ideology:** Disagreements on future of Russia, whether or not to depart from Stalinist policies.
- **Policies:** Industry, agriculture – particularly success of Khrushchev's Virgin Lands scheme.
- **Range of support:** For example in Party, country and from military, e.g. Marshal Zhukov.

b You should produce your own mind-map for this activity. For an example of how to start a mind-map see page 22.

🏅 🅐 Assess the Validity of This View

a and b You should produce your own mind-map for this activity. For an example of how to start a mind-map see page 22.

c Your answer might include reference to:
- Leadership struggles of 1954, in which Khrushchev's proposals were less radical than Malenkov's (i.e. develop heavy and light industry, and implement Virgin Lands Scheme, rather than Malenkov's 'new course' to change collective farm policy, reduce peasant taxes, invest more in consumer goods).
- Khrushchev's reversal of Stalinist policies from beginning of 1956 (releasing prisoners and attacking the police and the gulag system).
- Khrushchev's Secret Speech (Feb 1956) (blaming Stalin for the purges and terror, betraying Leninist principles and harming socialist progress; questioning Stalin's war leadership).
- Limitations to Khrushchev's reformist principles (continued support for economic controls, strong leadership, a single party, elimination of factions; suppression of uprisings triggered by his speech; refusal to take action against those responsible for the crimes he had denounced).

🔍 Key Question

Khrushchev's rise to power
- **Influence of ideas and ideology**: Concept of importance of Party allowed Khrushchev to use Party to climb to power (e.g. his use of Central Committee to prevent moves against him in 1957) ; discussion of strong central control versus collective power returned (temporary collective leadership ended when Khrushchev rose to power); legacy of 'ban on factions' allowed Khrushchev to eliminate rivals as being being 'anti-Party' (e.g. Beria in 1953, other opponents in 1957).
- **Importance of other factors:** Power struggle among the leaders, weaknesses of opponents; initial success of Virgin Lands Scheme.

De-Stalinisation
- **Influence of ideas and ideology:** Stalinism deemed a betrayal of Leninist principles; harming socialist progress.
- **Importance of other factors:** Need to establish control; need to justify new economic and political policies e.g. decentralisation; need to repress opposition.

Political and party change
- **Influence of ideas and ideology:** Political change included some decentralisation of power to the localities and democratisation (weakening the bureaucracy and giving more responsibility to the people); renewed emphasis on the Party increased importance of Party and government institutions; Party membership expanded with more working class members; role of local soviets extended; some power moved from central ministries to provincial authorities.
- **Importance of other factors:** Khrushchev's background, personal ambition and determination to differentiate himself from his predecessor; need to retain control.

🌐 Apply Your Knowledge

You should produce your own diagram for this activity.

Chapter 22

🌐 Apply Your Knowledge

Industry

Stalin, 1945–53
- **Successes and achievements:** Most heavy industry targets of Fourth and Fifth Five Year Plans (1946–50 and 1951–55 respectively) met; by 1950 USSR was stronger than before the war and second only to the USA in industrial capacity.
- **Failures and limitations:** Central planning too complex; managers avoided improving output (to prevent a rise in targets the following year); targets did not reflect consumer demand; inefficient use of resources demanded increased investment.

Khrushchev, 1953–64
- **Successes and achievements:** Significant growth in industrial output in many sectors (e.g. coal, electricity and consumer goods); living standards improved.
- **Failures and limitations:** Decentralisation measures added bureaucracy (his system would be abandoned in 1965); quality of life remained poor; heavy spending on armaments and the space race distorted the economy; the USSR failed to overtake the USA economically; the economic growth rate fell between 1958 and 1964.

Agriculture

Stalin, 1945–53
- **Successes and achievements:** Output increased as a result of Fourth Five Year plan.
- **Failures and limitations:** Peasants were left with little; farming practices were held back by inaccurate (ideological) scientific theories.

Khrushchev, 1953–64
- **Successes and achievements:** Early success of Virgin Lands Scheme; overall increase in production (e.g. in cereals except maize and in meat and milk).
- **Failures and limitations:** Following Fifth Five Year Plan production still lagged behind industry and by 1955 it was still lower than in 1940; problems of organisation (e.g. constant price changes, interference in farm management by Party officials) and distribution; peasants still preferred to work on their private plots rather than the collectives; lack of skills and money to maintain machinery and tractors; failure of Virgin Lands Scheme failed when land became overworked; new crops not always suitable and sometimes detracted from growth of wheat.

🏅 🅐 Assess the Validity of This View

a You should produce and consider your own list for this activity.

b A paragraph on the success of leaders in addressing the problem of land ownership and use might contain:

- An opening sentence that sets out your argument in relation to the question.
- References to the following:

Lenin
- Moved from peasant control (Oct 1917) to War Communism (1918–21) to NEP (1921); Trying to feed soldiers and workers and counter problems of peasant-hoarding, eventually allowing peasants to sell surpluses.

Stalin
- Introduced collectivisation which was outwardly successful but dekulakisation removed successful farmers; grain and livestock destroyed; collectives often poorly organised and lacking equipment; incentives for peasants to work hard disappeared; millions starved in the famine (1932–33); grain output did not rise above 1927 until after 1935.

Khrushchev
- Allowed peasants to set own targets; raised prices, reduced quotas and taxes; encouraged cultivation of new lands/crops (Virgin Lands Scheme). But success limited: peasants preferred to work own plots; Virgin Lands became overworked; new crops proved unsuitable.

🔍 Extract Analysis

a
- *Khrushchev was a committed Marxist.* Opposes.
- *Khrushchev acted in response to circumstances.* Supports.
- *Agricultural improvement was more important to Khrushchev than industrial growth.* Opposes.
- *Khrushchev did not believe in competing with the capitalist world.* Opposes.
- *Khrushchev made lavish promises about future economic growth in 1959.* Supports.
- *In 1964, Khrushchev promised that consumer goods and agricultural investment would be prioritised.* Supports.
- *Khrushchev produced economic success.* Opposes.

b
- **Overall argument:** Khrushchev was a pragmatist who aimed to improve agriculture and industrial output, so that socialism and communism would successfully compete with capitalist countries but he ultimately failed.
- **Contextual evidence supporting:** Some decentralisation; policies such as Virgin Lands Scheme and Seven Year Plan to develop industry, focusing on consumer goods, show attempt to carry out aims.
- **Contextual evidence opposing:** Although pragmatic, Khrushchev worked within the basic tents of communism, central planning prevailed and essence of Stalinism persisted.

🔍 Key Question

a and b You should produce your own mind-map and use it to assess the question for this activity.

Chapter 23

🌐 Apply Your Knowledge

a **Valid**
- Khrushchev's decentralisation policies were disliked by Central Party officials.
- Khrushchev was blamed for the handling of the Cuban missile crisis.
- Khrushchev represented the reformers and angered those who wanted to restore 'Stalinism' and police rule.
- Khrushchev was opposed by senior military figures.
- Khrushchev liked to 'meddle' in areas where he had limited expertise.

Invalid

- Khrushchev launched the Virgin Lands Scheme to try to improve USSR's agricultural output.
- There were violent nationalist demonstrations in Tblisi in protest against Khrushchev's de-Stalinisation speech.
- Cultural dissidents were committed to greater democracy, toleration, and civil rights.

b • You might argue that Khrushchev's personality was more important, referring to accusations against him ruling in a 'one-man style'; interfering where he lacked expertise; failing to take advice; nepotism; embarrassing behaviour at home and abroad.

- Alternatively you might conclude that it was the failure of his policies that caused his downfall, e.g. the failure of the Virgin Lands Scheme, problems with his policies to decentralise industry, and relaxation of cultural control that allowed the younger generation to question the Communist system.

- Whichever way you argue, make sure you support your judgement with detailed evidence.

Assess the Validity of This View

a **Opposition from within the Party** was **more dangerous** to the leader than the **opposition of cultural dissidents** in the years **1945 to 1964.'** Assess the validity of this view.

The word '**dangerous**' will require clarification. Dangerous in what respects?

b **'Danger' from opposition of cultural dissidents**

- **1945–53:** Limited opposition possible during Zhdanovshchina; cultural dissidents persecuted or went into exile.
- **1953–64:** Writings, Western influences (e.g. in pop culture) spread of secret press (*tamizdat* and *samizdat*), poetry readings – encouraged underground subversion.

'Danger' from opposition from within the Party

- **1945–53:** Leningrad Case (1949); Mingrelian Case (1951–52).
- **1953–64:** Struggle between reformers (e.g. Bulganin), and pro-Stalinists (e.g. Molotov and Malenkov; attempt of the 'anti-Party' group to oust Khrushchev in 1957 and his overthrow in 1964.

c Evidence would suggest a greater threat from within the Party than from cultural dissidents outside. You might include:

- The danger to the leader came primarily from potential loss of authority – the actions of Stalin in 1945–53 showed a paranoia regarding Party control; Khrushchev faced a genuine challenge – which ultimately unseated him.

- The 'danger' to political authority from cultural dissidents was minimal; given the Communist agents of repression (again, particularly under Stalin) there was very little they could do – hence underground organisations with limited explicit support. Nevertheless, their existence and Western contact posed a longer term 'danger' to socialism.

Plan Your Essay

a **Evidence to substantiate that opposition from cultural dissidents was ineffective:**

- During wartime (1941–45) the relaxation of restrictions on culture to foster an atmosphere of national reconciliation effectively eliminated opposition from cultural dissidents.
- From 1946, the Zhdanovshchina effectively stamped out cultural dissidence.
- Under Khrushchev (1953–64), cultural dissidence was better able to flourish.

Evidence to substantiate that opposition from Party members was effective:

- 1941–53: None: country united in war; opposition became treason.
- 1953–56: Resulted in the removal of several potential leaders (e.g. Beria, Malenkov 1953, 1954, Bulganin 1958).
- 1964: Succeeded in bringing about Khrushchev's downfall.

b You should use the points you have identified in the earlier part of this activity to help you write your conclusion.

Key Question

You should produce your own timeline for this activity. For an example of a good timeline see page 9.

Chapter 24

Apply Your Knowledge

a, **b** and **c** You should produce your own 'diamond 9' for this activity.

Assess the Validity of This View

a You should produce your own chart for this activity.

b and **c** You might decide that the economy of the USSR was in a much stronger position in 1964 than it had been in the 1930s. If so, you could substantiate your argument with points such as the following:

- **1930s:** USSR adjusting to change.
  - **Industry:** Five Year Plans failing to meet targets; over-emphasis on heavy industry and 'showpieces'; shortage of skills; weakened by trials of managers and hostility to foreigners; figures distorted although there was substantial growth taking place.
  - **Agriculture:** Collectivisation causing hardship, shortage of tractors and agricultural equipment, farming practices still backward.

- **By 1964:** USSR a strong industrial nation, although problems of supply (central planning) still existed.
  - **Industry:** Second only to the USA in industrial capacity (and had narrowed the gap with the USA too); consumer goods more common, although still behind West; improvements in communications, transport and technology.
  - **Agriculture:** Improvements such as increased mechanisation, new crops, although there were still problems with agricultural output (e.g. failure of Virgin Lands Scheme meant that grain had to be imported from the USA).

Extract Analysis

a • **Supporting phrases in the extract**
  - 'especially in the ending of the Terror and the raising of the general standard of living'
  - 'His political, economic and cultural accomplishments were a great improvement over Stalin'.

• **Supporting contextual evidence**
  - Khrushchev's de-Stalinisation policies brought greater personal freedom for Soviet citizens, including a reduction in influence of the police and greater cultural freedom.
  - His focus on the modern industries and consumer goods led to economic growth in those areas.
  - Living standards were raised, thanks to greater availability of consumer goods, housing initiatives, lowering of taxation, improvements in pensions, working hours and moves towards equal pay, increased influence allowed for trade unions, and improved educational provision, medicine and welfare services and transport.
  - His focus on technology and space science perpetuated the USSR's reputation as a great military power.

b • **Supporting phrases in the extract**
  - 'further improvement was not forthcoming'
  - 'the attempted solutions were insufficient to effect the renovation of the kind of state and society he espoused.'

• **Supporting contextual evidence**
  - Many of his reforms were half-hearted and ill thought-through, e.g. decentralisation of industry and agriculture.
  - Although social conditions improved, high-ranking Party officials retained privileges, and living standards were still significantly lower than in Western industrialised states.
  - He did not encourage independence for the nationalities, and restrictions on the Churches were reimposed.

c **Overall argument:** Khrushchev's political, economic and cultural achievements were huge, but his reforms still fell short of what the USSR needed.

Your answer might take the view that the argument is strongly convincing in that it backs up the overall argument by means of the phrases quoted in **a i)** and **b i)** above, and that these are supported by the points suggested in **a ii)** and **b ii)** above.

Revision Skills

You should produce your own cards, poster or timeline for this activity. For an example of a good timeline see page 9.

Glossary

A

anti-Semitic: being prejudiced against and persecuting Jews

autocratic: having no limits on a ruler's power

B

bureaucracy: a system of government in which most of the important decisions are taken by state officials rather than by elected representatives

burzhui: anyone considered a hindrance to worker or peasant prosperity

C

capitalism: private enterprise, which includes making money out of a 'capital' investment

Central Committee: elected by the Party congress and, in turn, elected the Politburo between each Party congress

Cheka: the name given to the Bolshevik Secret Police

Comecon: the Council for Mutual Economic Assistance, established in 1949 to coordinate the economic growth of countries inside the Soviet bloc

D

democratic centralism: communist idea of democracy whereby members of the local soviets were elected who, in turn, chose those who would sit on higher-level soviets and the All-Russian Congress of Soviets

Dual Power: whereby Russia was governed by an alliance of the Provisional Government and the Soviet

duma: an elected governing assembly

E

emancipation: freeing from bondage

G

Gosplan: the State General Planning Commission (1921–91); helped coordinate economic development and, from 1925, drafted economic plans

Great Turn: the move from NEP to the Five Year Plans and collectivisation of agriculture entailed a move to central planning and a 'command economy'

gulags: economic colonies where millions of prisoners were used to dig mines and canals, build railways and clear forests

I

indirect voting: a citizen elects a delegate to vote on their behalf

intelligentsia: the more educated members of Russian society, including writers and philosophers with both humanitarian and nationalist concerns

K

kolkhoz: a collective operated by a number of peasant families on state-owned land

komunalki: communal family dwellings formed of formerly private apartments that were resettled shortly after the revolution

Komsomol: the All-Union Leninist Young Communist League, the youth division of the Communist Party which was represented in its own right in the Supreme Soviet

kulak: a prosperous landed peasant

L

landowning elite: those who owned land and who were a privileged minority in Russian society

M

mir: a peasant commune

N

nationalisation: taking businesses out of private hands and placing them under state control

nomenklatura: a category of people who held key administrative positions in areas such as government, industry, agriculture, and education, appointed by the Communist Party in the region

O

Orthodox Church: following a split in the Christian Church in the 11th century, the Eastern Orthodox Church developed its own beliefs and rituals

P

Pan-Slavism: a belief that Slav races should be united

pogrom: an old Russian word which means 'round up' or lynching; after 1881 it gained the special connotation of an attack on Jews

police state: a state in which the activities of the people are closely monitored and controlled for political reasons

Politburo: the highest policy-making government authority under Communist rule

Presidium: Stalin re-named the Politburo as the Presidium in 1952; this name was retained until 1966

proletariat: urban working class

proletarianisation: to turn the mass of the population into urban workers

purge: literally a 'cleaning out of impurities'; forcible expulsions from the Communist Party in the 1920s; in the later 1930s, the removal of anyone deemed a political enemy

R

reaction: implies actions and policies that are backward looking in an attempt to restore the past

Red Guards: loyal, volunteer soldiers who had been recruited from the factory workers in the city

Russification: forcing everyone within the Russian Empire to think of themselves as 'Russian', by enforcing the Russian language and culture

S

serf: a person who was the property of the lord for whom he or she worked

socialism: the political and economic theory that the means of production, distribution and exchange should be owned by the community as a whole and that people should work cooperatively

socialist economy: one in which there is no private ownership and in which all members of society have a share in the State's resources

soviet: workers' council; the one in Petrograd (known as the Petrograd Soviet) was the most important

Sovnarkom: the cabinet, made up of the important ministers who, between them, would run the country

show trial: a trial that took place in front of the general public, usually for 'propaganda' purposes

V

Veshenkha: the Council of the National Economy

volost: a peasant community consisting of several villages or hamlets

W

war credits: the raising of taxes and loans to finance war

Whites: the forces ranged against the Bolshevik 'Reds'

Top revision tips for A Level History

Tsarist and Communist Russia

The History revision tips on this page are based on research reports on History revision and on the latest AQA examiners' reports.

General advice

☐ Make a realistic revision timetable for the months leading up to your exams and plan regular, short sessions for your History revision. Research shows that students who break down their revision into 30- to 60-minute sessions (and take short breaks in between subjects) are more likely to succeed in exams.

☐ Use the **progress checklists** (pages 3–4) to help you track your revision. It will enable you stick to your revision plan.

☐ Eat healthily and make sure you have regular amounts of sleep in the lead-up to your exams. This is obvious, but research shows this can help students perform better in exams.

☐ Make sure your phone and laptop are put away at least an hour before you go to bed. You will experience better quality sleep if you have had time away from the screen before sleeping.

Revising your History knowledge and understanding

☐ Using a variety of revision techniques can help to embed knowledge successfully, so don't just stick to one style. Try different revision methods, such as: flashcards, making charts, diagrams and mind-maps, highlighting your notebooks, colour-coding, re-reading your textbook or summarising your notes, group study, revision podcasts, and working through the activities in this Revision Guide.

☐ Create a timeline with colour-coded sticky notes to make sure you remember important dates relating to the six Russian Breadth Study key questions (use the **timeline** on page 9 as a starting point).

☐ Make sure you understand key concepts for this topic, such as autocracy, liberalism and Marxism. If you're unsure, attend your school revision sessions and ask your teacher to go through important concepts again.

☐ Identify your weaknesses. Which topics are easy and which are more challenging for you? Give yourself more time to revise the challenging topics.

☐ Answer past paper questions and check the answers (using the AQA mark schemes) to practise applying your knowledge correctly and accurately to exam questions.

Revising your History exam technique

☐ Review the **AQA mark scheme** (page 8) for each exam question, and make sure you understand how you will be marked.

☐ Make sure you revise your skills as well as your knowledge. In particular, ensure you know how to approach the extracts question. Practise identifying the overall interpretation in extracts.

☐ Find a memorable way to recall the **How to master your exam skills** steps (pages 6–7) – it will help you plan your answers effectively and quickly.

☐ Ask your teacher for the examiners' reports – you can find out from the reports what the examiners want to see in the papers, and their advice on what not to do.

☐ Time yourself and practise answering past paper questions.

☐ Take mock exams seriously. You can learn from them how to manage your time better under strict exam conditions.

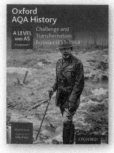

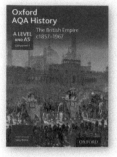

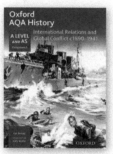

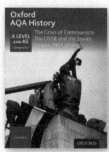
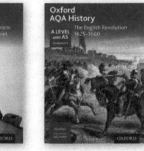

   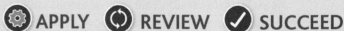
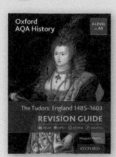